The Split in Israel

Through a Psychiatrist's Eyes

From shock to reset

VOLUME 3

Dr. Michael Ritsner

Table of Contents

CHAPTER 22: THE DEEP STATE

"Bureaucracy consists of officials, aristocracy of idols, and democracy of idolaters."

George Bernard Shaw

Introduction

Institutional social schizophrenia: we have a government that bears responsibility but has no authority, and a "deep state" that has authority but bears no responsibility for the failure of 7 October.

The term "institutional social schizophrenia" is a metaphor (a concept) describing the disintegration of unity in society and its institutions, analogous to the splitting of personality in clinical schizophrenia, manifesting in conflicts, contradictions, and the inability to act as a unified whole, which leads to social tension.

The "deep state" is not a secret society in masks; it is an administrative tumor that has grown through all the organs of power. The uniqueness of our deep state lies in the fact that it has been legalized. Thanks to the doctrines of Aharon Barak, the official ceased to be an executor of the will of the people and became its overseer. We have a classic case of the splitting of state consciousness: a minister signs an order, but the "legal advisor" freezes it, citing his own internal convictions. This is power that does not pass through the ballot box, which means it is accountable to no one.

In the history of Israeli politics, especially in the period following Aharon Barak's judicial revolution of the 1990s, there arose a phenomenon that a significant portion of society calls the "deep state." This is an unelected, powerful bloc of senior officials including the Supreme Court, the State Prosecution, the Legal Advisor to the Government, and the upper echelons of security and the media. Possessing great administrative power, these people conduct affairs, each in their own sphere, not necessarily in accordance with elected politicians: ministers, Knesset committees, and the prime minister. The struggle with this deep state became the central axis of Israeli political life, reaching its apogee during the rule of Benjamin Netanyahu. It is being waged by the elected political leadership (the Knesset and the Government) against the left-liberal deep state, with the goal of restoring the sovereignty of the people, whose power was usurped by unelected officials. The conflict has unfolded on several fronts.

1. The struggle for judicial reform and the criminal case against the prime minister.
2. The struggle for accountability after the failure of 7 October and the dismissal of the intelligence chiefs.
3. The conflict over the narrative and control of public opinion, in which the left-wing media are accused of ideological bias.

In essence, this is not merely a political confrontation but an existential conflict over who possesses supreme power in Israel: the democratically elected representatives of the people, or the unelected legal and bureaucratic elite.

The "Deep State"

The "deep state" (or "state within a state") is a branching network structure within state organs, institutions, business, the media, and the armed forces. Some of these are the subject of separate chapters (8, 11, 15, and 16). In this chapter I shall attempt to view the "deep state" from above, as it were.

From a Political Thriller

Night in Tel Aviv. In a half-dark office on an upper floor of a building on Kaplan Street, only a desk lamp burns.

Gali Baharav-Miara *puts down the receiver after a conversation with a former head of the Shin Bet. "They are trying to push the reform through again," she says quietly. "But we will not allow it. The court is the last line."*

At the same time in Jerusalem **Netanyahu** *looks at his phone screen: a message from a trusted advisor — "The legal advisor has again blocked the appointment." The prime minister grits his teeth. "This is not merely bureaucracy. This is war. And they are not playing by the rules of democracy."*

The "deep state" is two-headed: it is led in equal measure by the Supreme Court and by the Prosecution with the absolute power of the Government's Legal Advisor, who at present is Gali Baharav-Miara.

***

The army, police, and security services are, according to law, in direct subordination to the government. Nevertheless, security officials who ignore the will of the legislator have

expressed readiness to execute the decisions of the Supreme Court. In this sense, former IAF commander Eliezer Shkedy, former Inspector of Police Roni Alsheich, and former Shin Bet chiefs Yoram Cohen, Nadav Argaman, and Yuval Diskin spoke out in this vein as far back as spring 2023.

***

Who Enters the "Deep State"?

Institution / Sphere	What They Are Suspected Of
Judicial system (Supreme Court)	Undermining the authority of the Knesset
State Prosecution	"Tailoring" cases against politicians
Legal Advisor to the Government	Undermining the authority of the right-wing government
Legal elite and NGOs	Direct contacts with European foundations and American structures
Senior bureaucracy	Sabotage of government decisions
Army leadership	Political pressure; "left-wing bias"
Media and cultural elites	Creating a left-wing public climate
Academic sphere	Advancing liberal ideology
High-tech and business oligarchy	Dictating to the state how to behave through threats of capital withdrawal

This very turn of events was foreshadowed by Aharon Barak in 2016, speaking at Haifa University: "What will happen if the head of government says that the ruling of the court is unlawful and should not be obeyed? My answer: that is a coup, that is a putsch, and in that situation, everything will be decided by tanks, decided by the commander-in-chief."

The deep state operates on the principle of collective circular loyalty. It is a triumvirate:

The legal apex (the Supreme Court and the prosecution) creates prohibitive norms.

The security bloc (the army leadership and Shin Bet) sabotages government decisions under the pretext of "professional assessments."

The media provides informational cover, destroying anyone who dares to challenge this caste.

This is a closed cycle of elite self-reproduction. If you are not "one of their own," the system will expel or destroy you through fabricated cases. This is precisely why any attempt at reform is met with such furious, almost animal, resistance. It is possible that individual blocs are not fully integrated into the closed system, but I have no doubt that there are active interconnections between them, conditioned by their commonality of goal and motive.

What Are Their Motives?

1. *They consider themselves "guardians of the state."*
2. *Not to allow elected politicians to change the rules of the game.*
3. *To preserve the left-liberal environment in the courts, the media, the army, academia, and so on.*

4. *For them, "right-wing, national, religious" is the danger of Israel becoming a theocracy and a threat to their power.*
5. *Preservation of monopoly without the loss of resources, careers, or international contacts.*
6. *To preserve themselves and "the right Israel," acceptable to the West in the model of "liberal democracy with judicial supremacy," rather than national majority democracy.*

SERIOUS MATTERS OF THE DEEP STATE

(From a Political Thriller:)

Midnight. *The underground car park of the Supreme Court. Two silhouettes in the shadow of the columns. One is a tall judge in an overcoat; the other, a prosecutor with a briefcase.*

Judge: *(whispering) "Deri will not pass. We will block the appointment on grounds of 'reasonableness.'"*

One of them: *"And if the Knesset votes?" "Then we will find a reason. As always. The main thing is not to let them change the rules."*

The headlights of a car flash in the distance. They part silently.

In the car the judge dials a number: *"Are the protests ready? Let them come out into the streets immediately after the ruling." The line goes dead.*

***

In the Israeli context the deep state is usually associated not so much with the army or intelligence services as with the legal and bureaucratic apparatus, which is considered unaccountable to elected power. Critics argue that the deep state, or the "legal junta," engages in serious, odious activities that undermine democracy and sovereignty.

- The deep state uses subjective doctrines (such as "extreme unreasonableness") to annul laws of the Knesset and to block political appointments (as in the case of Aryeh Deri).
- The legal elite has arrogated to itself the right of veto, turning judges into political overseers and thereby decapitating the democratically elected government.
- The Legal Advisor to the Government is accused of systematically blocking any significant reform that the government attempts to advance that does not conform to the deep state's liberal agenda.
- The Elor Azaria case: the harsh prosecution of a rank-and-file soldier for an error in the field, which was perceived as a demonstration of the force of "legalism" over the army.
- *The legal apparatus betrayed rank-and-file soldiers but covers for elite layers who share its political agenda. This creates double standards that destroy trust in the law.*
- The use of loyal legal experts and media to create an illusion (for example, that the protest was spontaneous and apolitical) that contradicts the facts (a pre-planned operation).
- *Allowing the protest movement to commit "lawlessness" (blocking roads, threatening national security) without legal consequences, in order to maintain pressure on the government.*
- *Making every effort to transform the country from Jewish into universally inclusive.*

- *Since the prime minister's announcement of the freezing of the reform, the assertion that the left governs the country even when the right wins elections has been convincingly documented.*

In sum, the serious matters of the deep state constitute a complex of actions directed at the dismantling of the principle of majority rule and the replacement of the political will of the elected people with the will of the unelected legal-bureaucratic apparatus.

How Lawyers Captured the IDF

This text reveals the mechanism by which the army was transformed from an instrument of war into an instrument of legal bureaucracy. Here I shall describe how "advisors" became more important than commanders.

The Legal Exclusive:

The Army Under the Supervision of a "Sacred Caste"

An officer with a lawyer behind him. By 2023 a unique and dangerous situation had developed in the IDF: not a single serious operational measure was taken without the visa of the Legal Advisor (known in Hebrew as the PATZAR). This phenomenon received the name the "Legal Exclusive." Its essence is simple: the lawyers arrogated to themselves the right to determine not only legality but also the "reasonableness" of military actions.

"From a personal letter of a reserve lieutenant colonel sent to friends after 7 October: My dears, I still cannot believe it. For years we reported: Hamas is training at the fence, cutting the wire, preparing tunnels. Commanders wanted to strike pre-emptively, but each time a call came from the legal department: 'No immediate threat. Await the PATZAR visa.' We waited. And on 7 October they

came. I lost half my platoon in the first hours. ***Now I ask myself: who is more to blame, the terrorists or those who tied our hands with 'international law'? The lawyers won. And we lost."***

The Concept of "Sterile War"

Under the influence of Baharav-Miara and the judicial system, the army came to be dominated by the doctrine of "purity of arms," brought to the point of absurdity.

Prohibition on pre-emption: any attempt to strike at Hamas forces in preparation encountered a wall of legal checks. "Is there an immediate threat?" "Is the response proportionate?"

The Gaza example: residents of the border kibbutzim reported for years on Hamas training right at the fence. The army wanted to suppress these positions, but the legal echelon blocked the orders, arguing that firing at "unarmed" persons (even if they were cutting the fence) would provoke international lawsuits against officers.

Lawyers as "Censors"

The legal takeover had a deeper layer as well. General Staff officers began to fear not the enemy but the Commission of Inquiry. In 2023, at the peak of the "Kaplan" protests, the legal system gave the military to understand: if you act harshly against internal protesters or against external enemies without our approval, you will be left without protection. This created an atmosphere of "learned helplessness." Generals began to speak the language of lawyers, using the term "international legitimacy" more often than "operational victory."

The Schizophrenia of Subordination

A paradox arose: the Chief of the General Staff formally reports to the Minister of Defense and the government, but in practice to the Legal Advisor. When the government demanded offensive plans, the army (through its legal departments) found thousands of reasons why these were "impossible" or "illegal." This was the "Legal Exclusive" in action: a situation in which unelected officials in robes paralyzed the will of those who wear epaulettes.

Legal oversight was transformed from an insurance policy against war crimes into a straitjacket for the entire army. On 7 October the IDF did not strike pre-emptively not because it could not, but because the system had been programmed to wait for "legal authorization" that would never have arrived in time.

The concept promoted by, among others, David Ben Yehuda (a critic of "legalism") is based on the gradual expansion of the powers of legal advisors. The Government's Legal Advisor controls the government, while the Military Advocate General controls the army, the police, the Shin Bet, the Prison Service, the Police Internal Investigations Department (MAHASH), and the judicial guard. It would be logical for the Military Advocate General, like all other military personnel, to report to the Chief of the General Staff, who in turn reports to the government's representative, the Minister of Defense. It turns out that the Military Prosecutor is subordinate, in general, to the Government's Legal Advisor.

It emerged that a whole succession of failed Chiefs of the General Staff created this monstrous system: Benny Gantz, Gadi Eisenkot, Aviv Kochavi, and Herzi Halevi. They allowed the legal apparatus to seize control of the IDF. With one hand they reduced divisions, brigades, and battalions, cutting the ground forces, while with the other they created a monster subordinate to no one in the security system, not even the government.

Until the 1990s the Military Advocate General (MAG) was primarily an advisor on legal matters and the head of the military prosecution. His task: to ensure the lawfulness of the army's actions. Gradually, with the support of the Supreme Court, the powers of the MAG expanded from legal advice to mandatory directive instruction. The MAG was transformed from an advisor into a co-commander (or even the supreme commander in the legal sense). Commanders, from platoon leader to Chief of the General Staff, began to fear making decisions without prior approval or legal cover, dreading investigation and criminal prosecution.

The principal lever of the takeover is the threat of international prosecution and the imposition of an "ideal" ethics of war. The military prosecution began requiring that every military operation, every strike, and every action at a checkpoint be "legalized" in advance and conform not only to Israeli but also to international humanitarian law. "Fear of The Hague": the legal corps, supported by the Supreme Court, instilled in the IDF the belief that the only protection against the International Criminal Court (ICC) was excessive legal purity (that is, the renunciation of decisive actions that might be interpreted as "war crimes"). The army began to spend enormous resources on legal accompaniment rather than on combat readiness. A commander in the field, instead of acting according to the situation, had to think about legal consequences.

The Elor Azaria case became the culmination of this takeover. The legal corps harshly prosecuted a soldier for an error in a combat situation, thereby sending a clear signal to the entire army: we are more important than you. This paralyzed the will of commanders and soldiers to act decisively, because they understood that the Israeli legal system would betray them first in order to protect itself from international criticism. The legal apparatus sacrificed the security of soldiers and the state for the sake of its own moral and international legitimacy. The final effect of the "takeover" was a complete shift of IDF priorities.

- Priority was shifted from Victory and Security to legal purity and procedural compliance.
- The weakening of fighting spirit and the loss of resolve (inability to make tough, unpopular but necessary decisions) became one of the factors leading to conceptual blindness and the failure of 7 October.

How Did This Happen?

Here is what Lieutenant Colonel Dubi Yudkin recounts:

2012. Chief of the General Staff: Benny Gantz. The military prosecution adopted a provision whereby the Military Prosecutor would no longer report to the Chief of the General Staff but to the Government's Legal Advisor. And Benny Gantz nodded in agreement.

2012. The office of Chief of the General Staff Benny Gantz. On the desk: the prosecution's new provision. The Military Prosecutor no longer reports to the Chief of the General Staff. Gantz looks out the window at the soldiers drilling.

An advisor whispers: *"It is merely a formality, General. For protection from The Hague."*

Gantz signs. He does not know he has just handed over the keys to the army. The camera pulls back: in the corridor a young female prosecutor waits — the future Legal Advisor. She smiles.

2013. Chief of the General Staff still Benny Gantz. The prosecution adopts a new provision: all lawyers and prosecution personnel no longer report to the Chief of the General Staff but only to the Military Prosecutor, who in turn reports to the Legal Advisor. This is undeniably subversive activity against the IDF, but Benny Gantz does not comprehend the consequences and does not halt the process.

2014. Chief of the General Staff: Gadi Eisenkot. A new provision: the military police now reports directly to the prosecution, and the Chief of the General Staff has no right to intervene in investigations or instructions. Eisenkot does not intervene.

2018. Still Eisenkot. The prosecution prohibits opening fire in the perimeter at the Gaza and Lebanon borders. This allowed terrorists to approach the fence again and again, ultimately leading to the death of soldier Barel Hadaria-Shmueli, of blessed memory.

2021. Chief of the General Staff: Aviv Kochavi. In the framework of the project to construct a barrier in Gaza, the prosecution halts the laying of mines at the fence, arguing that this contravenes an international convention that Israel has not even signed. This absurd step allowed terrorists to approach the fence on 7 October and in preceding incidents.

2023. Chief of the General Staff: Herzi Halevi. *The female prosecutor permits soldiers to participate in demonstrations: something that had been forbidden throughout all 77 years of the state's existence. This divided the people and undermined the country's security.*

2024. Still Herzi Halevi. *The Military Prosecutor writes a letter in Hebrew and English asserting that the IDF is committing* *war crimes in Gaza. The publication of the letter undermined the international legitimacy of Israel and the morale of soldiers.*

2024. A slanderous story against IDF soldiers concerning events at Sde Teiman emerges. The worst Chief of the General Staff in history supports the female prosecutor and not the soldiers. Shortly thereafter, fabricated footage allegedly depicting events at Sde Teiman "leaks" into the media and accumulates 96 million views worldwide. The Chief of the General Staff orders the prosecutor to investigate the incident, but nothing is done in 15 months, despite the investigation being straightforward.

Nowhere in developed Western armies do prosecutors possess such broad, directive powers that in practice allow them to command the army rather than merely to advise it. In most democratic countries the role of the military prosecutor is separated from the chain of command, and they generally do not have the power to block the operational decisions of commanders. The difference between the Israeli model and the models of other countries lies in the fact that in Israel the Military Advocate General became not merely a legal advisor but a mandatory legal veto on many operational and command decisions.

Whereas in all the armies of the world military prosecutors are supervisors of legality and justice, in Israel they have been transformed into active co-commanders and political arbiters. This is the essence of the accusation of the "legal capture" of the IDF.

The Resignation of the Chief of the General Staff

The Chief of the General Staff of the Israel Defense Forces (IDF), Herzi Halevi, publicly accepted responsibility for the catastrophic failure of October 7, 2023. In a letter addressed to Prime Minister Benjamin Netanyahu and Defense Minister Israel Katz, he stated: "On the morning of October 7, under my command, the IDF did not fulfill its mission to protect the citizens of Israel. My responsibility for this terrible failure accompanies me every day and will accompany me for the rest of my life." Lieutenant General Herzi Halevi was not dismissed, although his continued tenure represented the principal source of tension between the political leadership and the military establishment.

The Demand for Halevi's Immediate Resignation Was Based on the Following Arguments:

- He bore the highest operational responsibility for IDF readiness and its response to the attack. The decisions he made in the hours and days preceding October 7 were erroneous and contributed to the catastrophic failure of the defense.
- The failure of October 7 exposed the inadequacy of the military doctrine, which relied on a technological barrier and intelligence, for which the General Staff was responsible.
- In Israeli tradition, leaders who have presided over major military failures are expected to accept symbolic responsibility by resigning, as occurred following the Yom Kippur War.
- Halevi found himself at the center of the crisis involving reservists, particularly pilots who threatened to refuse service in response to the judicial reform. Critics accused Halevi of inaction or even covert tolerance of the "blackmail" by reservists. This was cited as evidence of the political partisanship of the senior military command, which was perceived as aligning itself with the "Kaplanists" and the "legal elite."

The Situation Surrounding Halevi Was Tense, Yet He Remained in His Post, Becoming a Point of Conflict Between Political Leaders and Military Elites:

- The principal argument against dismissing Halevi was that during active combat operations in the Gaza Strip and on the northern front, changing the commanding officer was inadvisable. His dismissal could have undermined military unity and operational effectiveness at a critical moment.
- The military establishment and many former generals actively defended Halevi, insisting that his dismissal would have been politically motivated and harmful to the country.
- Leaks circulating constantly in the media pointed to a conflict between Halevi and the Prime Minister over war strategy, humanitarian aid, and the future role of the IDF in Gaza.
- Government supporters perceived Halevi's persistent refusal to resign as political insubordination, while his supporters believed he was demonstrating "leadership" by protecting the army from political interference.

In the end, Herzi Halevi departed from his post as a necessary consequence of the failure, but the process was prolonged to the maximum possible extent due to political struggle. His successor was Major General Eyal Zamir, appointed in February 2025 and assuming office in early March.

The Dismissal of the Shin Bet Director

The dismissal of Ronen Bar was necessitated by his direct responsibility for the catastrophic operational failure: the inability of the Shin Bet to prevent the mass invasion by Hamas from the Gaza Strip.

- The Shin Bet is responsible for counterterrorism operations and Israel's internal security, as well as for the collection of operational intelligence in areas adjacent to Israel, including Gaza and the West Bank.
- Bar and his agency failed to detect and did not report the strategic decision by Hamas to launch a full-scale invasion, nor the large-scale preparations for it, including training and weapons stockpiling.
- The Shin Bet failed to respond swiftly and neutralize the infiltrating militants in border communities and IDF bases. Although the Shin Bet possesses operational capabilities and rapid response forces, their deployment was insufficient and delayed, allowing militants to rampage through communities for hours.
- On October 16, 2023, Ronen Bar stated: "Despite a series of actions we undertook, we failed to create an adequate warning to prevent the attack. Responsibility for this lies with me. This is a time of war, not of investigations. But when that time comes, I will be the first to participate in the investigation."
- This statement reinforced the demand for resignation: if a leader has acknowledged his own fault, he must step down.

The resignation of Ronen Bar, which occurred in October 2025, was unprecedented in its public and politicized character. The events surrounding Bar's dismissal took the form of a clash between political and professional elites, rather than an ordinary resignation of a subordinate.

- The resignation was not presented as Bar's own decision but appeared to be a forced dismissal initiated by the political leadership, specifically the Prime Minister, under public pressure.

- In the run-up to the resignation, the media was flooded with insider leaks from security circles. These leaks, reportedly from Bar's supporters or from within the security establishment itself, were intended to shift blame for the failure onto the political echelon, specifically Netanyahu personally, or to cast doubt on the timing of the dismissal.
- The security establishment and its supporters in the media portrayed Bar as a "scapegoat" whom Netanyahu was "sacrificing" in order to divert attention from his own responsibility for the strategic failure.
- Rather than simply submitting a resignation letter and disappearing from the public sphere, as is customary for heads of intelligence services, Ronen Bar issued what amounted to a "political testament" or farewell address, which was widely circulated.
- In this address, he confirmed his personal responsibility, for which he was given credit, but simultaneously made clear that full responsibility must also be attributed to the political leadership.
- This public and imperious departure, accompanied by a call for investigation, was perceived as a final shot and a political condemnation of the Prime Minister, behavior characteristic of a political leader rather than a subordinate official.
- The political leadership insisted on the resignation, but disputes continued over the timing and the wording.

- In the end, his departure was exploited politically by both sides: the government declared that it had fulfilled the public's demand, while the opposition contended that it was insufficient, too late, and merely an attempt to cover tracks.

FROM A POLITICAL THRILLER

October 2025. The Last Day of Ronen Bar.

He exits the Shin Bet building for the final time. In his hands is a folder marked "Top Secret."

Journalist: *(rushing forward) "Mr. Bar, is this a sacrifice by Netanyahu?"*

Bar: *(stopping, looking into the camera) "Responsibility lies with everyone. Especially with those who ignored warnings for the sake of politics."*

Montage: footage from October 7, burning homes, weeping mothers.

Bar (voiceover): *"I am leaving. But the system remains." A car carries him into the night.*

Thus, the resignation of Ronen Bar was "dirty" because it became a fierce public confrontation between an official and the political authority to which he is legally subordinate. This is how the deep state behaves in Israel.

The Attempt to Dismiss the Legal Advisor to the Government

The assertion that it was necessary to dismiss the Legal Advisor to the Government, **Gali Baharav-Miara,** represented one of the most central and sharply contested political demands on the part of the governing coalition and its supporters. The principal cause of this demand lay in a fundamental conflict of authority and ideology between the elected executive branch and the senior legal bureaucracy.

The accusations against the Legal Advisor to the Government, who is an unelected official, were as follows:

1. Blocking Government Policy

The Legal Advisor holds veto power, or at the very least the power of a binding opinion, over all legislative initiatives and governmental decisions. Baharav-Miara systematically blocked key reforms and appointments that the government considered essential. She reversed or delayed administrative decisions made by ministers on the basis of her own subjective legal interpretations, employing, for instance, the doctrine of "reasonableness." Rather than defending the government in court, she functioned as a "prosecutor within the government," thereby creating a paralysis of executive authority.

2. Conflict of Interest and Politicization

Baharav-Miara acted not as an impartial legal counsel but as an ideological adversary and a part of the "deep state." She was disloyal to the political agenda of the government that had appointed her. While the Legal Advisor is appointed by the government, her role requires her to serve the entire state rather than the coalition. She abused her authority by imposing her own political agenda upon the government through legal opinions, rather than simply interpreting existing law.

FROM A POLITICAL THRILLER

December 14, 2025. The Supreme Court Chamber. Seven Judges in Black Robes.

Chief Justice: *(reading the ruling) "The dismissal is unlawful."*

Camera cuts to Gali Baharav-Miara in the hall. A faint smile crosses her face.

Montage: Netanyahu's office.

Ben-Gvir: *(striking the table with his fist) "We ignore this! I am ordering the police..."*

Levin: *"We cannot. That would be a coup."*

Netanyahu: *(gazing at a portrait of Ben-Gurion) "They think they have won time. But the war is only beginning."*

Outside, demonstrators chant: "De-mo-cra-cy!"

3. Refusal to Defend the Prime Minister

This was a particularly acute point in the context of Benjamin Netanyahu's criminal trial. Gali Baharav-Miara is obligated to represent the government and its ministers, but she stated plainly that she could not represent Netanyahu in his criminal cases, since her own position requires upholding the rule of law while the Prime Minister stands as a defendant. For government supporters, this was perceived as outright betrayal and a refusal to defend the head of the elected authority, intensifying the sense of political persecution.

FROM A POLITICAL THRILLER

Cabinet Office of the Prime Minister, August 2025. The Door Slams Shut.

Yariv Levin: *(placing a folder on the table) "We vote on the dismissal of Miara. Now."*

Netanyahu: *(nodding) "She has paralyzed the government."*

Ben-Gvir: *(entering) "Finally!"*

But within an hour, a call arrives from the Supreme Court: "Temporary injunction."

Netanyahu: *(staring out the window at demonstrators with flags) "They think they have won. But this is only the beginning."*

And across the city, Miara smiles: "The court will protect the law. Even from them."

***

In 2025, Benjamin Netanyahu's government made several attempts to dismiss Gali Baharav-Miara, who has held the post of Legal Advisor to the Government, equivalent to Attorney General, since February 2022. She was the first woman to hold this position and frequently clashed with the coalition over the judicial reform, the conscription of ultra-Orthodox men, the war in Gaza, and the criminal case against Netanyahu. The chronology of key events was as follows:

March 2025: Justice Minister Yariv Levin initiated dismissal proceedings. The government unanimously expressed a vote of no confidence, accusing her of "abuse of power" and creating obstacles to the cabinet's functioning.

June and July 2025: The government established an alternative ministerial committee, including Itamar Ben-Gvir, Bezalel Smotrich, and others, bypassing the independent appointments committee known as the Grunis Committee. The committee recommended dismissal.

August 4, 2025: The cabinet voted unanimously for immediate dismissal. However, the Supreme Court immediately froze the decision through a temporary judicial order.

September and October 2025: The Supreme Court recommended returning to the lawful procedure through the Grunis Committee, but the process stalled.

December 14, 2025: An extended panel of the Supreme Court, consisting of seven judges voting unanimously, annulled the government's dismissal decision, ruling it unlawful on the grounds of retroactive modification of the dismissal mechanism, the absence of substantive justification, and violations of administrative law. Gali Baharav-Miara continues to serve.

Some ministers, among them Shlomo Karhi, called for ignoring the court's ruling, but as of December 15, 2025, Baharav-Miara remains in her post.

The Legal Advisor to the Government holds a role unique to Israel. She not only advises the government but also serves as head of the prosecution. Unlike many other countries, where these roles are separated, in Israel the Legal Advisor fulfills a dual function: chief prosecutor of the state and legal counsel to the government. It is precisely this fusion of functions that generates constant conflict, rendering the position excessively powerful and susceptible to accusations of political bias.

The Rulings of the Legal Advisor

Smadar Shmueli accused Miara of failing to respond to a range of critical matters. **The following is a summary of the Legal Advisor's reported positions on key issues:**

1. Law granting immunity to IDF soldiers and police officers who participated in the events of October 7: AGAINST
2. Law on the death penalty for terrorists: AGAINST
3. Law on the deportation of terrorists and their families: AGAINST
4. Tightening detention conditions for security prisoners: AGAINST
5. Operation of the Sde Teiman detention facility: AGAINST
6. Use of the Shin Bet to combat crime in Arab society: AGAINST
7. Relaxation of restrictions on opening fire: AGAINST
8. Preventing the provision of state-appointed lawyers to "Nukhba" terrorists: AGAINST
9. Immediate sealing of a terrorist's home at the request of Minister Ben-Gvir: AGAINST
10. Revocation of residency of the inciting Mufti Sabri: AGAINST
11. Law permitting the closure of the Al-Jazeera television channel: AGAINST
12. Opening an investigation into inciting calls by Arab sector Knesset members to violence against Israel: AGAINST

13. Process of removing Shin Bet Director Ronen Bar from office: AGAINST
14. Allowing the Prime Minister to interview candidates to replace Ronen Bar, pursuant to a Supreme Court ruling: AGAINST
15. Opening an investigation into the leak of a fabricated video from the Sde Teiman base: AGAINST
16. Appointment of Major General Zini as head of the Shin Bet: AGAINST
17. Law on holding "Nukhba" group terrorists accountable: AGAINST
18. Bill on the establishment of a state investigative committee: AGAINST
19. Decision on the mass evacuation of the population of Gaza: AGAINST
20. Expansion of emergency powers of the Defense Minister without legislative authorization: AGAINST
21. Easing of detention conditions for "Nukhba" terrorists, including the provision of additional food and fruit: IN FAVOR
22. Requirement that every strike in the sector be assessed in accordance with the principles of distinction, proportionality, and precaution: IN FAVOR
23. Decision on the supply of food and medicine to Gaza during active hostilities: IN FAVOR

This list was generated with the assistance of the Grok-4 large language model (xAI, 2025) and broadly corresponds to the publicly known positions of Israel's Legal Advisor to the Government, Gali Baharav-Miara, on matters of national security and related laws and decisions, based on her official opinions, statements, and court submissions from 2023 to 2025.

She repeatedly clashed with Netanyahu's right-wing coalition, blocking or criticizing initiatives she considered to be in violation of the law, human rights, international law, or the principles of proportionality. This is confirmed by Israeli media sources, including The Times of Israel, Haaretz, and The Jerusalem Post, as well as by international sources and her own letters and opinions.

This pattern reflects her role as a "guardian of the law." She frequently defended the government in international forums, including matters related to aid for Gaza, while blocking initiatives put forward by the far-right ministers Ben-Gvir and Smotrich, which led to the attempts to dismiss her.

FROM A POLITICAL THRILLER

Morning in a Kibbutz near the Gaza Border. A Radio Plays in the Kitchen.

The announcer reads the news: "The Legal Advisor is against again: against the death penalty for terrorists, against the deportation of families, against the tightening of prison conditions..."

Grandmother: *(wiping her hands on her apron) "Against everything that might save us?"*

Grandfather: *(sighing) "She is in favor of humanitarian aid to Gaza, in favor of proportionality. But when they came on October 7, where was that proportionality?"*

Son: *(silently, staring at a memorial by the road) "Mama, why is she always against us?"*

***

The Factory of Meaning

The political left could never have maintained its hold on power, despite consistently losing ground demographically and electorally, without control over the "factory of meaning," that is, the institutions of education and media.

The Creation of the "Rootless Man"

The education system, particularly at the university level, became an incubator for what critics call "the Conception." The academic environment spent decades advancing post-Zionist narratives. Future officers, journalists, and lawyers were taught that nationalism was an atavism, and that "universal values" and international law stood above the right of a people to self-defense. Programs in "conflict resolution" displaced the study of military victories. Students were taught to understand the "enemy's narrative," which in practice translated into an inability to recognize the absolute evil of October 7. From an early age, the belief was instilled that the Supreme Court was the country's only moral compass, standing above the will of the people. This produced a generation of "obedient executors" for whom the opinion of the Legal Advisor was more important than a combat order.

The Mechanism of "Social Schizophrenia" in Action

When education and the media operate in tandem, an effect of collective hypnosis emerges. People saw Hamas drilling at the fence, yet the media told them: "This is merely theater."

People saw the failure in Gaza, yet the media told them: "Netanyahu is to blame for the absence of a political horizon." As a result, on October 7, Israelis awoke not in their own country, but in a reality they had been forbidden to see for years.

The information blockade created by the alliance of academia and media became the "soft power" of the deep state. It transformed Israeli society into a hostage of intellectual censorship, where critical thinking was declared a threat to democracy and blind faith in the "enlightened elite" became the sole mark of patriotism. On October 7, this wall collapsed, burying beneath it the illusions that had been so carefully cultivated over the years in university lecture halls and television studios.

FROM A POLITICAL THRILLER

The Deep State Media Front

Screenshot from an Anonymous Channel, 'The Truth Without Filters,' December 2025:

"Friends, here is a fresh leak from the newsroom of Channel 13. An editor writes to a journalist: 'Today the focus is on Netanyahu's guilt in the leaks; minimize the responsibility of the generals.' And in another chat: 'The protests for the hostages should be shown as a popular movement; do not mention the funding from the United States.' This is not journalism. This is the front of the deep state. While we are at war, they are waging war against us here."

***

The media front is the critically important and possibly the most influential element in the struggle between the elected government and the deep state. In Israel, this struggle is conducted primarily between the political majority and the traditional mainstream media, which are ideologically and structurally aligned with the left-liberal elite. The struggle on the media front proceeds along two main lines: narrative and control.

1. The Conflict of Narratives and the Shaping of Public Consciousness

The majority of traditional media outlets, including leading newspapers, major television channels, and key news websites, function as a single ideological mouthpiece, shaping public opinion against the government. The media systematically demonizes Benjamin Netanyahu and his supporters, ignoring their achievements and exaggerating their mistakes. This was manifested in the unprecedentedly negative coverage of his criminal cases. As an example, the accusation of "leaks" from the prosecution to journalists, as discussed in Case 4000, was viewed by critics as a coordinated campaign to discredit Netanyahu before the delivery of a judicial verdict.

The media justifies and minimizes the radical actions of the "Kaplanists," including road blockages and threats by reservists. Television channels frequently described road blockages as "popular resistance" or "high-quality protest," rather than focusing on lawbreaking and anarchy, which intensified the sense of double standards. After October 7, the government accused the media of maintaining its primary focus on the guilt of the political leadership while minimizing the professional accountability of the heads of the intelligence services and the IDF, who are part of the old establishment and the deep state.

2. The Struggle for Control and Containment

The government and its supporters have taken active steps to weaken or neutralize what they characterize as the left-liberal media deep state. The government actively supports and develops new, more right-leaning media outlets, such as Channel 14, which openly declares its support for the coalition and serves as the ideological counterpart to the traditional channels. The goal is to break the monopoly on narrative.

There have been attempts to legislate influence over media regulation or to expand ministerial authority over the media council, which critics characterized as "politicization" and an "assault on freedom of the press," while the government called it the "democratization" of the media space. The government and its supporters make active use of social media platforms, including X and Telegram, to communicate directly with their electorate, bypassing the traditional media outlets they consider hostile.

FROM A POLITICAL THRILLER

The Newsroom of Channel 13, 11:00 p.m. The Editor-in-Chief Bursts into the Editing Suite:

Editor: *"We change the lead story. The leak from the Prime Minister's office goes to the front page. The generals' accountability goes to the end of the broadcast."*

Journalist: *"But the facts..."*

Editor: *"Facts are what we decide to show."*

The screen splits in two: on the left, the headline reads "Netanyahu Undermined Security"; on the right, an alternative channel displays "Deep State Conceals the Failure of October 7."

A viewer at home flips between channels. In his eyes, there is exhaustion. He no longer knows whom to believe.

***

The principal argument of the deep state has always been the same: "We are professionals; we know better than politicians." On October 7, this myth was drenched in blood. It emerged that the "professional caste," which had spent all its time fighting its own government and the judicial reform, had missed the enemy at its very doorstep.

The deep state lost the fence, lost the intelligence, and lost the public's trust. Yet instead of resigning, its members deployed their resources to shift the blame onto the political leadership. This is the supreme form of bureaucratic cynicism: to hold full power in matters of security, yet when failure arrives, to hide behind the backs of those whose work they had obstructed.

The Result of the Media War

The struggle on the media front has led to the intensification of social schizophrenia in Israel. Israeli citizens now inhabit two entirely opposing informational realities. Traditional media focuses on threats to democracy, corruption, and the trial of Netanyahu. Alternative media and social networks focus on the government's achievements, the struggle against the deep state, and what they characterize as the unjust persecution of the Prime Minister.

In this war, the media are not neutral observers but active participants in the conflict over the future of Israel.

The Origins of the Conflict: Before October 7, 2023

Factor	Deep State Objective	Government Objective
Criminal cases	Neutralize Netanyahu through legal prosecution (cases 1000, 2000, 4000).	Delegitimize the judicial system by accusing it of political hatred and fabrication of cases.
Judicial reform	Preserve their unlimited powers (judicial oversight, the 'reasonableness' doctrine).	Limit the power of the HCJ and restore the sovereignty of the Knesset (the elected authority).
Protests	Overthrow the government through the 'Kaplanist Intifada,' using civil disobedience and blackmail with reservists.	Suppress the protest movement, declare it a coup and anti-democratic anarchy.

The Struggle for Power

The essence of Israel's most profound political crisis is the conflict between the elected government, led by Benjamin Netanyahu, and the unelected deep state, comprising the senior legal, security, and media elites. This is an existential struggle for power and national identity, which reached its apex following October 7.

Several factors defined the conflict prior to October 7. Regarding criminal cases: the deep state's goal was to neutralize Netanyahu through legal prosecution, using Cases 1000, 2000, and 4000; the government's goal was to delegitimize the legal system by accusing it of political bias and fabrication of cases.

Regarding judicial reform: the deep state's goal was to preserve its unlimited authority through judicial review and the "reasonableness" doctrine; the government's goal was to limit the power of the Supreme Court and restore the sovereignty of the Knesset as the elected authority.

Regarding the protests: the deep state's goal was to topple the government through the "Kaplanist intifada," using civil disobedience and blackmail through reservists; the government's goal was to suppress the protest movement by declaring it a putsch and anti-democratic anarchy.

The Apex of the Crisis: After October 7, 2023

The catastrophe of October 7 did not bring this war to an end; rather, it transferred it into a phase of struggle over blame and responsibility.

The Current State of Affairs: End of 2025

The struggle remains in a state of trench warfare, in which neither side has achieved complete victory. The government succeeded in replacing the heads of the security forces, specifically those of the IDF and the Shin Bet, and improved coordination and the working atmosphere. The government failed to fully neutralize the Legal Advisor and did not achieve full restoration of its sovereignty, continuing to operate under legal pressure and the threat of court intervention. The reputation and authority of the deep state have been severely undermined by the failure of October 7, the admission of error by the heads of the intelligence services, and the ongoing investigation concerning the Military Advocate General. This calls into question their moral superiority and impartiality. Society has remained ideologically divided. The deep state lost its security symbols, specifically Bar and Halevi, but retained legal leverage through the Supreme Court and the Legal Advisor, continuing its war against the elected authority.

The Supreme Court: The Principal Danger

Jurist Dr. Chaim Shayn commented on the bleak remarks made by former Supreme Court President Aharon Barak concerning the end of Israeli democracy.

> *"Aharon Barak is right that Israeli democracy is in danger, because a small group that was never elected is attempting to seize power and govern Israel in a clearly undemocratic manner. This group, which has been concentrated in the Supreme Court for generations, believes that voters are limited in their intelligence, incapable of making decisions and governing the country, and therefore the judicial system must make decisions in their place. That is the end of democracy. Those who threaten democracy are those who believe they were destined to hold power by birthright, although they were never elected."*

Shayn continued: "When an elected body, the Knesset or the government, attempts to pass laws and advance initiatives, and the Supreme Court, using its authority as the highest judicial organ, obstructs this, it constitutes an attack on democracy. It is impossible to govern a country when an elected body is forced to ask itself what decision several Supreme Court justices would have made on every issue it attempts to resolve. That is not democracy. The Knesset was elected to lead; the government was elected to lead; and in a democratic country, there can be no competition for leadership."

"What concerns Israeli leftists, and Supreme Court justices among them, most of all, is that a man named Benjamin Netanyahu, who was presumed to belong to their camp, an educated man who speaks excellent English, suddenly appears alongside a group they regard as beneath them and seizes the country of 'their fathers,' and they are not prepared to forgive this. That is why they exert every effort to harm him. They have been doing this for years, and yet it does not help them, and he is re-elected at every election. I believe the right will win a major victory in the next election as well. This drives them to madness, and they exert every effort to prevent it."

This war, which has become the driving force of Israeli politics, is far from over.

***

FROM A POLITICAL THRILLER

November 2024. Underground Command Post.

The War Is Ongoing.

Netanyahu meets with the coalition.

Smotrich: *"Now is the right time. The people can see who is responsible for the failure."*

Ben-Gvir: *"We bring back the reform. In full."*

Montage: in Baharav-Miara's office, a stack of petitions to the Supreme Court. She calls the Chief Justice: "If they touch even a single article, we block everything."

Voiceover: *"After October 7, they thought the deep state was broken. They were wrong."*

Conclusion: Myth or Eternal Guardian?

In the end, the "deep state" is like that proverbial father-in-law in the Jewish joke: no one has ever seen him, yet everyone is certain it is he who is responsible for the over-salted soup, the car that will not start, and Netanyahu's continued hold on power. Some cry: "It exists! Here is the proof: Gali Baharav-Miara has once again blocked the law on the deportation of terrorists' families!" Others shrug: "These are simply independent institutions doing the work the law requires of them." And still others add in a whisper: "Quiet, it can hear us." The truth, as always, lies somewhere in the middle.

The deep state is not a secret lodge in the basement of the Knesset, where judges, generals, and legal advisors drink coffee and decide the fate of the country. It is rather the inertia of the system: the bureaucracy, the courts, the army, and the intelligence services, which have grown accustomed to operating according to rules written before the current ministers had learned to read. When revolutionaries come to power and seek to overturn everything in a single night, this inertia suddenly transforms into the "deep state." When the same people have held power for decades, this same inertia magically becomes the "healthy conservatism of institutions."

The conflict with the "deep state" is a battle for Israel's very right to be sovereign. Either power will return to those chosen by the people, or Israel will remain the hostage of a caste of the "enlightened," leading the country toward the abyss while confidently holding a helm they broke long ago. The end of 2025 shows: the people are beginning to awaken, but the deep state still hopes that the rain in Jerusalem will wash away the traces of their betrayal.

So, dear readers, if tomorrow Gali Baharav-Miara is finally dismissed, or conversely, Ben-Gvir is removed from office for defying the court, do not rush to cry "Victory!" or "Conspiracy!" She has transformed herself from a consultant into a dictator with veto power. This is the essence of the "deep state": the creation of a body that stands above the law while claiming to protect the rule of law. The system of checks and balances has been transformed into a system of strangleholds and blockades.

Simply remember: the deep state is a mirror. It does not reveal what hides in the dark corridors of power; it reveals how ready we ourselves are to live by the rules we considered sacred only yesterday.

The deep state is a virus in the operating system of the state. It has convinced half the population that defending the bureaucracy is itself a form of patriotism. October 7 became the moment when the "deep state" collided with a reality it could neither "litigate" nor "commentate away" in a television studio. Terrorists do not recognize the jurisdiction of the Supreme Court.

Imagine: A Retired Shin Bet Official Sits in the Studio of Channel 12 and Declares:

Retiree: *"Netanyahu is destroying democracy!"*
Host: *(nodding) "Absolutely!"*
A viewer at home thinks: "And who destroyed the fence on October 7?"
Retiree: *"We are the guardians of the state!"*
Viewer: "Guardians? You nearly lost it!"

And so it goes, every evening. The deep state is not a myth. It simply loves television airtime very much.

***

Truly, the Israeli deep state is a powerful factor in the schizophrenia of society: it is capable of paralyzing an elected government, creating a situation in which the decisions of the cabinet and the Knesset are not implemented, while conducting its own policy in the interests of the liberal left elite. In doing so, the deep state represents a threat to democracy and to the country's ability to confront its existential enemies. Its activists obstruct Israel from being a strong Jewish state.

Retirees from the deep state, drawn from the media, the army, the Shin Bet, the courts, and the prosecution, constitute the leading group of Kaplanists, putschists, and commentators on the studios of left-leaning channels 11, 12, and 13. This is a genuine information ring. Former Shin Bet directors and generals, trained at the "right" foundations, create in studio settings an illusion of expert consensus. The ordinary citizen hears the same thing from ten mouths and falls into a state of induced submission. To disagree with the opinion of this caste is to be declared "an enemy of democracy." This is a classic inversion of meaning.

The phenomenon of "retirees in studios" constitutes an information blockade. Former intelligence chiefs, trained at the "right" Western foundations, create an illusion of expert consensus. The ordinary citizen sees on television ten individuals adorned with epaulets and decorations, all saying in unison: "Netanyahu is a security threat." This is induced submission: the authority of rank deployed as an instrument of political manipulation. These people no longer serve the state; they serve the System, which guarantees their caste the preservation of its privileges.

However, not all retirees belong to the deep state! Take care of your nerves. For even if the deep state does exist, it certainly does not read your tweets. At least not officially.

FROM A POLITICAL THRILLER

End of 2025. Jerusalem in the Rain.

Netanyahu stands on the balcony of his residence, gazing at the lights of the city.
Voiceover (his thoughts): *"They lost the fence. They lost the intelligence. They lost the trust. But they still hold the courts."*
The camera rises higher: the city is divided. One half displays the flags of Israel; the other carries placards bearing the words "Rule of Law."
Voiceover: *"The war is not over. The next move belongs to the people."*

The screen goes dark: "To be continued."

CHAPTER 23
THE LEFT DOCTRINE OF THE ARMY

Introduction

This is the story of how the IDF was transformed from a fearsome "machine of destruction" into a "high-tech police force with a humanitarian inclination."

The left doctrine of the army is not a planning error. It is a deliberate amputation of aggression. The IDF was taught to be ashamed of its strength. And on October 7, the enemy came precisely for that: for our bashful, Harvard-educated generals who, until the very last moment, believed in the "rationality of evil."

The Israeli Army was taught for decades that victory was impossible and that escalation was evil. The old doctrine of Ben-Gurion, which called for transferring war to enemy territory and achieving its complete defeat, was replaced by "conflict management." The IDF ceased to be a sword and became a shield, and moreover a shield constrained by legal limits. Generals were taught to believe that a "smart" fence and electronic sensors could replace fighting spirit and the will to go all the way. This was technological fetishism, behind which lay a fear of the political responsibility required for genuine victory.

Israel's military doctrine, formulated in the late 1940s and early 1950s under the leadership of David Ben-Gurion, was grounded in harsh realism: the Arabs would not accept the existence of a Jewish state, and therefore the goal of defense was not merely to repel aggression but to construct a system of deterrence so powerful that the enemy would not even contemplate war. Given the absence of strategic depth, limited resources, and the numerical superiority of the adversary, the doctrine encompassed three key pillars: deterrence, early warning, and decisive victory, with the mandatory transfer of combat operations to enemy territory, including a preemptive strike when necessary. This was not an abstract theory; precisely this logic underpinned the brilliant victory of the Six-Day War.

Imagine the year 1967. The Six-Day War. Israeli tanks racing across the Sinai, aircraft delivering preemptive strikes, Arab armies annihilated within days. This was a victory built on the doctrine of David Ben-Gurion: deterrence through fear, early warning, and decisive victory with the transfer of battle to enemy territory. Ben-Gurion, despite political differences, had adopted Vladimir Jabotinsky's idea of the "Iron Wall," an impregnable force behind which the Jews would build their state.

But in the 1990s, everything changed. How did the "liberal virus" paralyze the military instinct? The Oslo Accords brought with them the euphoria of a "New Middle East." Shimon Peres promised peace through concessions. This wave penetrated the offices of IDF generals. The army, always apolitical, began to view Palestinian terror not as an existential threat but as a "manageable risk." Territories became "disputed," and concessions became the path to reconciliation. Thus was born the "left conception": a retreat from preemptive strikes and a reliance on restraint instead of victory. The military leadership ceased to see the enemy for what it was, namely a predator, and began to see it as it was convenient to describe in liberal salons: a socioeconomic problem. The emphasis shifted from "destruction of the enemy's force" to "high-tech monitoring." It was believed that a camera on a fence was more important than a finger on a trigger. The army was transformed not so much into a shield as into an instrument of the political process. The culmination was the catastrophe of October 7, 2023.

This chapter tells the story of how the illusory peace-loving "left doctrine" penetrated the innermost sanctum of Israeli security, why it weakened the army's readiness, and how attempts to return to the classical principles of Ben-Gurion and Jabotinsky clash with the inertia of the system. For in the end, as history has shown, the Iron Wall works only when it is truly made of iron, and not of diplomatic illusions.

From the Iron Wall to the Illusions of Peace

The idea of the "Iron Wall," an impregnable force behind which the Jews would build their state, originated with Vladimir Jabotinsky, whose 1923 essay predicted that peace would come only when the Arabs became convinced of the impossibility of destroying Israel. Ben-Gurion, although a political opponent of the revisionists, adopted this iron logic in matters of security and made it the foundation of the IDF.

However, in the 1990s, under the influence of the Oslo Accords, a quiet but profound shift occurred in the supreme command of the army. The "peace process," that euphoria of a "New Middle East" promised by Shimon Peres, penetrated the offices of generals. The army, traditionally apolitical, began to perceive Palestinian terror not as an existential threat but as a "manageable risk," amenable to negotiation and concessions. Arab states? They were supposedly no longer dreaming of a dash to the sea. Territories? They were "disputed," and could and should be surrendered for the sake of peace, since the partner across the table was now "moderate." Thus was born what right-wing critics called the "left conception" in the IDF: a retreat from preemptive strikes, a reliance on containment rather than decisive victory, and the belief that concessions would diminish rather than whet the enemy's appetite. The army was transformed into an instrument not only of defense but of the political process, with tragic consequences whose culmination was the failure of October 7, 2023.

The Doctrine of Deterrence

Traditional Israeli deterrence doctrine was built on a simple principle: the enemy must fear even the thought of an attack. This implied not passive defense but the active creation of an "Iron Wall," a military force so powerful that aggression became suicidal. Preemptive strikes, the transfer of war to enemy territory, decisive victory: all of this worked in 1967, when Israel destroyed a coalition of Arab armies in six days.

In the 1950s through the 1970s, the IDF was a machine of victory: preemptive strikes, transfer of combat to enemy territory, no illusions about "peace now." The army was an instrument of survival.

But after Oslo in the 1990s, the doctrine began to evolve, or to degrade. The "peace process" brought hope for a "new Middle East" in which concessions would lead to reconciliation. The senior IDF command, previously strictly apolitical, gradually absorbed this ideology: Palestinian terror was not an existential threat but a "manageable risk"; Arab states no longer dreamed of a "dash to the sea"; territories could be surrendered for the sake of peace.

Thus was born what in Israel is known as the "Conception," an analogue to the ill-famed "conception" that preceded Yom Kippur 1973: the transition from deterrence through victory to deterrence through restraint. Instead of eliminating the threat, it was to be "managed": economic concessions to Gaza in the form of work permits and supplies, "quiet for quiet," periodic "mowing the grass" operations, limited operations to trim Hamas's wings without uprooting the organization.

The army began to position itself not only as the nation's shield but as a progressive social institution. Women were integrated into combat roles, with mixed battalions such as "Caracal" from the 2000s onward and female tank crews on the Merkava from 2017 to 2022. The focus was placed on being the "most moral army in the world," with legal oversight of operations and concern about international courts. Ground forces were reduced in favor of technology: the "smart fence," missile defense systems, and drones, rather than a mass of troops on the border.

Officers observed all of this. Many discussed it privately: "We are guarding the process, not winning." Some resisted, warning of unpreparedness, as General Yitzhak Brick had done for years. Within the General Staff, an environment developed in which an officer's career depended not on his boldness in battle but on his "correct" views. Those who spoke of victory, like General Yitzhak Brick, were declared alarmists and marginalized. The result was that instead of warriors, the system produced "security managers" in uniform. The system promoted those who accepted the new reality: careers depended on adaptation to "restraint," inclusion, and international legitimacy. Those who protested loudly often left the service or failed to rise. A quiet selection: the army remained professional, but its priorities had shifted.

This "Left Conception" Led to a Chain of Changes in the IDF:

The integration of women into combat units, with a focus on gender equality, LGBT rights, and minorities, was promoted as social progress. However, critics, including retired generals, argued that this diverted resources from pure combat training and lowered standards in the name of "inclusion."

The IDF increasingly became an arbiter in internal disputes, ranging from the judicial reform to the evacuation of settlements. Generals made public statements on political matters, which undermined the image of an apolitical "people's army."

The IDF's legal corps, headed by figures such as Yifat Tomer-Yerushalmi, acquired veto power over operations due to concerns about the Hague Tribunal. Field commanders began to "look over their shoulders at the prosecutor," fearing investigations for "disproportionality," which is directly accused of slowing decisive action.

Political correctness in recruitment and the integration of ultra-Orthodox men and Arabs were worthy goals, but in the view of critics, they diluted the fighting spirit and cohesion of elite units.

A classic example was the policy of "something to lose": Hamas was given an economy so that it would "become moderate." The result was that over fifteen years, Hamas built an army under the IDF's nose, while deterrence was eroded.

FROM A POLITICAL THRILLER

The General's Seminar

A Scene Describing the Cognitive Gap Between Reality and Doctrine.

Setting: *The Conference Room of the General Staff (The Kirya). The smell of expensive coffee. On the tables, tablets displaying charts on the "economic stability of Gaza."*

Characters: *A Public Relations (PR) officer (a young ambitious girl) and the Combat Colonel (a division commander of the "old school").*

PR officer: *"Colleagues, we must understand: the concept of 'decisive victory' is outdated. In the twenty-first century, war is a question of legitimacy. If we strike too hard, we will lose the support of Biden and Brussels."*

Colonel: *"But Hamas is digging tunnels directly beneath our posts! My scouts can hear the sound of jackhammers!"*

PR officer: *(condescendingly) "That is the 'sound of industrialization.' They need to feed their people. Sinwar is a rational actor. He understands that Qatari money matters more than war. Our task is not to provoke them. We are building a 'smart fence' that will make war impossible."*

Colonel: *"You are relying on sensors? What if they disable them five minutes before the attack? Who will be shooting?"*

PR officer: *"The legal department will be shooting, if we violate 'proportionality.' We must cultivate the 'humane soldier.' Our army is, above all, values."*

Colonel: *(quietly) "Our army is, above all, survival. When they pour through that 'smart fence,' your values will not stop a bullet."*

PR officer: *(making a note in his pad) "Colonel, you display 'outdated thinking.' You need to complete a course at the Wexner Foundation on the subject of 'The Army in Civil Society.' You do not fit the modern conception."*

And this "left conception" did not remain confined to the offices of generals. It seeped into the public sphere, where the army began to position itself not only as the nation's shield but as a progressive social institution worthy of headlines in the liberal press. In the Oslo era and the years that followed, the IDF actively promoted the image of the "most moral army in the world," in which combat readiness coexisted with an emphasis on inclusion and tolerance.

The left-wing press enthusiastically covered stories about the integration of people with special needs: the program "Special in Uniform," launched in 2014, allowed young people with **Down syndrome and other disabilities** to serve in auxiliary roles on bases, in kitchens, and in logistics. Soldiers such as Ortal Butvia from 2020 to 2023 and Sergeant Zohar Silok became the subjects of media reports: "A Girl with Down Syndrome Serves in the IDF!" ran the headlines in JNS, NDTV, and even on the IDF's Facebook page. Noble? Without question. Yet many asked: does this not distract from the primary mission, namely victory over the enemy? The dominant focus of the press coverage of the IDF was striking.

Schizophrenia Through Feminism and Social Marketing

The IDF of the Oslo era became a prisoner of its own pursuit of moral superiority in the eyes of the West. Even more conspicuous were the female tank crews. From 2017 to 2018, a pilot program was launched, and from 2022 onward, permanent all-female crews operated Merkava IVs along the Egyptian border. The press was jubilant: "The First Women in Tanks!" "A Historic Breakthrough in Gender Equality!" Chief of the General Staff Aviv Kochavi praised them: "They will fulfill the mission professionally and successfully."

Then came October 7, 2023: these very crews, from the Caracal Battalion, were the first to engage Hamas near Kibbutz Holit and Sufa, and distinguished themselves by destroying dozens of terrorists over seventeen hours of continuous combat. The Times of Israel, Haaretz, and Ynet sang their praises: "Female Tank Crews Saved the Kibbutzim!" "The World's First Female Tank Crews in Real Combat." The case of the Caracal Battalion and the female tank crews was the pinnacle of tragic irony.

The girls demonstrated extraordinary courage and proved that they could fight like lions. But their heroism became a smokescreen for systemic failure. The press seized upon this "feminist breakthrough" in order to avoid answering the question: why were the tank crews left alone against hundreds of militants? Why did the "industry of progress" substitute itself for the "industry of defense"?

Hamas came to kill not "gender quotas" but Jews. Inclusion did not blind the enemy; it blinded us. The heroism was unquestionable, but it simultaneously underscored the irony: while the press celebrated "inclusion," combat readiness in the "quiet" sectors, including Gaza, was atrophying.

If an army becomes too "progressive" for magazine covers, it risks becoming insufficiently lethal for the battlefield. After all, Jabotinsky's "Iron Wall" is not a wall made of rainbow flags and press releases about tolerance. This evolution from "victory at any cost" to "management and inclusion" is a classic example of how the Oslo ideology, through the schizophrenia of consciousness at all levels of society, dissolved the classical doctrine of a victorious army and the nation's instinct for self-preservation.

FROM A POLITICAL THRILLER

War of Posts and Real Blood

A Scene Exposing the Gap Between the Press Release and the Reality at the Fence.

Setting: *The IDF Spokesperson's Department. A modern office, monitors displaying social media engagement statistics.*

Characters: *A PR Officer (a young and ambitious woman) and a Lieutenant Colonel Operations Officer (covered in dust, just arrived from the border).*

PR Officer: *(cheerfully) "Look, our post about the female tank crews has received 50,000 reposts in the United States! We are breaking stereotypes! Even CNN wants to do a feature about the 'most feminist army in the world.' This is a huge success for Israel's image."*

Lieutenant Colonel: *(grimly) "You would do better to produce a feature about the fact that these girls at the border are short of ammunition and that surveillance operatives are reporting suspicious holes in the fence."*

PR Officer: *(dismissively) "Why be so negative? Fear and 'holes' don't sell. People need positivity. They need to see that we are part of the Western world, that we have inclusion, that we are 'just like them.' This is our principal defense: international sympathy."*

Lieutenant Colonel: *(quietly) "Our principal defense is when the enemy is afraid to lift his head. But right now the enemy is watching your posts and laughing. He sees not tanks; he sees a 'social experiment.' And when he decides to put it to the test, your reposts will not cover the infantry."*

The consequences became visible on October 7: the "Conception" collapsed. Hamas showed no fear of the IDF's power, because it had observed weakness. Israel had been deterring itself, not the enemy. Following the catastrophe, many voices, including experts from JISS and MEF, have called for a return to the classical approach: victory instead of management, preemptive strikes instead of "mowing the grass."

But inertia is powerful: even in 2025, debates continue as to whether "restraint" should be wholly abandoned or whether doing so would lead to escalation. For in the Middle East, fear is the strongest currency, but the illusions of peace come at a steep price.

Thus, the "left doctrine" transformed the IDF's traditional role from that of an "army oriented toward victory and security" into the role of a "social and liberal institution." The price proved excessive.

From the 'Small Army' to Vulnerability

One of the key tendencies driven by the Oslo "peace" doctrine and stringent budgetary austerity was the systematic reduction of the "mass" of ground forces and reserves from the 1990s onward. This was not accidental: following the collapse of the Soviet Union and the diminution of the threat from regular Arab armies, generals became convinced that Israel could afford to transition to a model of a "small, smart, and technological army." The emphasis was placed on aviation, intelligence, cyber capabilities, and precision weapons, rather than on massive armored divisions and millions of reservists.

The process began under Ehud Barak, both as Chief of the General Staff in the 1990s and as Prime Minister, continued under Dan Halutz with his emphasis on the air force, and subsequently intensified under Benny Gantz from 2011 to 2015, Gadi Eisenkot from 2015 to 2019, and Aviv Kochavi from 2019 to 2023. These Chiefs of the General Staff consistently reduced the regular ground forces, the number of tanks and artillery pieces, and the reserve brigades, reallocating budgets toward "smart" systems: Iron Dome, cyber units, drones, and multilayered missile defense.

Specific Facts Regarding Reductions, Based on Open Sources:

Tanks: In the 1990s, Israel possessed thousands of tanks including reserves. By 2023, the active fleet had been reduced to approximately 2,200 to 2,500 units, primarily Merkava variants of various models, with hundreds in reserve or storage. Major General Yitzhak Brick accused Gantz of "crossing a red line" by removing hundreds of tanks from the service inventory of the ground forces.

Artillery and Reserves: Regular career officers and soldiers were reduced, with a target of 40,000 career personnel. Reserve training was cut and brigades were disbanded. The Kochavi "Tnufa" (Momentum) plan emphasized "multilayered" integration across air, sea, and cyber domains, but at the expense of mass on the ground.

Total Strength: Active personnel stood at approximately 169,500 in 2023; reserves numbered approximately 465,000 on paper, but the actual combat readiness of the reserves before October 7 was assessed as "average" or below average, due to reduced training exercises.

Israel obtained a high-technology army, the best in the world in missile defense, intelligence, and precision strikes, but with critically diminished capacity for prolonged ground operations, the holding of territory, and mass mobilization. When "mass" was needed for the rapid suppression of an invasion, there simply was not enough.

The concept of the "small and smart" army proved to be a lethal illusion. In the pursuit of economy and technology, left-wing reformers destroyed the mass of ground divisions, believing that aviation and special forces would resolve all challenges.

October 7 demonstrated: no sensors can replace a soldier in a trench. When the "smart fence" fell within fifteen minutes, it became clear that behind it lay emptiness. The doctrine of "deterring" Hamas through economic incentives was not a strategy; it was a capitulation of reason before comfort. We built an army for parades and precision operations, then found ourselves facing an existential war of annihilation.

The lesson of October 7, 2023 served as a tragic confirmation: the sudden Hamas attack, involving approximately 3,000 terrorists, paralyzed the south for hours. Regular forces were dispersed and insufficient; reserves mobilized a record approximately 300,000 personnel, with initial turnout exceeding 120 percent due to shock, but this took time, and kibbutzim and bases were held by civilian response teams and individual soldiers. The shortage of manpower on the border, reduced patrols, and faith in "technology," specifically a fenced barrier with sensors that Hamas simply bypassed using bulldozers, had left the country vulnerable before a low-technology but mass invasion.

The period of the 1990s under the leadership of Y. Rabin, S. Peres, and E. Barak saw the elimination of part of the tank divisions and budget cuts, along with the idea of the "small and smart army." The period from 2000 to 2010 under A. Sharon and E. Olmert saw the disbanding of reserve formations and the diminishment of the role of mass ground forces, with an emphasis on special forces, the air force, and missile defense, specifically Iron Dome. The period from 2015 to 2020 under the Gideon Plan, led by G. Eisenkot, saw a reduction of the reserves by approximately 100,000 personnel, a reduction of career military to approximately 40,000, and the elimination of tank and artillery battalions, with resources transferred to cyber and intelligence. The period from 2020 to 2025 under A. Kochavi and H. Halevi saw shortened service periods, a reduced number of reservists, and a further shift of emphasis toward drones and missile defense.

Criticism from retired generals, including Brick and HaCohen among others, had been sounding for years: 'We fed the illusion that drones and missile defense could replace tank divisions.' After October 7, the IDF began the reverse process: expanding the reserves, returning tanks from storage, and creating new brigades. But the price had already been paid. The illusion of the 'small army' collapsed beneath the treads of reality.

In the end, the generals had dreamed of a "small, smart army," something like an iPhone: thin, shiny, and expensive. But on October 7, Hamas placed a call: "Hello, is this reality? Your iPhone has no signal in Gaza, because there are bulldozers there instead of Wi-Fi." It turned out that in a war in the Middle East, sometimes what is needed is not a smartphone but a good old tank, large, loud, and in sufficient numbers that the enemy does not even consider making a call.

The Foundation of Brainwashing

How did it come about that the entire officer corps suddenly began speaking the language of left-wing NGOs? The answer lies in the promotion system. Through structures such as the Wexner Foundation, the senior officer corps underwent a process of "cleansing" from national values. Officers were taken to Harvard not to teach them to fight but to instill in them "liberal sensitivities." As a result, an ideological incest developed within the General Staff: only those who believed in the "rationality of the enemy" and the "necessity of a Palestinian state" were permitted to advance. Those who, like General Yitzhak Brick, cried out about the unpreparedness of the ground forces, were declared marginals and reactionaries.

The Wexner Foundation is an American philanthropic organization founded in 1983 by billionaire Leslie Wexner. The foundation's official mission is the development of leadership qualities among Jewish professionals and volunteers in North America and among senior public servants in Israel.

Principal Programs:

The Wexner Heritage Program: A two-year intensive program for volunteer leaders of Jewish communities in North America, combining the study of Jewish history, texts, values, and leadership skills. The Wexner Graduate Fellowship and Davidson Scholars Program: Support for graduate students and professionals in Jewish education and community service. The Wexner Field Fellowship: A three-year program for Jewish professionals in the middle age range of thirty-seven to fifty years, with a focus on leadership and Jewish learning. Programs for Israel: These previously included the Wexner Israel Fellowship, comprising internships at Harvard Kennedy School for Israeli officials, and Wexner Senior Leaders for senior civil servants. Many of these programs sent promising Israeli IDF officers, police officials, Shin Bet employees, and Foreign Ministry personnel for training in the United States.

The Foundation presents itself as pluralistic and non-political, emphasizing investments in "strong Jewish leadership" and connections between North America and Israel.

Critics Accuse the Foundation of:

A left-wing bias, arguing that the programs promote "liberal" or "anti-democratic" ideas and encourage officials to disregard the directives of elected politicians. Interference in Israel's internal affairs, as the Foundation funded the training of hundreds of Israeli IDF generals and agency heads, which in the view of critics creates a network of influence loyal to external interests. Cooperation with left-wing organizations, with alleged connections to groups such as Breaking the Silence cited. The Foundation is accused of advancing left-wing progressive ideas, ignoring national interests, and undermining the government.

The program is accused of ideological indoctrination through the imposition of a specific ideology, the suppression of critical thinking, and the silencing of dissent: participants are immersed in the American progressivism of Harvard, with an emphasis on "human rights," "proportionality," "dialogue," and "liberal values," which dissolve the firm doctrine of Ben-Gurion and Jabotinsky. The result is that generals return with a belief in "manageable risk" rather than decisive victory, in "quiet for quiet" with Hamas, and in the idea that technology can replace "mass" of troops.

How the Foundation Reprogrammed the Army

October 7 was not merely the negligence of individual generals or intelligence operatives. It was the culmination of a systemic shift in the thinking of the IDF's elite, which had been taking place for decades under external influence. And the key channel of this influence was the Wexner Foundation program. This was not simply education. It was the recruitment of Israel's elite under the guise of an academic program.

The curriculum featured lectures on "liberal leadership," "rethinking the nation-state," "models of minority rights in armed conflicts," and "the transition from military response to civil mechanisms." The values inculcated were humanism over force, retreat over victory, and capitulation as moral superiority. This amounted to the ideological dismantling of the elite: generals were explained that war was an outdated anachronism; officers were instilled with the belief that a soldier must "not violate rights"; judges were programmed to regard international law as more important than Israeli law; future ministerial cadres were convinced that Israel was merely one among many and must "stop considering itself exceptional."

The result was an elite programmed to lose, officials trained in capitulation, and an army mentally disarmed long before the breach, whether physical or ideological, occurred.

The Wexner Injection: A Forge of Obedient Generals

One of the most effective technologies for altering the DNA of Israeli command was the Wexner Foundation. Under the guise of a prestigious internship at Harvard, the best IDF officers, police commanders, and civil servants were for years immersed in the "sterile" environment of left-liberal academicism. This was a classic intellectual colonization. An officer accustomed to the harsh logic of war in the Middle East was placed in an atmosphere where he was taught that force is weakness and national pride is an atavism. Instead of tactics for the elimination of the enemy, they were taught "theories of inclusivity" and "dialogue in conditions of conflict." Upon returning, the "Wexner graduates" formed a closed caste within the General Staff. If one had not passed through this filter, if one did not share their "progressive" agenda, the path upward was closed. We obtained a military leadership more concerned with how it appeared in the eyes of Cambridge professors than with how to defend the border with Gaza. This was not merely "education"; it was a viral attack on the chain of command. These were the very men who, on October 7, in the first critical hours, could not take the decision to respond with force, because their minds had been paralyzed by years of training in humaneness toward those who had come to kill them.

Among the alumni of the Wexner Foundation are hundreds of generals, intelligence operatives, judges, and officials, by various estimates between 500 and 650 individuals, whose decisions shaped the strategy of the state. **The Wexner Foundation was raising a new elite:** not warriors but bureaucrats, not strategists but humanists. Instead of force, restraint. Instead of victory, a ceasefire. Instead of an army, a "society of dialogue." Instead of an enemy, a "partner in the peace process." They disarmed the IDF mentally, long before the enemy breached the fence. They studied in the wrong place and learned the wrong things. Their goal was not the defense of Israel but its dismantling. And they nearly succeeded.

In 2023, Ben-Gvir, as Minister of National Security, prohibited police officers from participating in Wexner Foundation programs, calling the foundation "radically left-wing" and part of the "deep state." Politicians directly blamed "Wexnerites" for "reprogramming" the elite, from the politicization of the army to the blindness that preceded October 7. The program concluded in 2024, following a break with Harvard over anti-Israel protests, but its network of former students remains powerful.

So, while ordinary soldiers sweat on training grounds, the IDF's elite flies to Harvard to drink coffee with professors who teach that "strength is not tanks but dialogue and inclusion." They return, and suddenly Hamas is not a "strategic threat" but a "partner in conflict management." The Wexner Foundation is as if an American uncle decided to "improve" the Israeli army by gifting it a year in a liberal summer camp. The result? October 7 showed that the enemy was not impressed by Harvard diplomas. He simply came with machine guns.

In the end, the "reprogramming" was not a conspiracy in a basement but a quiet erosion: through prestigious fellowships, networks, and "soft power," the army's elite absorbed ideas alien to the classical doctrine. The consequences are still being dealt with to this day.

FROM A POLITICAL THRILLER

Diploma Versus Gunsight

Setting: *The Office of a Senior Official in the General Staff. A diploma from a prestigious foreign program hangs on the wall.*

Characters: *A General Who Is a Graduate of the Program and an Operations Officer.*

Officer: *"We are recording anomalous activity at the border. Hamas has deployed equipment. Aviation must be scrambled for a show of force."*

General: *(stroking the framed diploma) "Listen, that is overly linear thinking. In my last seminar in Boston, we examined the model of 'reducing friction through economic incentives.' If we scramble planes, we will destroy trust."*

Officer: *(astonished) "Trust with whom? With terrorists?"*

General: *"With the process. We must think in twenty-first-century categories. Hamas is transforming. They want stability. My diploma confirms that force-based methods in such cases are counterproductive."*

Officer: *"General, your diploma does not know how to shoot. And they do."*

The IDF Stopped Winning

Society asks why the IDF no longer achieves decisive victories as it did in 1967. The answer lies in a combination of political, legal, and ideological factors.

Under Aharon Barak, the Supreme Court began actively intervening in military decisions, imposing limitations on targeted eliminations and requiring mandatory approval for the demolition of houses. This effectively "tied the hands" of commanders and ruled out total victories.

The senior officer corps, thoroughly imbued with a left-liberal worldview through the Wexner Foundation and similar channels, consistently preferred "conflict management" and "containment" over decisive victory.

The IDF was no longer fighting regular armies but hybrid, guerrilla structures such as Hamas and Hezbollah, which used civilians as shields.

Military prosecutors oversaw combat operations. Soldiers were taught to "fight humanely" for the sake of international legitimacy rather than for the sake of victory. Any decisive action immediately triggered investigations and media scandals.

Summary:

- Previously, in 1948, 1967, and 1973, the emphasis was on short wars with decisive victory. From the 1990s onward, the emphasis shifted to "conflict management": the minimization of risks, "containment," and international legitimacy. War became a tool for maintaining the status quo.
- *The IDF assumed the role of a political actor rather than a military machine. An example: in 2005, the army itself participated in the expulsion of Jews from Gush Katif instead of preparing for victory over the enemy.*
- Excessive oversight by military prosecutors in combat operations. Soldiers were taught to "fight humanely" to avoid accusations. Every step was reviewed by the media and international organizations.
- Instead of destroying the enemy, the emphasis was placed on protective technologies.
- After 1973, and especially after Lebanon in 1982, the Israeli elite became afraid of large-scale ground operations.
- **The IDF became an "army for conflict management and defense" rather than an army for decisive victory.**

Who Is Responsible?

- Left-wing governments under Rabin, Peres, Barak, and Olmert bet on peace processes, transforming the army from a force of victory into a "guardian of the process."
- Right-wing governments under Sharon and Netanyahu preferred "containment over victory."

- *The senior IDF leadership became a club of generals who, after leaving the army, moved into politics or business. Their motivation was not victory but "stability" and "international legitimacy."*
- *Legal restrictions on the conduct of war, including lawsuits, threats of the Hague Tribunal, and internal investigations, caused soldiers and officers to fear taking decisive action. Any mistake by the army immediately became a media scandal.*
- Leadership preferred to "minimize losses and risks" rather than fight to the end.

Thus, responsibility for the IDF ceasing to win falls on erroneous strategic decisions, judicial and international pressure, left-wing elites that implanted "humanism instead of victory" into the army, a General Staff that transformed into a bureaucracy, politicians who agreed to management instead of decisive war, and the division of society and elites.

FROM A POLITICAL THRILLER

Safe Degree of Betrayal

How Military Prosecution and Left Doctrine Tie the Commander's Hands.

Setting: *The Command Post of the Gaza Division. On the screens: preparations by terrorists for a breach, one week before October 7.*

Characters: *A Young Major (field commander) and a Legal Advisor in the rank of Captain.*

Major: *"Look at the thermal imager. They are training to capture the watchtower. These are not 'farmers.' Give me authorization for* *a preemptive strike on their training camp while they are all gathered in one place."*

Legal Advisor: *(calmly leafing through a directive) "Major, on what grounds? They are on their own territory. They have the 'right to conduct exercises.' If we open fire, it will be interpreted as escalation."*

Major: *"What escalation? They will be in our bedrooms tomorrow!"*

Legal Advisor: *"You are thinking in terms of 'war,' but we are currently in a mode of 'maintaining stability.' According to the General Staff doctrine, Hamas is a 'restrained force.' Your aggression will destroy months of work to transfer Qatari funds to them. Do you want to be the one who starts a war over 'suspicious maneuvers'?"*

Major: *"I want to be the one who protects the kibbutz!"*

Legal Advisor: *"Protect it upon actual violation of the border. And do not forget: every shot must be 'proportionate.' If a civilian cook happens to be in the camp, you will face a court martial. The left doctrine is not just words, Major. It is your accountability before the Hague."*

The Ideological Filter

The assertion that there are no right-wing generals in the General Staff is explained by a deliberate political purge and ideological selection that began during the Oslo period of the 1990s.

The Beginning of the Purge, 1995

After generals subjected the Oslo Accords to a rigorous military analysis, the left-wing leadership decided to "change the command" and exclude those who refused to blindly accept the Oslo Doctrine.

The IDF underwent a structural left-wing revolution that led to a conscious selection of leadership cadres according to criteria that excluded traditionally right-wing views. The starting point was the suicide of **General Moti Gur** in 1995, with the official version citing cancer. Gur's death coincided with the Oslo period and the deepest social division. His passing symbolized the disappearance of the old Zionist guard, which was willing to fight for every inch of land, yielding its place to a new generation of leaders more inclined toward compromise and politics. **Within the military and political establishment, Gur was one of those who expressed serious doubts about the military aspects of Oslo.** The reaction of the Israeli left-wing leadership to the strategic studies of the generals in 1995 was decisive: 'If the military command refuses to accept the complete transformation of Israeli military strategy, a strategy the army had forged through 45 years of bloody combat, then we will change the military command.' In the Israeli army, the socialists launched a political purge. **From the time of the Rabin government to the present day, all generals appointed to the General Staff have held extremely left-wing political views.** All the most talented military commanders who refused to blindly accept the Oslo Doctrine were blocked at the rank of colonel, or at most brigadier general. They were pushed into the reserves, without promotions in rank, without the ability to influence army strategy. The Chief of the General Staff under Rabin was Ehud Barak. The political purges Barak conducted in the army completely transformed the composition of the General Staff.

All senior officers from the rank of colonel onward were selected on the basis of loyalty to the progressive ideas instilled

through the Wexner Foundation leadership program courses. Officers of a right-wing orientation ceased to be promoted above the rank of lieutenant colonel. In order to advance, it was at minimum required to complete a course in progressivism at a university.

The expression of left-centrist views was perceived as "state-minded thinking." The expression of right-wing ideologically motivated views was regarded as "politicization" and slowed career advancement.

Many senior officers, including Barak, Lipkin-Shahak, Halutz, Gantz, and Ashkenazi, after demobilization joined centrist and left-centrist parties, forming a powerful coalition advocating "security through separation." From their perspective, the Arabs were civilians who needed to be protected; it was better for a thousand Israeli soldiers to die than for a single civilian to be harmed. Therefore, before an offensive, artillery fire should not be used. Homes of terrorists should not be bombed; they should first be warned.

This artificial selection weakened the IDF, making it wholly dependent on left-wing political ideology and bureaucracy, which ultimately rendered the army vulnerable to the October 7 attack.

The Failure of the Defense Doctrine

The failure of the IDF's defense doctrine, which became apparent following the catastrophe of October 7, 2023, was fundamental and multilayered. The doctrine that had dominated Israel's southern frontier for approximately two decades proved incapable of withstanding a large-scale, combined attack. This failure can be summarized as the collapse of the doctrine of "Deterrence, Barrier, and Technological Superiority." Three key elements that formed the basis of border security with the Gaza Strip came under severe criticism.

A. The Collapse of the Deterrence Doctrine

The doctrine assumed that Israel could achieve long-term deterrence of Hamas and other factions by employing a combination of precision military strikes in response to rocket fire and an economic incentive in the form of work permits in Israel and humanitarian assistance. The goal was to maintain "calm in exchange for Gaza."

Hamas exploited this policy to complete its preparations and accumulate resources, disguising its true intentions. Israeli leadership fundamentally misinterpreted the prolonged period of quiet and Hamas's economic interest as an absence of desire to launch a full-scale war, underestimating its jihadist ideological goal.

B. The Failure of the Barrier Doctrine

The IDF relied on a technologically advanced "smart" barrier, featuring underground sensors, cameras, and automated targeting systems, as an impenetrable physical defense. The idea was that the barrier would replace sufficient numbers of personnel on the ground.

As documented by retired Major General Yitzhak Brick, who served as IDF Ombudsman for ten years, it was under the influence of the Barak doctrine that the IDF reduced several reserve divisions and cut its artillery forces in half. Entire armored brigades were disbanded. Between 2003 and 2017, the reserves were cut by 80 percent and the corps of junior officers was effectively gutted. The bulk of the IDF budget and almost all US military assistance were redirected to the air force as the strategic branch of the "small, technological, and lethal" Israel Defense Forces.

Hamas systematically studied the weaknesses of the barrier. On the day of the attack, the barrier was easily and rapidly breached using bulldozers, motorcycles, and drones. The absence of multilayered defense and the minimal number of soldiers at key positions meant that a breach in one place immediately led to the seizure of vast stretches of territory.

C. The Failure of the Technological Intelligence Doctrine

The primary emphasis was placed on technology for information gathering, including signals intelligence, sensors, and cameras, rather than on classical human intelligence networks. Israel considered itself untouchable due to its technological superiority.

Hamas deceived the technological system by using communications blackouts, old-fashioned communication methods, and simple camouflage techniques such as decoys and dummy equipment. The Shin Bet and Military Intelligence fell victim to "conceptual blindness": they filtered out warning signals because those signals did not conform to the dominant conception that Hamas did not want war.

The Left-Wing Nature of the IDF Doctrine

Excessive influence of lawyers. Undue attention by military lawyers to "legality" and "proportionality" in order to avoid accusations of war crimes constrained commanders, making them less decisive and more bureaucratic. Military prosecution was transformed into an oversight body that paralyzed the initiative of commanders. By 2023, the IDF had reached a point at which the fear of the Hague Tribunal had become stronger than the fear of defeat. Soldiers were instilled with the belief that "the purity of arms" was more important than the completion of the mission. This turned the army into a hostage of legal advisors who dictated which targets could be fired upon and which were "disproportionate."

The redistribution of combat forces and resources toward social needs, such as the expansion of female combat positions in Gaza, which required the reallocation of soldiers, distracted the army from its core combat tasks and lowered the overall professional standard.

In the end, the defense doctrine failed because it was too dependent on technology and insufficiently supported by manpower and readiness for decisive action.

General Yitzhak Brick

Major General (Reserve) Yitzhak Brick, who served as IDF Ombudsman for ten years, is known as the principal denouncer of problems within the IDF. He gave candid interviews after despairing of convincing Israel's leadership to address the army's problems.

Brick's Prophecy

"Alongside a barrage of 5,000 rockets, 8,000 commandos equipped from head to toe and trained for the mission of entering by land and capturing several populated communities... They will carry out a massacre there. What is unclear about this?... The army will not be there. The army is too small today!"

"Brick's Prophecy" of July 2023 refers to the warnings of retired Major General Yitzhak Brick, former IDF Ombudsman. This prophecy was confirmed in a terrible manner on October 7. Who is Yitzhak Brick?

Yitzhak Brick is a combat officer who participated in the Yom Kippur War of 1973 and is known as a harsh critic of the state of the Israeli army. Since 2018, he repeatedly published reports and articles warning of systemic problems in the IDF: shortages of training, outdated equipment, bureaucracy, a decline in the combat capability of ground forces, and general unreadiness for a multi-front war. He is often called the "prophet" or "Cassandra" of the Israeli army, because his warnings were ignored by the senior command and by politicians for years.

In July and August of 2023, against the background of protests against the judicial reform and internal divisions in Israel, Brick intensified his warnings. He wrote and spoke in the media, arguing that Israel was not prepared for a real war on multiple fronts simultaneously, including Gaza, Lebanon, Syria, and Iran. He stated that the army relied on technology while ignoring basic soldier training, ammunition stocks, and reserve mobilization. He further argued that the internal division caused by the judicial reform was weakening the army and could lead to catastrophe. Brick was convinced that a "very serious malfunction" had occurred in the IDF's organizational and command culture, one that could "destroy Israel like a nuclear bomb." However, he was consistently dismissed.

- Conflict with Gadi Eisenkot: When Brick submitted a devastating report on the unpreparedness of the northern border, Chief of the General Staff Gadi Eisenkot replied that "inspections are not Brick's job" and later did everything possible to ensure that the report was not transmitted to parliamentary committees or to the Cabinet. Eisenkot could not accept a report showing that the IDF had been "set back thirty years."

- Commanders to whom Brick reported shortages of forces and outdated equipment, such as soldiers conducting surveillance via smartphones, responded: "Make do with what you have, and if you cannot, get out." They preferred not to know about the problems in order to avoid taking responsibility.

Brick's Predictions for a Regional War on Five Fronts:

- Massive bombardment of 3,000 rockets and drones per day, causing severe destruction in the rear.
- Chaos and hysteria among the population, which had not been prepared.
- Rampaging Arab rioters within Israel, in cities such as Acre, Lod, and Haifa, armed with 400,000 weapons.

After the Hamas attack of October 7, 2023, when serious failures in intelligence, defense, and mobilization became apparent, many recalled Brick's words. His warnings proved prophetic: the army was indeed unprepared for such a scenario, which led to thousands of casualties and a protracted war. Israeli media published headlines such as "What Wasn't Brick Listened To?" and "Brick Had Warned."

How Herzi Halevi Weakened the Army

Herzi Halevi served as IDF Chief of the General Staff from January 2023 to March 2025. He permitted the politicization of the army during the protests. Amid mass protests, thousands of reservists, including air force pilots and elite units, announced their refusal to serve in protest against the judicial reform. Halevi did not take firm measures against the "refusers," such as dismissals or disciplinary punishments, which undermined the discipline and combat capability of the army. Instead of declaring that "the army is above politics," he began to empathize with the "pain" of the refusers. This amounted to a psychological demobilization.

When the supreme commander justifies insubordination, the army ceases to be a structure and becomes a debating club. On October 7, that debating club encountered an enemy that does not debate.

The main points of criticism, based on public statements and media reports, are as follows:

- The IDF failed to prevent the largest attack in Israel's history, resulting in approximately 1,200 killed and approximately 250 taken hostage.
- Underestimation of the threat from Hamas, excessive reliance on technology such as the fence and intelligence rather than ground force preparation, and the ignoring of warnings.
- The army was "lulled to sleep" by Hamas's actions and was not prepared.
- Instead, Halevi emphasized the need for unity and warned of the risks that social division posed to the army. This was a "softness" and sympathy toward the protesters, many of whom were from the left-wing and centrist camps.
- Politicization: accusations of a "left-wing bias" and resistance to investigations, including conflicts with the State Comptroller.

- Personnel decisions: the promotion of officers despite the failures of October 7, which led to the blocking of appointments by the Defense Minister.
- He did not require air force and ground forces bases to be prepared for defense against drones, precision missiles, and militant infiltration. Bases remained vulnerable to weapons theft and sabotage.
- He invested the bulk of American foreign military assistance, more than 18 billion dollars, in the purchase of aircraft but allocated almost nothing to ground forces, less expensive air defense systems, and thousands of Israeli-made attack drones.
- He drove the IDF to the most severe personnel crisis in its history. While previously 100 to 120 officers left each year, during his tenure 900 captains and majors expressed a desire to resign, as noted by Yitzhak Brick on July 13, 2024, indicating a qualitative and quantitative collapse of the career army.

Halevi's tactics are frequently described as militarily "inept," focused on limited incursion and the preservation of international cover. They did not lead to the final destruction of Hamas, since militants recovered in areas from which the IDF withdrew. Halevi, supported by Defense Minister Yoav Gallant, was leading the army and the people of Israel "toward the abyss."

Generals Versus Politicians

The central paradox of the Israeli security system is the blurred boundary between military strategy and high politics. In Israel, military leaders, who often belong to the left-wing elite, carry enormous authority and are inevitably drawn into politics. But their mentality of "following orders" adapts poorly to the politics of "compromise."

The fundamental difference in thinking between generals and politicians, which manifests in their goals, methodology, planning horizon, and attitude toward risk, explains why successes on the battlefield rarely translate into successes in the political arena. In Israel, where military leaders often carry enormous authority and are part of the secular elite, their mentality of "following orders" adapts poorly to the politics of "compromise," which creates internal tension.

Social Schizophrenia as Dissonance

The term "social schizophrenia" describes a deep cognitive and values-based dissonance between the ideology followed by the military command and the objective needs of the nation in the area of security. In the context of this chapter, this dissonance manifests at three levels.

A. Dissonance Between Values and Mission

- The IDF perceives itself as a "social institution" and an "avant-garde of liberalism," embracing gender equality, minority rights, and legal purity.
- An army must be a machine oriented exclusively toward decisive victory and the physical elimination of threats.
- The army is torn between the requirement to "fight humanely" in order to avoid courts and international criticism, and the necessity of being lethal enough to defeat the enemy. This split,

according to critics, renders it ineffective and leads to failures such as October 7.

B. Dissonance Between Vision and Facts

- The elite believes in "deterrence," the "peace process," and technological superiority as encapsulated in the Barrier Doctrine. It is subject to "conceptual blindness" and refuses to accept data that contradicts this worldview.
- There exist clear, repeatedly demonstrated facts regarding the army's unpreparedness, its reduction in manpower, and the radical ideology of the enemy in the form of Hamas.
- The senior command deliberately filters out inconvenient facts, ignoring Brick and ignoring the "Jericho Wall" plan, in order to preserve the desired "image of success." This leads to the country living in false confidence about its security while professionals are sounding the alarm.

C. Political Division

- Within the IDF there is an inclination toward left-centrist pragmatism and an alienation from "right-wing" and traditional views, visible in ideological selection and the "Generals' Party."
- A growing proportion of society and the government lean toward right-wing, ideologically motivated views, meaning security through the holding of territories and decisive victory.
- An army that by definition should be an apolitical instrument of the entire state is perceived by a significant part of society, especially after the events of October 7, as part of an opposition left-wing clique that is fighting the country's political leadership through protests, criticism of Netanyahu, and the judicial

reform, which undermines public trust and makes strategic unity during wartime impossible.

Thus, the left doctrine of the IDF is perceived as a trigger that creates a paralyzing split, or schizophrenia, between the ideal and the reality, between the leadership and the objective threat.

Shadows on the Quiet Border

June 2023. The Negev Desert, the Egyptian border, the area of Mount Harif. The heat presses down from the morning like a vise. The guard post is a concrete cube with narrow embrasures, a wire fence with sensors stretching for hundreds of kilometers. It is always quiet here. "The calmest border," they say in the IDF. Drug smuggling, yes, it happens at night. But war? There is no war.

Sergeant Lia Ben-Nun, nineteen years old, from Rishon LeZion, and Staff Sergeant Ori Yitzhak Ilouz, twenty years old, from Safed, began their shift on Friday evening. A twelve-hour patrol at a mixed post, a young man and a young woman. This was the norm in border battalions such as "Caracal" and "Bardelas": integration, equality, social progress. They checked the communications at 4:15 in the morning. All was quiet. Then silence.

An Egyptian policeman crosses the border through an emergency passage in the fence. He is armed. He approaches closely. He fires on the sleeping soldiers. Lia and Ori are killed on the spot, without firing a single shot in response. Their bodies are found only several hours later. Shortly afterward, in a firefight, a third soldier, Staff Sergeant Ohad Dahan, twenty years old, is killed attempting to stop the attacker. The Egyptian is shot dead. An IDF investigation later revealed: long shifts of twelve hours in the heat, a shortage of manpower on the border, and a state of relaxed vigilance because of the peace treaty with Egypt dating from 1979.

The posts were mixed in order to promote equality. But at the critical moment, vigilance was dulled.

Officially, it was classified as a terrorist attack. But this tragedy became a symbol of how an army, once oriented exclusively toward the elimination of threats, gradually transformed into an institution in which social goals, including the integration of women, inclusion, and "morality" in the eyes of the world, began to compete with the primary task: to kill enemies efficiently and without hesitation.

The Main Directions of IDF Reform

The failure to prevent the Hamas attack revealed systemic problems: excessive reliance on technology, underestimation of ground forces, intelligence errors, and the absence of preparation for a multi-front war. Reforms are being discussed in Israeli media, expert circles, and within the army under the leadership of Chief of the General Staff Eyal Zamir, who took office in March 2025.

1. Strengthening Intelligence and a Culture of Thinking

- Mandatory study of Arabic language and Islamic culture for all intelligence personnel, including cyber and technical specialists. A special department was created for this purpose in 2025.
- The revival of the principle of "Ipcha Mistabra" (consideration of alternative scenarios): intellectual openness, skepticism, and debate in intelligence work.
- Combating groupthink: avoiding the dominant "conception."

2. Balance Between Technology and Ground Forces

- Expansion of ground troops: the creation of new units, enlargement of infantry and armored forces.
- Strengthening border defense and air defense: expansion of border protection units, modernization of systems against low-altitude threats such as drones and paragliders.
- Modernization of the navy and cyber units: focus on artificial intelligence, electronic warfare, and signals interception.

3 Personnel and Structural Changes

- Large-scale reshuffling and dismissals: Zamir in 2025 initiated a "purge" of senior officers responsible for October 7, acknowledging the systemic failure.
- Reform of officer training: new programs with a focus on real combat experience.
- Expansion of reserves: a plan to maintain 60,000 reservists in service from 2026 onward, with efforts to draft ultra-Orthodox men to grow the human resources pool.

4 Other Proposals

- Restoration of ammunition stocks, logistics, and mobilization capability.
- Improvement of coordination between branches of service and with the civilian sector.
- Political depoliticization of the army: avoiding the influence of internal divisions, as exemplified by the 2023 protests.

Reforms are being implemented gradually due to budgetary constraints and ongoing threats. Full reform depends on the establishment of a state commission of inquiry, the creation of which remains a subject of contention.

Conclusion

"The ship has been repaired, the water no longer penetrates, and it sails safely to the secure shore under the guidance of a stubborn captain who has overcome countless difficulties and dangers."

Arik Ben Simhon

The ideology of Oslo, through the mechanism of schizophrenia, transformed the army into a showcase of liberal achievements.

We learned to be the "most moral" in Haaretz reports but forgot how to be the most terrifying in Sinwar's eyes. On October 7, reality returned, shattering the stage sets of the "progressive" social project. ***The "left doctrine" created a situation in which the army feared its own people and its "right-wing" government more than it feared the enemy beyond the fence.*** The IDF stopped winning not because it ran out of rockets. It stopped winning because its mind was infected with the virus of doubt. The left doctrine transformed the army from an instrument of the nation's survival into an instrument of self-flagellation.

We lost at the moment when we decided that "morality" in the face of murderers was more important than protecting our own children. The tragedy of October 7, 2023 was the result of thirty years of ideological and strategic drift by the IDF, beginning with the Oslo Accords.

The IDF abandoned the Zionist doctrine of decisive victory in favor of the "left doctrine" of containment and conflict management. The army was transformed into a "social institution" burdened with liberal values, excessive legal oversight, and dependence on technology.

This shift led to a systematic reduction of ground forces and reserves, which critically weakened the country's ability to repel a large-scale invasion. The failure of the "smart" barrier and the "conceptual blindness" of intelligence were a direct consequence of this hypertrophied faith in technology and the false certainty that Hamas had been deterred.

The General Staff succumbed to an ideological filter through political purges that prevented officers who did not share left-centrist pragmatism from reaching senior positions. Warnings from professionals such as General Yitzhak Brick were deliberately ignored in favor of maintaining an "image of success."

The IDF on October 7 was a reflection of the deep social schizophrenia of the elites. *An army deprived of the right to win by its own leadership was doomed to this blow. Generals who saw Netanyahu as a greater threat than Sinwar committed professional suicide.*

Israel's revival will begin only when the spirit of crushing the enemy returns to the army and when lawyers and "progressive" professors are expelled from the operational planning headquarters. The ultimate decision between victory and defeat does not lie in tactics but in political will. As long as generals wage a war of "limited incursion" to minimize risks and casualties, only strong political leadership can define unambiguous goals and provide the international protection necessary to achieve them.

For the revival of Israel, it is necessary to conduct a fundamental revision of the defense doctrine, restore to the IDF its original mission of achieving decisive victory and ensuring security, and restore the strategic balance between the political leadership that defines the goals and the military command responsible for their effective execution.

PART V. FAILURES AND VICTORIES

CHAPTER 24
ON THE EVE OF THE INVASION

"Truth should be delivered as one delivers a coat, not thrown in the face like a wet towel."

Mark Twain

Introduction

The Gaza Strip is a territory on the eastern coast of the Mediterranean Sea covering 363 square kilometers. In accordance with the UN Partition Plan of 1947 for Palestine into Arab and Jewish parts, it was intended, along with the West Bank of the Jordan River, to form part of the Palestinian Arab state. However, as a result of the attack by Arab countries on Israel in 1948, the Gaza Strip was occupied by Egypt, and in 1967, during the Six-Day War, it was liberated by Israel. Between 1993 and 1995, Israelis and Palestinians concluded a series of agreements, the Oslo Accords, under which self-governance was introduced in the West Bank and the Gaza Strip, and the Palestinian National Authority was established. In 2005, as part of Prime Minister Ariel Sharon's "unilateral disengagement" plan, the residents of Jewish settlements were expelled and the Israeli army was withdrawn from the Gaza Strip and from some areas of the West Bank. In June 2007, Hamas seized power in the Gaza Strip by military force, declaring its intention to establish an Islamic state there. Its goal is the destruction of Israel.

The "Era of Blindness" is the term that best describes the condition of the Israeli military-political establishment in the years and months preceding October 7, 2023. In Israeli parlance, this became known as "the Conception." It was a period of collective cognitive dissonance, during which real threats were ignored in favor of a constructed intellectual model. In the context of my analysis, this represents the apex of "social schizophrenia" afflicting the country's elite, which lived and acted in detachment from reality, and in defiance of it.

"On the Eve of the Invasion" is not merely a description of the failure of October 7, 2023; it is a narrative about intellectual paralysis. This is perhaps the most tragic section of the book. Here we move from an analysis of "inner demons" to the moment when they finally obscure the vision of those who were obligated to stand guard. *'Hamas has become pragmatic': this was the principal mantra of the deep state, an induced self-deception. Intelligence saw the facts, including the training, the tunnels, and the weapons acquisitions, but interpreted them through the prism of its own desires. When reality contradicts the conception, the conception wins, and reality is discarded as 'noise.'*

The Collapse of October 7

The "Era of Blindness" ended at 6:30 in the morning of October 7, when reality breached the "smart fence" and the intellectual constructs of the elite within a matter of minutes. It emerged that while Israel was occupied with the schizophrenia of consciousness and judicial disputes, its enemy had been preparing a medieval massacre, using Israel's own self-confidence against it.

The tragedy of October 7, 2023 was not merely an operational failure but the culmination of a deep strategic and ideological delusion that had dominated Israel for two decades. It was an era in which the supreme military and political leadership, afflicted with "conceptual blindness," replaced the doctrine of decisive victory with the soothing but illusory conception of "Deterrence, Barrier, and Technological Superiority." Military Intelligence AMAN and the Shin Bet ceased to be analytical centers and became a sect of "Witnesses of Silence."

This conviction was founded on three fatal errors: first, an overestimation of its own technological potential, reducing defense to a "smart" fence; second, a catastrophic underestimation of the ideological motivation of the enemy, meaning the belief that Hamas was interested in "economic management" rather than jihad; and third, a systematic reduction of ground forces and logistics, which made the IDF "small but lethal" only on paper and left it unprepared for a war of attrition or a massive invasion.

While Major General Yitzhak Brick had for years been warning of a "serious illness" in the IDF's organizational culture, the senior command and the political cabinet ignored these signals.

Hamas Became Pragmatic

The central idea of the "blindness" was that Hamas had allegedly evolved from a terrorist organization into a sovereign government that valued its hold on power and economic benefits, including money from Qatar and work permits in Israel. Hamas was believed to have been "intimidated" by the IDF's power following previous operations. Any military exercises by militants near the fence were perceived as "posturing" for internal consumption rather than preparation for an actual invasion. The most dangerous hallucination is the one you have paid for yourself.

"The Conception" was not merely an error but an induced self-deception of the highest order.

AMAN analysts looked at Hamas's preparations for a massacre and said: "They are simply extracting more money from Qatar." This is a classic case of cognitive distortion, in which the mind filters out any threat if it requires leaving the comfort zone. The system found it more convenient to believe in a "rational" Sinwar than to admit that a machine for the murder of Jews was being constructed in the south.

Technological Arrogance

Israel came to believe that modern technologies could fully replace physical presence and human intuition. A wall costing billions of shekels, equipped with sensors, cameras, and remotely operated machine guns, created the illusion of absolute impermeability. Command assumed that the "fence" would provide real-time warning, which allowed for a reduction in the number of personnel on the border.

Internal chaos as a smokescreen. The entire year of 2023 unfolded under the sign of the "Kaplanist Intifada." Intelligence resources within the Shin Bet and AMAN and the attention of the senior leadership were consumed by the internal confrontation, the protests, and the threats of reservists to refuse service.

For Yahya Sinwar, the internal division of Israel looked like "decomposition from within." He observed that the army was drawn into political debates and that society was divided. This convinced him that Israel was at the weakest point in its history.

Ignoring Small Signals

The most tragic aspect of the blindness was the systematic ignoring of warnings from below. Female soldiers serving on the border for months had been reporting unusual Hamas training exercises, including the rehearsal of kibbutz capture and fence destruction. Their reports were mocked or ignored by senior officers who were in the grip of the "Conception." This was social schizophrenia: the reality on the ground did not correspond to the theory in the headquarters.

The Role of Legalism in the Blindness

Critics such as David Ben-Yehuda add another layer to this: legal fear. Legal restrictions prevented preemptive strikes against groups of Hamas militants training near the fence, since they "did not represent an immediate threat" according to international law as interpreted by the Military Prosecution. The army was so preoccupied with ensuring the "legal purity" of every action that it lost the hunter's instinct necessary for survival in the Middle Eastern region.

Thus, the catastrophe of October 7 was predetermined by a failure of will and an unwillingness to know the truth, transforming from an unthinkable scenario into an inevitable one.

A History of Military Operations in the Gaza Strip

Since the year 2000, Israel has conducted ten major military operations in Gaza, after each of which costly reconstruction work was carried out. A brief overview of these operations was compiled by the Telegram channel "Alexei Zheleznov," with the author identified as Gali Eira.

Operation Rainbow, 2004. Dates: May 18 to 23, 2004. Objective: the elimination of armed groups in Rafah. Result: smuggling tunnels were destroyed, with casualties on both sides. Damage: 298 homes destroyed, roads and infrastructure damaged. Estimated damage: 50 to 80 million dollars.

Operation Autumn Clouds, 2006. Dates: November 1 to 7, 2006. Cause: mass rocket fire from Gaza. Result: reduction of Hamas activity, destruction of infrastructure in Beit Hanoun. Damage: not specified.

Operation Hot Winter, 2008. Dates: February 29 to March 3, 2008. Cause: intensification of rocket attacks. Result: a short-term reduction in combat activity. Damage: destruction of infrastructure in Gaza; the precise sum was not published, but it is estimated that Hamas could have received up to 500 million dollars for reconstruction.

Operation Summer Rains, 2008. Dates: June 27 to November 27, 2008. The operation was triggered by the events of June 25, when Palestinian militants attacked an Israeli army post near Kibbutz Kerem Shalom, killing two soldiers and abducting Corporal Gilad Shalit. Three thousand Israeli soldiers were deployed in the operation, whose declared objective was the liberation of Shalit, opposed by approximately 9,000 militants. During the fighting, which involved ground forces supported by aviation and artillery, 400 Palestinians were killed according to Palestinian Ministry of Health data. The Israeli side lost five soldiers and six civilians. Gilad Shalit was released only in 2011 in exchange for 1,027 Palestinian prisoners. Damage: precise data are absent, but 6.2 billion dollars were requested for the reconstruction of Gaza.

Operation Cast Lead, 2008 to 2009. Dates: December 27, 2008 to January 18, 2009. Cause: rocket fire on Israel. Result: a major military operation with airstrikes and ground intervention, with heavy losses among militants. Damage: World Bank assessment of 4 to 6 billion dollars; UN assessment of 10 to 15 billion dollars.

Operation Pillar of Defense, 2012. Dates: November 14 to 21, 2012. Cause: intensification of rocket attacks. Result: airstrikes on Hamas infrastructure and the elimination of leadership figures. Damage: 1.2 billion dollars, of which 542 million represented direct losses and 700 million indirect losses. Between 2 and 4 billion dollars were requested for reconstruction.

Operation Protective Edge, 2014. Dates: July 7 to August 26, 2014. Cause: the murder of three Israeli teenagers and rocket fire. Result: a ground operation, destruction of tunnels, and significant destruction in Gaza. Damage: according to the UN assessment, reconstruction required 7.8 billion dollars.

Operation Guardian of the Walls, 2021. Dates: May 10 to 21, 2021. Cause: mass disturbances in Jerusalem and rocket fire. Result: destruction of Hamas tunnels and elimination of militants. Damage: World Bank assessment of 350 to 570 million dollars; between 2 and 4 billion dollars were requested for reconstruction.

Operation Shield and Arrow, 2023. Dates: May 9 to 13, 2023. Cause: rocket fire and provocations by Islamic Jihad. Result: targeted strikes on militant leaders and a temporary de-escalation. Damage: no reliable data.

Operation Iron Swords, 2023 to 2025. Dates: from October 7, 2023, ongoing. Cause: the Hamas attack, the abduction of hostages, and rocket fire. Result: heavy losses for Hamas and

Hezbollah and counterterrorist operations in several countries. Damage: World Bank assessment of 30 to 40 billion dollars; UN assessment of up to 100 billion dollars.

FROM A POLITICAL THRILLER

The Meeting at the Mirror

A Scene Describing the Consensus of Generals and Politicians Before an Operation.

Setting: *A bunker beneath the General Staff ('the Pit'). On the screens: a map of Gaza with marked targets.*

Characters: The Prime Minister, the Chief of the General Staff, and the Head of the Shin Bet.

Prime Minister: *(wearily) "Tel Aviv is under fire again. How much time do we need to clear the northern sector?"*

Chief of the General Staff: *"Three weeks on the ground. But I do not recommend going deep. Our lawyers are talking about the risk of a humanitarian catastrophe, and the West will hit the brakes within five days. Let's simply 'mow the lawn.' We destroy 30 percent of their rocket launchers, blow up a couple of tunnels, and exit under Egyptian guarantees."*

Head of the Shin Bet: *"Agreed. Sinwar is under stress right now. If we don't finish him off, he will understand that the rules of the game have not changed. He will receive his money from the Qataris, and we will get two years of quiet. This is pragmatic."*

Prime Minister: *"And what happens in two years?"*

Chief of the General Staff: *(shrugging) "In two years, we will 'mow' again. We have excellent intelligence; we see everything. The Iron Dome technology allows us to play this game indefinitely."*

Head of the Shin Bet: *(quietly) "The main thing is that the lawn does not turn into a jungle while we are looking the other way."*

Prime Minister: *"All right. I approve the operation. Call it something heroic for the press."*

Chief of the General Staff: *(without long reflection) "Let it be called 'Limited Retribution.'"*

Head of the Shin Bet: *"Agreed."*

The Doctrine of Mowing the Lawn:

The Art of Cultivating a Catastrophe

"Mowing the lawn" was not a strategy; it was a refusal of strategy. Instead of surgically removing the tumor of Hamas, the Israeli establishment decided that the tumor could be persuaded to grow proportionately. This was compulsive repetition. Every two to three years, we entered Gaza, lost soldiers, destroyed tunnels, and then withdrew, giving the enemy the opportunity to build them anew, only deeper and stronger. The conviction that 'Hamas is better than chaos' became the principal intellectual error of the decade. We were feeding the tiger, hoping it would only eat on schedule.

Israel repeatedly applied force that did not lead to the elimination of the threat. Behind these operations lay a doctrine known as "mowing the lawn," and its authorship can be attributed to a broad consensus in the Israeli military-political establishment, including a number of generals and prime ministers.

"Mowing the lawn" is an informal but broadly accepted doctrine of conflict management that dominated Israeli policy toward Gaza from the moment of withdrawal from the strip in 2005.

Its goal was not complete and final victory, meaning the destruction of Hamas and the overthrow of its rule, but the periodic reduction of its capabilities and the restoration of deterrence for a defined period.

Israel acknowledged that the overthrow of Hamas was politically undesirable due to the risk of chaos or the rise to power of an even more radical group, and militarily too costly.

A major operation was conducted when Hamas or other factions crossed a "red line," such as rocket fire on major cities or the construction of large tunnels. The task was to destroy the maximum number of militants, infrastructure, weapons depots, and tunnels.

Operations were to be conducted regularly, like lawn mowing, to prevent Hamas from rebuilding its capabilities to a level representing an existential threat.

The doctrine took shape in the 2000s and was supported by the majority of prime ministers and chiefs of the General Staff: Ehud Olmert during Cast Lead in 2008 to 2009; Benjamin Netanyahu during Pillar of Defense in 2012, Protective Edge in 2014, and others; and the chiefs of the General Staff of the period from 2007 to 2023, including Gabi Ashkenazi, Benny Gantz, and Gadi Eisenkot, who were the executors of this doctrine, believing it to be the only pragmatic method of managing Gaza without full military control.

Hamas was building its strength. But behind this lay political and military calculations. Netanyahu and his allies believed that "mowing the lawn" was sufficient to maintain quiet while there was no better political solution. Generals Gantz and Eisenkot believed that "mowing the lawn" was the only option available given the current political deadlock and international pressure.

The doctrine of 'Mowing the Lawn' collapsed on October 7, 2023.

The scale of the attack showed that Hamas had used the periods following each "mowing" to create a threat of strategic proportions, including thousands of rockets, an extensive tunnel network, and a breach of the perimeter. The price of refusing a full victory proved higher than the price of full occupation or the search for a genuine political solution. Thus, before October 7, Israel's strategy was not to defeat Hamas but to manage its existence, periodically weakening it.

The Failure of the Doctrine

The motivations behind the doctrine and their explanations were as follows. Regarding the deterrence of demographic risk: Israel did not want to take full control of Gaza, since this would have meant taking charge of 2.3 million Palestinians, threatening the Jewish majority and the democratic character of the state. Regarding the avoidance of a political vacuum: Israel feared that the overthrow of Hamas would lead to complete chaos, resulting in Gaza becoming either a base for even more extremist groups such as ISIS, or Israel being forced to govern the strip for decades. The prevailing view was that "Hamas is evil, but it is controlled evil." Regarding threat management: the military leadership believed that the Iron Dome system and periodic strikes could keep the rocket threat at an acceptable level, inflicting damage but not paralyzing the economy and the country's way of life. Regarding international pressure: large-scale ground operations aimed at the full overthrow of the authorities had always provoked unprecedented international pressure, which forced Israel to stop short of complete victory.

The Road to Casus Belli

The "disengagement" of 2005 and the violent deportation from Gaza led to the consolidation of Hamas's power, whose declared goal is the destruction of Israel.

The subsequent seven counterterrorist operations by the IDF between 2006 and 2021 were conducted in response to rocket fire that grew steadily more powerful. In parallel, the threat to internal security was growing, as demonstrated by the Arab pogroms in Lod in 2021.

The government, the army, and the intelligence services relied on defense and technology. The Iron Dome saved lives but did not resolve the problem of Gaza and, in the view of critics, undermined the legitimacy of the IDF to conduct a major ground operation necessary for destroying Hamas's rule.

It was clear to many that such an operation would be long and costly. In order to start a "real war," a casus belli, a formal pretext for the declaration of war, was needed. What happened on October 7, 2023 was a monstrous episode that not only served as a casus belli but shook not only Israelis but their enemies as well.

Hamas's Preparation for the Massacre

Documents discovered on Hamas computers in the Gaza Strip reveal that the organization had penetrated the surveillance cameras and computers of nearby communities and gained access to confidential information years before the attack.

The terrorists had access to and were capable of the following:

- accessing the surveillance cameras of communities;

- obtaining the contact lists of rapid response fighters and security guards;
- documenting the meetings of heads of governing bodies;
- mapping state institutions and essential facilities;
- collecting personal data on officials;
- monitoring the heads of governing bodies and security personnel;
- accessing internal mail since 2016;
- preparing detailed target files for each community;
- and planning attacks on central facilities.

"The level of precision and detail is surprising," says a former Shin Bet official. The documents show that planning for the attack began at least as early as 2016.

FROM A POLITICAL THRILLER

Eyes in Your Bedroom

A Scene Emphasizing the Horror of Informational Defenselessness.

Setting: *Hamas headquarters in a tunnel beneath Gaza. Dozens of monitors broadcasting live video from Israeli community cameras.*

Characters: A Hamas Technical Officer and a Nukhba Special Forces Commander.

Officer: *(pointing at a screen) "Look, this is the camera above the gate of Kibbutz Be'eri. The guard changes at 6:00. At 6:15, he goes for coffee. The rapid response group: here are their phone numbers; we intercept their messages."*

Commander: *"And what about Israeli intelligence? Can they not see that we are in their network?"*

Officer: *(smirking) "They are too busy with the 'judicial reform.' Their 'deep state' is looking for enemies in the Knesset rather than in their surveillance cameras. They are confident that we are 'pragmatists.' They send us Qatari money, and with that money we buy access to their servers."*

Commander: *(studying the list of council heads) "We will kill them in their own homes. They built a 'smart fence,' but they forgot that we are already inside their homes through their own computers."*

Officer: *"Tomorrow they will update their antivirus. But tomorrow will not come for them."*

The IDF investigation states that the gap between what Hamas actually represented and how it was assessed in Israel began to grow several years after Operation Protective Edge in 2014. Around the same time, Hamas concluded that the only way to succeed was to launch a surprise attack and catch the IDF off guard.

The Jericho Wall Plan

In 2018, Israeli intelligence received the first version of the attack plan, which later evolved into the "Jericho Wall" plan. Yahya Sinwar had begun developing it a year earlier, immediately after being elected leader of Hamas in the strip. The plan envisioned the capture of the Gaza Division headquarters, the penetration of large forces into Israeli territory, the seizure of border areas, killings, and kidnappings. In Israel, these plans were not taken seriously, and Sinwar was considered a pragmatist who valued the benefits of Israel's "conflict management" strategy, including the advantage over the Palestinian Authority on the West Bank where Hamas was gaining popularity in contrast to the weak Fatah.

In 2022, a new version of the plan, developed the previous year and already bearing the name "Jericho Wall," fell into the hands of Israeli intelligence.

The document described in detail, over dozens of pages, the invasion plan that was executed on October 7, 2023: a massive bombardment before the start of the attack; methods for breaching the separation fence; the capture of kibbutzim and military bases; and the use of drones to disable surveillance cameras and the "see-and-shoot" systems on the fence. According to the results of the army investigation, the command of the intelligence service of the Gaza Division, which was responsible for analyzing the document and presenting it to higher authority, did not connect the "Jericho Wall" to the earlier 2018 plans. Intelligence concluded that this was a new and immature plan that Hamas did not intend to execute. The Shin Bet likewise did not consider it a genuine operational guide.

Responsibility for understanding the situation in Gaza and the threats posed by Hamas lies with Military Intelligence AMAN and the General Security Service, the Shin Bet. The Shin Bet notes that its task is to prevent terrorist attacks, while warning of war is the army's responsibility.

The largest unit of military intelligence and of the entire IDF is the electronic intelligence Unit 8200. It is precisely on 8200 data that the IDF typically relies for threat elimination and targeted operations. In recent years, the unit had devoted far more attention to modern technologies and far less to classical intelligence methods, including the analysis of open sources, imagery intelligence, and even signals intelligence.

According to the army investigation, several months before the start of the war, when AMAN received information about Hamas exercises rehearsing the capture of communities, two female analysts from Unit 8200 compared this data with the "Jericho Wall" plan and concluded that the militants genuinely intended to execute it. Corroborating evidence included citations from the Quran used by the terrorists, which indicated the seriousness of their intentions. The exercises concluded with the phrase: "We have killed everyone."

This analysis was presented to the command of the 8200 Southern District section; however, the commanders, upon reviewing the conclusions, rejected them as unsound and did not transmit the materials to higher command and to the AMAN leadership.

> *"It was assumed that Hamas did not want war. And when any information did not fit within this conviction, it was either dismissed as erroneous or interpreted in an exclusively positive light," explains former Deputy Head of the Shin Bet Israel Hasson.*

The Shin Bet investigation states that the service had perceived the results of Operation Guardian of the Walls in 2021 as a clear Hamas victory and had warned the political leadership that the terrorist movement was not afraid of a confrontation with the IDF and continued to regard the destruction of Israel as its goal. However, this did not help the Shin Bet leadership to either correctly assess the "Jericho Wall" document or to understand the situation on the night of October 7.

According to Israel Hasson, this was partly a consequence of the fact that the last two heads of the service had come from its operational department: "The Shin Bet has an excellent operational department, but its task is to execute assignments. Tell it to retrieve a needle from the bottom of the ocean and it will retrieve it. However, it will not analyze why the needle ended up in that particular place at that particular time. But the capacity and drive for such analysis were necessary to understand Hamas's plans."

Both the current leadership of the Shin Bet and Israel Hasson identify the abandonment of human intelligence, known as HUMINT, as the principal cause of the failure.

Since 2017, when Yahya Sinwar exposed and executed several dozen Israeli agents, the Shin Bet had virtually no network of agents in Gaza. The remaining agents were either uninformed or had been turned. It goes without saying that had the Shin Bet possessed even a single agent within the Nukhba unit that carried out the October 7 attack, that agent's signal on the night before the assault could have completely changed the situation.

The existence of the separation fence between Israel and Gaza undoubtedly complicated the recruitment of agents and communication with them, but this is not a justification, as Israel Hasson is convinced: "Once I was in charge of the Shin Bet's Lebanon agents department. Believe me, recruiting agents in Lebanon was also not easy. **But HUMINT is the Shin Bet's principal advantage over military intelligence.** An agent does not even have to be a Nukhba fighter; he can be one of the dozens or hundreds of people surrounding each Hamas leader. And when Israeli SIM cards are activated in Gaza for the next time, he will inform the Shin Bet of what the holder of that SIM card is doing. And if the holder of a suddenly activated SIM card is not sitting as usual in front of the television, then perhaps the Shin Bet will not ignore that event, as it ignored it on the night of October 7."

The Plan for the Destruction of Israel

Secret messages from Hamas leaders captured in Gaza show that following Operation Guardian of the Walls, Hamas concluded that the destruction of Israel had become an achievable goal in the foreseeable future.

According to these documents, Hamas leader Yahya Sinwar requested 500 million dollars from Iran for the "destruction of the imaginary entity," and militants from Jordan and Syria were to join the attack. New research by the Center for Information and Intelligence on Terrorism, conducted by Dr. Uri Rost of Sapir College, shows how in recent years the ideology of the "destruction of Israel" was transformed from a distant religious vision into a practical strategy.

The documents contain internal correspondence and messages between Sinwar, senior leaders of Iran, and Hezbollah, asserting that "Israel has become more vulnerable than ever" and that the "resistance has grown stronger." Before Operation Guardian of the Walls in May 2021, Hamas was aware of its military and political limitations, and therefore the "destruction of Israel" remained a distant scenario. However, after the war, the military wing of Hamas published a book declaring: *"The defeat of the enemy has become a reality that one can touch with one's own hand." In September 2021, under the patronage of Sinwar, a conference titled "The Pledge of the End of Times: Palestine After Liberation" was held in Gaza, at which the Hamas leader declared: "We are moving toward a great strategic victory that will change the future of the region, the Islamic ummah, and the entire world... We see liberation with our own eyes and are preparing for what will come after it."*

FROM A POLITICAL THRILLER

The Price of the Question Is 500 Million

A Scene Describing the Interception or Analysis of Sinwar's Letter to His Iranian Supervisors.

Setting: *The Analysis Department of AMAN (Military Intelligence). Night. On the screen: a decrypted letter from Sinwar to the commander of the Quds Force.*

Characters: A Senior Analyst and a Translator Officer.

Translator: *(reading aloud) "'This imaginary entity is weaker than people think... We request 500 million dollars over two years for its ultimate eradication.' They are asking for 20 million a month for a 'great strategic victory.'"*

Analyst: *(stirring cold coffee) "Again this Eastern rhetoric. Sinwar always writes in the style of Islamic prophecies. He needs money to pay officials and to maintain clan loyalty. He understands, after all, that 500 million dollars will not be enough to defeat the IDF."*

Translator: *"But here it says 'the activation of all fronts' and 'a joint defense agreement with Hezbollah.' This sounds like a plan for a regional war."*

Analyst: *(yawning) "Sinwar is a merchant. He frightens the Iranians with grandiose plans so that they do not cut the budget. In reality he wants to buy a few hundred more jeeps and build new villas for his entourage. Write in the report: 'Hamas continues to use ideological rhetoric to obtain financing, remaining within the framework of pragmatic management of the strip.'"*

Translator: *"But what if he is not bargaining? What if he genuinely believes that we are an 'imaginary entity'? That we are weak? What then?"*

Analyst: *"Then he is a madman. And we do not build strategy on the plans of madmen. We build it on 'rational interests.'"*

One of the most important documents discovered was a message sent in June 2021 by Sinwar, Mohammed Deif, and Marwan Issa to the commander of the IRGC Quds Force special unit. It stated:

> *"This imaginary entity is weaker than people think. With the help of Allah, with your support, and with the assistance of our ummah, we are capable of eradicating it and liquidating it in the very nearest future... We believe in Allah and are certain that we are close to the fulfillment of the divine promise." In the same letter, the Hamas leadership requested 500 million dollars from Iran over two years: "To achieve these great goals, we need financial support in the amount of 20 million dollars per month over two years, amounting to 500 million dollars."*

In another document, dated January 2019 and prepared by Sinwar's office, analyzing Hamas's relations with Iran and their mutual interests, a single highlighted section bears the heading "What Do We Want from Them?" It specifies: "The conclusion of a joint defense agreement with the Quds Force, Hezbollah, and Hamas, in preparation for the war for the liberation of Al-Quds and the activation of all fronts against the common enemy, Israel. The development of a practical plan for a simultaneous attack from multiple directions."

Six Weeks Before October 7

What happened in the six weeks preceding the bloody Hamas attack on southern Israel? *This is the account of Colonel Chaim Cohen, commander of the northern brigade of the Gaza Division.*

First of all, he accused the IDF Chief of the General Staff of an absence of "basic information" about what was happening: "I will always ask where the air force was when the day of October 7 arrived. I will always ask how intelligence failed to warn of a surprise attack."

Cohen claimed that he had wanted to strike against the terrorist organization preemptively but was denied: "At that time there was shooting, explosions, and disturbances on the border fence, and the entire chain of command was patrolling the sector, including the Defense Minister himself. I recommended delivering the first strike, but the answer was**: 'Hamas is restrained.'"** Chaim Cohen stated that unknown elements within the army had conspired to place the blame for the October 7 massacre on him. He, however, went on the offensive: "At 3:30 in the morning I drove to the brigade, although the intelligence data were vague. I naively assumed that at least part of the IDF's command chain was thinking as I was, but unfortunately, I was wrong in the first hour of the battle.

At 6:29 in the morning, the gates of hell opened before the brigade, and I saw a wide breach at dozens of 'hot points' where hundreds of terrorists, paragliders, and inflatable boats were simultaneously present... I declared that we were in a state of 'surprise war.' I was struck by the enemy's ability to field a terrorist army for the attack without any intelligence warning."

"I only learned about the 'Jericho Wall' plan after the Ilana Dayan investigation, approximately a month later," Cohen added.

"I understood that I would have to try to stop thousands of terrorists while simultaneously managing dozens of events. That day, no one from the General Staff operations center bothered to open the communications networks. While the media was broadcasting an accurate picture of the situation from civilians, no one had the decency to consolidate it from the IDF's perspective in real time," the officer stated.

The Ignoring of Surveillance Reports

This is a classic example of how the "Conception," meaning the blindness of the leadership, comes into conflict with the facts on the ground. Here are the details of exactly how this happened and why the system preferred to remain blind.

What They Saw and Reported

Over the course of at least a year before the attack, female surveillance soldiers at bases along the Gaza border, especially at Nahal Oz, were recording anomalous activity. Hamas militants were training to blow up the fence and pass through it in pickup trucks and on motorcycles, multiple times a day. Models of Israeli surveillance towers and kibbutz gates were observed, with storm techniques being rehearsed. Militants were approaching close to the fence, photographing cameras, sensors, and gate locks. "Farmers," who were in fact Hamas scouts, were gathering information on IDF patrols and shift schedules.

How the Leadership Responded

Ignoring the reports was systemic. When the girls transmitted their reports to intelligence officers and unit commanders, they encountered the following reactions. They were told: "Your task is to record; interpretation will be done at higher levels." Their professionalism was questioned because of their age and rank. They faced condescension and sexism: their reports were called "overly emotional" or "female panic." For persistence, they were threatened with court martial for "violating subordination" and "spreading panic." Intelligence officers from AMAN insisted that Hamas was staging "a show" to extract money from Qatar but "in reality they are afraid and will not attack."

FROM A POLITICAL THRILLER

Cassandras in Headphones

A Scene Describing the Ignoring of Reports from Surveillance Soldiers (Tatzpitaniyot).

Setting: *Command post on the border with Gaza. Rows of monitors.*

Characters: A Young Surveillance Soldier and a Senior AMAN Intelligence Officer.

Surveillance Soldier: *(pointing at a screen) "Lieutenant Colonel, sir, look at sector four. They have been conducting exercises to blow up the fence for the third consecutive week. Today they deployed jeeps with machine guns. These are not 'farmers'; these are assault groups!"*

Officer: *(without looking up from his tablet) "Listen, girl, you see only a picture. We have 'deep understanding.' Hamas is currently busy distributing work permits for Israel. They need quiet. What you are seeing is 'theater,' a show for their internal consumption."*

Surveillance Soldier: *"But they are rehearsing the capture of the division headquarters! I can see a model of our building in their camp!"*

Officer: *(irritably) "Stop panicking. This is 'virtual reality.' Sinwar is rational. He is not suicidal. You attend to your sensors and do not interfere with the adults analyzing strategy. There is currently a 'period of stability' in Gaza. Both the Shin Bet and AMAN have confirmed this."*

Surveillance Soldier: *(quietly) "And what if your strategy is simply their camouflage?"*

Officer: *"Dismissed. And do not bring me these 'alarmist' reports again. They spoil the overall picture of success."*

The Culmination of the Blindness

Several weeks before October 7, the frequency of Hamas exercises increased to a critical level. The surveillance soldiers observed militants rehearsing the capture of entire replicas of Israeli communities. Experienced soldiers who had served for more than a year said: "Something unprecedented is being prepared." One of them later stated in an interview that she had submitted a report indicating that Hamas was rehearsing a scenario for the capture of the base. The officer's response was: "Hamas is a gang in slippers; they will never dare to attack an IDF base."

The Tragedy of October 7

When the attack began, the surveillance soldiers were the first to see the breach on their screens. It was they who began crying into the radio "Turkish Rider!" (the code for a border breach), but in many sectors help arrived too late.

The Nahal Oz base was one of the first targets. Hamas knew the exact layout of the control rooms. The majority of the female surveillance soldiers who had spent months warning of the attack were killed at close range or taken captive.

Why This Matters for the Analysis: This case is a vivid illustration of 'hierarchical schizophrenia.'

The break with reality: the lower ranks see the facts; the upper ranks see their theory, their "Conception." Elite arrogance: the leadership's confidence that the "deep state" and technology know better than "girls at monitors" deprived the system of immunity. Political background: in 2023, the generals' attention was dispersed among fighting the protests, debating the reform, and ensuring "legal purity." There were no resources left for a serious analysis of the "girls' reports."

This failure became a symbol of the end of the 'era of blindness.' It proved that even the most technologically advanced army is defenseless if its leadership is imprisoned in fictitious conceptions.

Chronology of Events on the Eve of October 7

- ♦ *June 13, 2021: Naftali Bennett becomes Prime Minister of Israel.*
- ♦ *October 2021: Aharon Haliva is appointed head of Military Intelligence.*
- ♦ ***October 2021: Ronen Bar is appointed head of the Shin Bet.***

- May 2022: Military intelligence analysts present the report "Jericho Wall" on Hamas's preparations for an attack. Haliva and the IDF do not take it seriously.
- *July 1, 2022: Yair Lapid replaces Bennett as Prime Minister.*
- **October 2022: Lapid transfers Israeli gas fields to Lebanon without the consent of the Knesset. This decision was supported by Aharon Haliva.**
- October 23, 2022 (one week before the new elections): the interim government of Yair Lapid, in violation of the rules, approved the appointment of Herzi Halevi as Chief of the General Staff. He takes office in January 2023.
- November 1, 2022: Likud wins the elections.
- **December 29, 2022: Benjamin Netanyahu becomes Prime Minister. Yoav Gallant is appointed Defense Minister.**
- 2023 (before October 7): Head of Military Intelligence Aharon Haliva receives reports about preparations for an attack in Gaza but ignores them.
- **October 6, 2023, 10:00 p.m.: The Shin Bet ignores the mass activation of Israeli SIM cards in Gaza, which could have indicated preparations for an attack.**
- The night of October 6 to 7, 2023: The Shin Bet and Military Intelligence continue to receive alarming signals without taking the necessary defensive measures.
- *Around 3:00 a.m.: Head of Military Intelligence Aharon Haliva, who was vacationing in Eilat, is awakened but decides not to take action until morning.*

- **Ronen Bar and General Staff officers fail to recognize the clear signs of a large-scale attack. Shin Bet and police special forces are directed toward the potential combat zone, but there was no warning about the deadly danger to the Nova music festival near Kibbutz Re'im.**

Political Appointments

Unfortunately, the current IDF is not what it was in 1967 and 1973. Since then, the IDF has adopted the "left doctrine," conducted a rigorous selection of colonels and generals, and retired those who did not accept it. The remaining generals were taught to control conflicts with enemies rather than to defeat them.

Brainwashed, peace-loving generals, humanists with progressive ideas, fear of prosecutors, and fear of the media are hardly capable of dealing with the aggressive and death-ready militants of Hamas.

Personnel appointments influenced the development of events on October 7: the attack was not prevented despite numerous warning signals. The government of two politicians, Bennett and Lapid, placed incompetent leaders in key security positions without understanding their unsuitability for ensuring the country's security. Lieutenant General Herzi Halevi, Chief of the General Staff, and Major General Yaron Finkelman, commander of the Southern Military District, failed to protect the country from the attack from the Gaza Strip on October 7, 2023.

The words of Herzi Halevi, "If we had believed it was possible, we would have acted differently," became for many Israelis a verdict on the entire system. This is not merely an acknowledgment of error but testimony to fundamental incompetence. A security professional is obligated to prepare precisely for the "impossible."

The appointments made during this period by the Bennett-Lapid government became a 'time bomb' under national security.

- The appointment of Herzi Halevi as Chief of the General Staff was initiated by Benny Gantz, Defense Minister in the Lapid government, in the middle of an election campaign, within weeks of the elections. The opposition, Likud, declared that such fateful appointments should not be made by a transitional government.

- *It appears that the "government of change" selected leaders who shared the liberal-technocratic paradigm, creating an intellectually homogeneous security bloc more susceptible to groupthink.*

- Halevi's words confirm that the IDF leadership lived in a reality in which the enemy acted according to the logic of "reasonableness" imposed by the legal and political establishment, rather than on the basis of its own religious-ideological doctrine.

- Yaron Finkelman, commander of the Southern District, was criticized for excessive faith in the "smart fence," which Hamas disabled in the first ten minutes of the attack using inexpensive drones.

- Halevi is accused of failing to hear the signals from below, including from the surveillance soldiers, because they destroyed the comfortable picture of "containment" that was being broadcast to the political echelon.

My analysis: this is an example of how the internal struggle of elites affects the country's defense capability.

1. Political appointments are a method of consolidating the influence of the 'liberal camp' in the security structures.
2. *The army leadership, feeling the support of the 'Kaplanists' and the legal elite, began to perceive itself as an independent political actor, as manifested in the story of the reservists' refusal.*
3. The outcome: instead of preparing for war with Hamas, the army leadership was immersed in the internal political conflict, which led to a loss of vigilance on the eve of October 7.

A Legal Thriller

How exactly was the procedure for the appointment of Herzi Halevi challenged in the Supreme Court, and what was the role of the Legal Advisor in this process? This story is one of the most instructive examples of what critics call "legal lawlessness" and the "double standards of the deep state." It demonstrates how the legal system can bend its own rules when this is beneficial for a particular political camp and the military establishment.

The Rushed Appointment: Legal Hacking of the System

The Behind-the-Scenes Story of the 'Emergency'

September 2022. Israel is in a state of protracted political crisis. The Lapid government is transitional; its powers are limited by law and by a longstanding tradition: no fateful appointments during an election period. This is the "golden rule" of Israeli democracy, designed to prevent departing authority from placing its people in key positions. However, in the offices of the Ministry of

Defense and the office of the Legal Advisor to the Government, an unprecedented maneuver was being prepared. The goal: the appointment of Herzi Halevi as the twenty-third Chief of the General Staff of the IDF.

The Secret File 'X.' In order to circumvent the law, Gali Baharav-Miara deployed a trump card that could not be challenged in open court: a "Secret Security Opinion." This document, prepared by the military establishment, contained arguments that today read like a horror film screenplay. The first claim was an "Iranian Window of Opportunity": at the end of 2022 and the beginning of 2023, Iran would reach the threshold of nuclear weapons capability, and the army could not wait a single day without a permanent commander. The second claim was "Unique Security Challenges": secret intelligence reports portended an "unprecedented escalation" on the northern borders. The third claim was a "Risk of a Power Vacuum": if Halevi was not appointed, the security system would be left suspended in midair in the face of an existential threat.

The Legal Battering Ram. Baharav-Miara used this data in the Supreme Court, asserting that the "difficulties of the transitional period outweigh formal prohibitions." The media repeated the narrative: "The army is above politics, and Halevi is the only one who can save us." This created a precedent of exceptionalism: if the system considers a situation to be an emergency, it can disregard the voter.

The Irony of Fate and the Bitter Outcome. It is now known that the very "secret challenges" for whose sake the rule was broken were slept through. The rushed appointment of Halevi did not save the country from the catastrophe of October 7 but produced a Chief of the General Staff who owed his position to a legal maneuver. This was the first crack in the "Shield of David" through which the poison of internal struggle and external aggression seeped in. The appointment became an act of "legal hacking": loyalty to "one's own" proved more important than professional vigilance.

The Transitional Government Rule

In Israeli law, there exists a tradition and a directive from the Legal Advisor: a transitional government must refrain from making appointments to senior positions. Previously, Legal Advisors had blocked the appointments of judges, police chiefs, and others for precisely this reason.

The Role of Gali Baharav-Miara

Despite the status of the Lapid government as transitional, Defense Minister Benny Gantz insisted on appointing a new Chief of the General Staff. Legal Advisor to the Government Gali Baharav-Miara took an unprecedented step: she issued a permit for the appointment, justifying it on grounds of an "emergency security situation" and "the need for stability in the IDF." She relied on a secret opinion prepared by the Legal Advisor of the Ministry of Defense, Itay Ofir, and supported by AMAN reports.

The key points of the "secret report" were: "2023 marks the beginning of a new strategic era"; "unique and exceptional security challenges" would begin precisely in 2023; "the price of error" in the absence of a permanent commander would be fatal; a delay of months in the appointment would cause "irreparable damage."

Why this appears cynical: Halevi was "needed immediately" to prepare for the "new era," yet it was precisely under his command that the army was unprepared for the most serious challenge of that "era," namely October 7. "Secret data" are used when they coincide with the interests of the "right" camp; when right-wingers invoke security, the same lawyers say: "The election period outweighs operational arguments."

The Supreme Court procedure unfolded as follows. The opposition, led by Netanyahu, declared the absence of any emergency justifying the urgency. Public organizations filed petitions with the Supreme Court demanding the annulment of the appointment. The Supreme Court unanimously rejected the petitions, citing non-interference with the discretion of the Legal Advisor when it is grounded in the professional opinions of defense structures.

The scenario of an elite conspiracy: the political interest of Lapid and Gantz was to appoint 'their' person; legal cover was provided by the Legal Advisor finding a loophole in the form of the 'secret data'; judicial legitimation was provided by the Supreme Court stamping its approval.

The Final Act of the Thriller:

1. The system 'hacked' the democratic safeguards for the purpose of expediting Halevi's appointment.
2. In the end, Halevi became the face of the greatest security failure in Israeli history.
3. Halevi's quote, 'If we had believed...,' sounds particularly scandalous against the backdrop of the legal fury with which he was pushed through as the 'only possible' savior.
4. *When the right wing attempts to appoint someone, the Supreme Court and the Legal Advisor say: 'Unreasonable! Election period!' When the left-centrist government appoints a Chief of the General Staff a month before the*

elections, the Supreme Court says: 'This is critically important for security!'

The Boomerang Effect:

- The precedent trap: by once permitting an appointment during an election period due to 'emergency,' the system opened a Pandora's box. In 2025, the government in conditions of war uses the same emergency argument for its own decisions, including personnel decisions.
- The battle for the post of Legal Advisor: attempts to dismiss Baharav-Miara encounter her thesis about the 'unreasonableness' of such a step, but critics remind her of the 'reasonableness' of Halevi's appointment in 2022.
- 'Secret data' against 'secret data': the current authorities rely on their own secret materials regarding the war and sabotage, and the Legal Advisor cannot challenge them without admitting that in 2022 similar information was manipulated.

The principal meaning: the collapse of trust in the law. For the right-wing camp, it is proof that the 'deep state' bends the law to suit itself. For the left-wing camp, it is fear of the vulnerability of the 'defender' of the system. For society: 'social schizophrenia,' in which the law has become a malleable material.

The Impact of the Legal Thriller on

the Army During the War of 2023 to 2024

A crisis of legitimacy in the eyes of soldiers. A part of the personnel, especially from the right-wing camp and religious Zionism, perceived Halevi as a creature of the "deep state." Questions arose: "Are we executing operational tasks or a political agenda?" This undermined trust in the General Staff's orders.

Conflicting chains of command. Cabinet ministers, including Smotrich and Ben-Gvir, openly criticized Halevi. This slowed strategic decisions, such as those concerning Rafah and the Philadelphi Corridor. The army felt the government's distrust, and the government felt the sabotage of its political goals.

The schizophrenia of governance. Against the background of the public war of elites against one another, soldiers experienced the sensation of chaos in the rear while maintaining iron discipline at the front.

Legal paralysis on the battlefield. The influence of military lawyers intensified: they participated in the approval of virtually every target, which slowed the pace of the offensive and increased risks for soldiers for the sake of "international purity." Soldiers feared that any error would become the subject of investigations by the very system that had pushed Halevi through.

The price of politicizing the army. Halevi became a "lame duck" from the first day of his appointment. The method by which he was pushed through the legal prohibitions deprived him of the moral right to demand unconditional trust at the moment of catastrophe. In 2024, this manifested as "heroism despite the command": outstanding tactical performance and strategic subjugation to "social schizophrenia."

Plans to Capture the Gaza Division Headquarters

The analysis of Hamas's plans for the capture of the Gaza Division headquarters at the Re'im base is a study of one of the most audacious and, unfortunately, successful parts of Operation Al-Aqsa Flood. The capture of the facility was critically important for the terrorists: it housed the "brain" of the defense of southern Israel, including the servers of the "smart fence," the officers making decisions about aviation and reserves. The breach of Re'im was a propaganda blow to the IDF's prestige.

According to documents and maps found on the militants, the plan was characterized by precision. First, the immediate "blinding" of the headquarters: suicide drones and snipers destroyed the communication towers and remote-controlled fire systems around the base. Second, the command lost the picture of the border: "white noise" at the moment of the breach by thousands of militants. Third, the assault involved elite Nukhba forces using powerful explosive charges and civilian jeeps to breach the gates, with paragliders to create chaos inside the perimeter. Fourth, the terrorists had detailed maps of the base, including officers' residential quarters on a Saturday morning, server rooms and communications nodes, and weapons rooms.

Why the Assault Succeeded:

- The base had minimal personnel; many officers were at home; holiday leave schedules worked to the enemy's advantage.
- Faith in the impenetrability of the fence meant that the headquarters was not prepared for a full-scale assault.
- The decision-making chain "froze" while waiting for orders from above when communications had already been lost.

The battle for the base lasted many hours. Soldiers and officers displayed personal heroism. But for the critical hours, the Gaza Division ceased to exist as a command unit, which allowed Hamas to operate unimpeded in the kibbutzim of Be'eri, Kfar Aza, and others: units on the ground were not receiving orders and were waiting for instructions from headquarters that was fighting for its own survival.

The Fall of the Brain and the Collapse of the Conception

The base, conceived as a high-technology nerve center, proved defenseless against the primitive but determined force of the enemy. While the defense establishment was immersed in "legal activism" and internal protests, the enemy was studying the architecture of Israeli security. The beheading of the division in the first hours of the attack demonstrated the critical vulnerability of a system in which technological arrogance had displaced basic vigilance and the belief in the "rationality" of the adversary had replaced readiness for combat.

Rules of Engagement

The legal thriller of October 7 began long before the first rockets. The rules of engagement were the quintessence of that very schizophrenia. The lawyers of the "deep state" created a system in which a soldier feared firing at a terrorist near the fence lest he trigger "international condemnation." We were protecting the "rights" of the enemy while depriving our own citizens of the right to life.

The Supreme Court and the Military Prosecution created a situation in which a soldier at the fence feared an "unarmed" terrorist with wire cutters more than death. This paralysis before the law became the key with which Hamas opened the border. Hamas studied our legal "schizophrenia" and made it part of its operational plan.

Legal Advisor to the Government Gali Baharav-Miara did not permit the Prime Minister to introduce new Rules of Engagement at the very beginning of the Hamas invasion. A dispute arose over the "legal packaging" and the legal basis for a large-scale military response.

Netanyahu's Demand

Approximately 7:00 to 9:00 a.m., October 7, 2023

In the first hours of the invasion, when the scale of the attack became clear, Prime Minister Netanyahu demanded immediate action from the IDF, including declaring a "state of war," which would legally change the regime of combat operations and grant IDF forces maximum authority to save lives, and changing the Rules of Engagement to the maximum degree, tightening and liberalizing them for soldiers fighting terrorists on Israeli territory so that they could act without excessive legal restrictions.

The intervention of Legal Advisor Gali Baharav-Miara and the Chief Military Prosecutor: they intervened, insisting on compliance with international and Israeli law.

- The effective "declaration of war" was rejected; the Legal Advisor demanded a decision by the Security Cabinet or the government as a whole, rather than a unilateral decision by the Prime Minister or Defense Minister.

- Only after 11:00 a.m. did the Security Cabinet formally approve the "commencement of military operations," which had already been underway for four hours and had cost many lives. Well done, Gali Baharav-Miara. Did it help at the Hague?

- The Legal Advisor insisted that even under conditions of invasion, any new Rules of Engagement must be clearly defined and legally authorized in order to ensure the legitimacy of actions and to protect soldiers from future prosecutions. The problem was that the massacre could not be stopped while waiting for the "legal packaging."

What was happening at 4 in the morning of October 7 was the apotheosis of the deep state's failure. When the warning lights went on at the Shin Bet and AMAN, instead of immediately scrambling aviation and the Gaza Division, the generals decided to "wait until morning." This was not an error; it was a paralysis of will. Having spent so long fighting the "Bibi dictatorship," when the real threat arrived, they proved incapable of action. They were too occupied with saving face for their Conception to save the lives of people.

The lawyers' intervention on the morning of October 7 did not prevent appeals to the Hague, meaning the International Criminal Court, which confirms the futility of the 'legal shield.' Despite the attempts of the Legal Advisor and the military prosecutors to formally secure the IDF's actions within a legal framework, this proved insufficient for international justice:

1. In May 2024, ICC Prosecutor Karim Khan requested arrest warrants for Israeli top leadership, including Prime Minister Benjamin Netanyahu and Defense Minister Yoav Gallant.

2. The accusations concern crimes against humanity and war crimes in connection with the war in Gaza, specifically actions that the ICC alleges led to famine and excessive civilian casualties.

3. The very fact of the issuance of warrant requests, despite the 'legal purity' of the October 7 procedures, shows that the international community and the ICC focus on outcomes and

proportionality, not on the formal side of the approval of Rules of Engagement.

4. Israeli legal doctrine relies on the principle of complementarity, meaning that Israel is capable of investigating independently, but the ICC, judging by the prosecutor's actions, believes that Israel either cannot or does not wish to effectively investigate these crimes.

Thus, the lawyers' intervention on October 7 proved powerless before international pressure. Absurdity is the most delicate word for assessing the decisions of Gali Baharav-Miara under these circumstances.

The Decision of the Chief of the General Staff

Chief of the General Staff Herzi Halevi refused to comply with Netanyahu and, following the Legal Advisor's instructions, confirmed the priority of "legal legitimacy" even under conditions of chaos and massacre. Halevi refused to immediately approve radically "free" Rules of Engagement corresponding to the actual combat situation. He understood that if the military were to act according to rules not authorized by the lawyers, he himself would bear command responsibility for possible violations in the future, whereas the Legal Advisor was providing a "legal shield" to the system.

The price of this decision was hundreds of killed and captured Israeli citizens for whom the "legal shield" was of no use whatsoever. If one is not to be judged for this, for what then?

The incident underscored the fundamental 'social schizophrenia' of the Israeli legal system, which becomes an 'obstacle' to executive power and the army in a moment of existential crisis. In other words: let the state perish, but the bureaucratic procedure of the 'legal shield' will be observed.

As a physician obligated to follow protocols, I have been in situations in which it was necessary to deviate from them. In critical cases, a physician has the right to depart from the standard in order to save a life and then answers for this decision before colleagues and courts.

But should a government lawyer with such power not be guided by the benefit to the state in a moment of mortal threat?

Let me recall: the total number of civilian and military casualties on October 7 was approximately 1,250 people. It is impossible to divide this number precisely by four-hour intervals, but it was during the interval from 7:00 to 11:00 a.m. that the most mass massacre occurred in the kibbutzim and at the Nova festival. Thank them indeed: they will no longer have need of legal protection. Chief of the General Staff Herzi Halevi appears unworthy of his soldiers and officers who heroically saved the lives of people and the country.

Summary:

- At 7:00 a.m., Netanyahu demanded a declaration of war and the introduction of corresponding Rules of Engagement.
- The Legal Advisor overruled this; the Chief of the General Staff refused to comply with the Prime Minister and executed the Legal Advisor's instructions.
- "Legal schizophrenia" is the precise definition of the absurdity in which bureaucratic and legal peacetime procedures intervened at a critical moment of war.

Conclusion

The 'Era of Blindness' is not a technical malfunction; it is ideological blindness. The liberal conception of 'proportionality' and the 'pragmatism of the enemy' disarmed Israel. October 7 was the moment when the 'wet towel' of truth, in Mark Twain's phrase, struck the nation in the face. We paid for illusions with the blood of those whom we were obligated to protect.

The catastrophe of October 7 was the collision of two hallucinations.

Sinwar's hallucination that Israel would collapse collided with the hallucination of our General Staff that Hamas had been "pacified." The one with knives in its hands won. This is a verdict on the era of "smart" containment. Either the army returns to reality and aggression, or the Conception will consume what remains of the country.

Israeli media before October 7 functioned not as a mirror of reality but as a filter of "correct" news: an informational "Iron Wall." Anyone who doubted the Conception or supported the reform was branded a "destroyer of democracy" or a "messianic fanatic." This deprived professional warnings from experts outside the "left camp" of airtime. The media created a conveyor belt of former Shin Bet and AMAN heads who in one voice insisted: "Hamas is restrained." Journalists stopped asking pointed questions and became part of the same "deep state." While the "Kaplanists" received round-the-clock airtime and glorification, alternative viewpoints were marginalized. This blinded society and destroyed "army unity" not through the efforts of the government but through media and the refusal to serve.

Israel knew about Hamas's plans: the Jericho Wall document of 2022 described the attack scenario but was deemed "unrealistic."

The blockade of Gaza radicalized the population, strengthening support for the organizations. The judicial reform of 2023 triggered mass protests, distracting the army and weakening vigilance.

The Primary Failure: Adherence to the Erroneous Conception of Deterrence

IDF strategists proceeded from the "rationality" of Hamas, meaning its interest in preserving power and economic benefits from Qatari money, and therefore concluded that there was no desire for a full-scale attack.

This led to a fatal imbalance: intentions were assessed while capabilities were ignored.

The Result: Strategic-Level Decisions That Turned into a Catastrophe

- Overestimation of the reliability of the "smart fence" and underestimation of tunnels and a ground breach led to the critical reduction of manpower on the border and the withdrawal of elite units to other directions.
- The reliance on high-technology intelligence, specifically AMAN and Unit 8200, with neglect of HUMINT and open-source intelligence, led to the ignoring of the surveillance soldiers' warnings.
- The unpreparedness of operational headquarters and the absence of adequate rapid-response plans for the October 7 breach led to a gap between plans on paper and the actual threat.

The Factors That Preceded the Catastrophe of October 7:

- The "schizophrenia" of society wrought by the "peace process" of Oslo.
- The violent expulsion of thousands of Israelis from Gaza in 2005.
- The political blindness of the "peace camp."
- The collapse of trust in institutions, including the Knesset, the government, and the Supreme Court.
- Protests organized "in military fashion," the "Kaplanist Nukhba."
- The "left doctrine" of the IDF, which led to the loss of offensive spirit.
- The systemic failure of the IDF, AMAN, and the Shin Bet on the night of October 7.

The failure of October 7 showed that the 'left doctrine' of the security services and the erroneous 'Conception' deepened 'social schizophrenia': the official reality diverged from the objective threat.

The Systemic Crisis Revealed:

- The 'devil's advocate' institution of doubt was reduced to an empty formality. Any officer who spoke of a possible Hamas attack was branded a "panic-monger." The inability to accept the principle of "ipcha mistabra" ("the opposite could become reality") paralyzed the country at the critical moment.

- Intellectual terror within the system: professionalism was sacrificed to loyalty to the Conception. When surveillance soldiers saw training exercises for the capture of kibbutzim, headquarters replied: "Do not interfere with our management of the quiet."
- The collapse of the deterrence doctrine: the ignoring of the radical ideology of Hamas; the involvement of military leadership in politics and its inclination toward "liberal proportionality" instead of ensuring the country's security.
- A "culture of lies and negligence" in the General Staff: professional warnings were replaced by the "virtual reality" of success.

Conclusion: Generals, officers, and soldiers are a necessary instrument of war. But only strong political leadership is capable of defining the ultimate goal and withstanding the pressure necessary for victory.

CHAPTER 25
THE CATASTROPHE OF OCTOBER 7

"If you are going through hell, keep going."

Winston Churchill

Introduction

The week of the Sukkot holiday at the beginning of October 2023 was characterized by the highest level of political tension and internal division in the country, despite an outward sense of calm and celebration. The principal driving force of the atmosphere was the large-scale protests against the judicial reform that the government was advancing. For nearly nine months, the country had been living in a state of permanent political crisis. The protests in Tel Aviv and across the country were directed against the "reasonableness" bill, which allowed the Supreme Court to adjudicate not according to the laws but according to its own concepts and to annul decisions of the government and laws of the Knesset.

As if in mockery, the "Kaplanists" called this a struggle to save Israeli democracy.

The Sukkah on Ayalon as a Symbol of Blindness

During the week of Sukkot, the protesters continued their targeted actions and blockades. The most symbolic incident was the blocking of the central Ayalon Highway in Tel Aviv, where demonstrators conspicuously erected a holiday sukkah on the roadway to demonstrate that the protest continued even during the holiday. This sukkah on the asphalt of Ayalon became a monument to national disorientation. While intelligence was receiving signals of "unusual activity" in Gaza, police resources and public attention were riveted to protecting the protesters from themselves. This was the apex of social schizophrenia: the country was waging war against the specter of "dictatorship" while real, medieval tyranny was raising its knife above it. Festive complacency, multiplied by political fanaticism, created the ideal "security vacuum." On the eve of the attack, on the night between Friday and Saturday, the country was in a state of complete religious celebration and rest, which contributed to a further decline in readiness and the departure of military personnel on leave.

Society remained sharply divided into two camps: supporters of the reform and its opponents among centrists and leftists. Against the backdrop of the protests, unprecedented calls for refusal of service were heard from reservists, particularly in the air force and elite units. This created critical tension within the IDF and reinforced the sense of internal weakness and division. Israel was focused exclusively on its internal conflicts. Everyone was clearly exhausted by the chronic confrontation.

Against the background of the political storm, the greater part of the country was immersed in the celebration of Sukkot, a traditional period of family rest, tourism, and general relaxation. Many families were on vacation, and a portion of the regular military and security service personnel were on leave or on duty with reduced vigilance.

The dominant conception of the "deterrence" of enemies provided a false sense of security.

The recent transfer of IDF forces to the West Bank and the emphasis on the technological barrier of the fence created a conviction that the border with Gaza was "the safest." The contrast between joyful gatherings in the booths and political enmity created an atmosphere of social schizophrenia that suddenly ended on October 7.

My wife Stella and I, together with friends, had booked two nights at a hotel on the Dead Sea and spent the fifth and sixth of October there with great pleasure. Having checked out in the first half of the day on October 6, we stopped on the way home to visit my brother in Ashdod. The meeting was warm and delicious: we had not seen each other for a long time, and Liza, his wife, cooks wonderfully. Satisfied with both the vacation with friends and the Dead Sea and the visit to my brother, we arrived home to Haifa by evening. Who could have known that this night would be the last peaceful one...

It was not my intention to present in this book a detailed picture of the Hamas attack and the fighting. No one in the country yet has such a picture, although fragments of the results of certain investigations have already reached the open press. These are what I will use, though I cannot vouch for their absolute accuracy.

As it turned out, there were operational warnings in the days before the attack, such as reports on the conclusion of Hamas exercises, but they were ignored because of the conceptual fixation. The attack began on Shabbat and on the holiday of Simchat Torah, a day when religious families gather and many military bases operate in a mode of minimal readiness.

Thus, Israel approached October 7 in a state of psychological exhaustion, ideological division, and collective blindness regarding the external threat, which provided the ideal cover for an unprecedented assault.

No One Expected the Attack

On the morning of October 7, 2023, Israel, blinded and stupefied by social schizophrenia, conflicts, and internal division, came to understand that its "real world" had been illusory.

The "Catastrophe of October 7," the "Black Saturday," is the most severe event in the modern history of the State of Israel, the bloodiest for the Jewish people since the Holocaust, and the largest terrorist attack in the world in terms of victims per capita. October 7 was not merely a tragedy or the greatest intelligence failure; it was a point of no return, a moment after which the previous explanatory models ceased to function. Israel woke up in a world where all the previous "security guarantees," moral compromises, and "fine-tuned deterrents" had proven to be fiction.

"Hamas does not want war and is not preparing for a large-scale attack."

This was the main "Conception," as it is called in Israel, from which the security services had been operating in recent years, especially after the underground barrier was built on the border with Gaza to protect the country from attack through tunnels. It strengthened particularly after Operation Guardian of the Walls in 2021. At that time, apart from rocket fire, Hamas made only cautious attempts to cross the border, all of which were successfully intercepted by the military. For Hamas, Operation Guardian of the Walls and the accompanying disturbances in cities with mixed Arab-Jewish populations became the final proof that the IDF was not so invincible, and that the Arab population of Israel was only waiting for a signal to join the terrorists' attack from within.

The government and the security structures considered the correct approach to be not the "resolution of the conflict" but the "management of the conflict."

Hamas was the enemy, but the goal was to create conditions for prolonged periods of quiet. The IDF and the political leadership of the country relied on intelligence analysis that proved to be wrong.

The Palestinian organization Hamas attacked Israeli territory on October 7, 2023, in order to disrupt the normalization of relations between the Jewish state and Saudi Arabia.

Hamas believed that the killing of large numbers of Israelis and the subsequent powerful Israeli strikes on Gaza constituted the necessary price of a "great achievement." The "resistance" planned to awaken the world and return the Palestinian question to the agenda. It was clear to the terrorists in advance that Israel would respond with strikes on Gaza and that many people would die. They were not wrong.

Risk Factors for the War with Hamas

The war between Israel and Hamas, which began following the attack of October 7, 2023, has many roots that had been accumulating over decades. These risk factors include geopolitical, internal, and ideological dimensions. I will enumerate them in order of risk, from high to low, drawing on analyses by experts, including US Congressional reports and BBC analyses. The assessments are subjective but are based on the frequency of mention in authoritative sources.

- *High risk: factors that directly provoke and sustain violence.*
- *Medium risk: factors that exacerbate tension.*
- *Low risk: indirect or long-term factors.*

The causal factor that made war practically inevitable was the unchanging strategic goal of Hamas: the destruction of Israel.

The conditional factor was Israeli policy of "managing the conflict" rather than resolving it. The remaining factors that led to the war of 2023 to 2025 can be divided into structural factors representing long-term risks, situational factors representing immediate catalysts, and the main trigger, which was the event that moved the situation from a state of high risk to a state of war.

Risk Factors

These elements created the necessary background of high tension and instability that allowed the trigger to fire.

Critical risk: *the trigger was the failure of intelligence and defense on October 7, 2023. The very fact of the successful, unprecedented in scale and brutality, Hamas invasion of Israel, which led to the deaths of approximately 1,200 people and the capture of hostages, constituted a direct act of war. The IDF's failure to contain the attack made a large-scale military operation the only possible political and moral response.*

Highest risk: the existential goal of Hamas, the complete destruction of Israel, was not subject to discussion. Hamas had accumulated significant military potential in the form of rockets and tunnels under Iranian leadership, waiting for the right moment for a decisive strike. The humanitarian and economic crisis in the Gaza

Strip, caused by years of Israeli and Egyptian blockade, created the ideal environment for the radicalization of the population and for recruitment. The absence of economic prospects strengthened readiness for violence. Before 2023, Israel for years adhered to a policy of "buying quiet" through Qatari money and work permits, and of deliberate containment, believing that Hamas "could be bought" and that this was better than occupation or a diplomatic impasse. This policy allowed Hamas to arm itself and prepare.

Medium risk: the deteriorating situation on the West Bank, the rise in violence by Israeli settlers, and the constant tension around Al-Aqsa Mosque served as ideological fuel for Hamas, which positioned itself as the "defender of Jerusalem and Al-Aqsa." The deep political and social split in Israel over the judicial reform in 2023 led to hundreds of thousands of reservists protesting, and the attention of the political and military leadership was diverted to internal unrest. Hamas perceived this as a sign of weakness and vulnerability. The irony and tragedy of that morning was that some of the "Brothers in Arms" who had for months held the country hostage with their refusal of service jumped into their cars and drove south to help: this was a spontaneous sobering, but paid for at a terrible price. However, even this heroism does not negate the fact that their prior blackmail had become for Sinwar the main indicator of Israel's "readiness" for the blow. They were extinguishing a fire they themselves had helped to fan with their calls for sabotage. The success of the Abraham Accords and the negotiations over normalization of relations between Israel and Saudi Arabia created a parallel concern: Hamas and Iran sought to disrupt the process by returning the Palestinian question to the center of the regional agenda through violence.

Low risk: the strengthening of Iran and its "Axis of Resistance," including Hezbollah in Lebanon and the Houthis in Yemen, created a strategic environment in which Hamas felt itself part of a larger, Iran-supported anti-Israel alliance.

The Hamas attack was not a 'sudden' event but the culmination of the enumerated factors.

The immediate motive was the desire to disrupt the normalization of Israel with Arab countries. In Israel, the word "Conception" long ago ceased to be an abstraction. It is not a plan or a strategy but a stable mental construct within which facts are interpreted so as not to destroy a pre-accepted picture of the world. The Conception is dangerous not because it forbids seeing the facts: it forbids drawing adequate conclusions from them.

Chronology of Events on October 7, 2023

This is a story not only of a planned Hamas military operation but also of a chaotic yet extremely brutal invasion by a "second wave" consisting of residents of Gaza. According to updated IDF data, approximately 6,000 people crossed the border that day: of these, 3,800 were elite Nukhba special forces, and the remaining 2,200 were civilians and militants of other organizations. Below is a minute-by-minute chronology of the catastrophe, with emphasis on the role of the "civilian" residents of Gaza.

The Breach and the Military Assault: 6:30 to 8:00 a.m.

6:29 a.m.: Hamas launches more than 3,000 rockets. Under cover of the salvos, drones destroy Israeli communications towers and the "smart fence" at 119 points.

6:40 a.m.: The first Nukhba units on motorcycles and paragliders enter Israeli communities and military bases, including Re'im and Nahal Oz.

7:00 to 7:30 a.m.: The beginning of the mass massacre at the Nova festival and in the kibbutzim of Be'eri and Kfar Aza. The militants operate according to precise maps, capturing hostages and killing defenders.

Between 6:30 a.m. and late evening on October 7, a void formed: not only military but also managerial. The state disappeared precisely when it was needed most. This pause cost hundreds of lives.

The Second Wave:

The Invasion by Gaza Residents, 8:30 to 12:00 p.m.

When it became clear that the Israeli army was not responding and the fence had been completely destroyed, a crowd from Gaza poured through the breaches. These were not only armed militants of the "second echelon" but ordinary residents: teenagers, men, and even elderly people.

9:00 a.m.: Video recordings show residents of Gaza entering Israeli territory on bicycles, carts, and on foot. They did not participate in battles with the army but actively joined in looting and violence.

10:00 a.m.: The role of the "civilians" becomes critical: they enter homes already "cleared" by the militants and begin removing electronics, furniture, and driving off livestock.

Participation in kidnappings: it was precisely the residents of the "second wave" who seized many hostages who were not on Hamas's original lists. In some cases, "civilians" simply grabbed children and women and dragged them into Gaza on motorcycles or tractors in order to later "sell" them to Hamas.

Documentation: residents of Gaza conducted live streams on social media, celebrating the massacre and mocking the bodies of the dead, creating the effect of a "national celebration" inside the strip.

FROM A POLITICAL THRILLER

Where Is the IDF?

A Scene Describing the Paralysis of the System in the First Hours of the Invasion.

Setting: *A living room in one of the kibbutzim. 7:30 in the morning. Outside, cries in Arabic and bursts of automatic gunfire are audible.*

Characters: The Head of the Household (a reserve officer) and His Wife.

Father: *(dialing a number convulsively) "Damn it, no one is picking up! The division headquarters has an answering machine! How is this possible?"*

Wife: *(pressing the children to her) "Where is the army? Where are the helicopters? For an hour now we have been hearing them break down the neighbors' doors!"*

Father: *(looking out the window at the burning fence) "They have broken through along the entire line. The only contact is the reservists' chat. The guys are writing that the bases have been captured and there is no communications. The generals in Tel Aviv are probably still thinking this is an 'incident at the fence.'"*

Wife: *"But we have a 'smart fence'! They told us it was impenetrable!"*

Father: *(bitterly) "The fence turned out to be smarter than those who managed it. Those who should have given the order spent too long studying 'humanity' and 'proportionality.' And now they are killing us in our bedrooms. I am taking my pistol. If they come in, lie down on the children."*

Attempts at Stabilization: 12:00 p.m. to Evening

1:00 p.m.: The IDF begins to recover. The first special forces groups enter battles inside the kibbutzim.

3:00 p.m.: Crowds of Gaza residents continue to move through the holes in the fence, transporting looted property. The army still does not control the perimeter.

7:00 to 10:00 p.m.: The IDF restores partial control over most communities, but looters from Gaza continue to hide in the strip, taking the last hostages.

"Civilian" Accomplices.

The catastrophe of October 7 erased the line between Hamas and part of the civilian population of Gaza. It later emerged that many Gaza residents who had worked in the kibbutzim for years had been providing Hamas with detailed plans of the houses and the locations of the families. Many hostages, including the Bibas family, were held not in Hamas tunnels but in the private homes of "ordinary" Gaza residents, including UNRWA teachers and doctors. This "nationwide" involvement was the most shocking discovery for Israel, completely destroying the belief in the possibility of peaceful coexistence under current conditions.

The Morning of October 7, 2023

The First Hours, Part One

At approximately 1:00 in the morning on the transition from October 6 to 7, the head of the Shin Bet was summoned to headquarters after receiving a report that in Gaza several dozen Israeli SIM cards had been activated, which are used for communications when attempting to cross the border. Shortly afterward, other signs of unusual activity in Hamas ranks appeared. The Shin Bet's report indicates that two days earlier, individual SIM cards had already been activated in the strip. The Shin Bet, lacking agents in Gaza, concluded that nothing was expected to happen.

However, given certain other alarming signals, the intelligence service allowed for the possibility that Hamas might undertake isolated attempts to attack or abduct Israelis and sent the "Tequila" special forces unit to the border.

The attack began at approximately 6:30 in the morning with a massive rocket bombardment of the center and south of Israel, which served as a diversionary maneuver. Several thousand Hamas militants and "uninvolved" residents of the strip broke through the border barrier, including through breaches made by explosives and bulldozers, and through tunnels. The main military bases of the IDF's Southern Command, including the Gaza Division, were captured or paralyzed, which knocked out the command center.

The militants penetrated dozens of border communities, including Be'eri, Kfar Aza, and Nir Oz, where they carried out mass killings, torture, rapes, and the burning of entire families.

6:29 a.m.: Netanyahu is notified of what is happening.

6:35 a.m.: Air raid siren in response to Hamas rockets.

7:00 a.m.: The Nova music festival near Kibbutz Re'im came under attack by Hamas militants. The assault led to an unprecedented massacre of adults and children.

7:40 a.m.: The IDF announced that Hamas militants had entered the south of Israel.

8:23 a.m.: Israel declared a state of military readiness.

8:34 a.m.: Israel announced the beginning of a counterterrorism operation named "Iron Swords."

7:00 to 12:20 p.m.: Hamas militants committed massacres in a number of Israeli communities, including Netiv HaAsara, Be'eri, Kfar Aza, Holit, Nir Oz, and others.

11:35 a.m.: Prime Minister Benjamin Netanyahu declared that Israel was in a state of war.

12:21 p.m.: The IDF began the operation to liberate its communities.

2:29 p.m.: The United States condemned the Hamas terrorist attack and confirmed its support for Israel.

The Combined Attack

The number of rockets and mortar shells on the first day of the war was cited as "approximately 4,500." With the beginning of the bombardment, sirens sounded in many parts of the country; however, subsequent analysis showed that all the strikes had two main objectives: IDF bases along the border with Gaza, and the air force bases of Nevatim, Ramon, Palmachim, and Hatzerim. The goal was to prevent the air force from striking the infiltrating militants and targets inside Gaza. And this goal was partially achieved.

The Hamas ground attack consisted of three main waves, in each of which the terrorists attempted to seize control of different territories in the south of Israel. The total number of participants was given as 6,000, and the number of breaches in the fence as "no fewer than 114." The terrorists operated as organized forces and employed advanced technological means.

As part of the third wave of the attack, an entire Nukhba company in ten pickup trucks was deployed. However, near the Gaza fence, all these pickup trucks carrying terrorists were destroyed by drone strikes. On the body of one of the terrorists was found a plan of the Tel Nof base.

October 7 was not merely a military defeat: it was the collapse of technological idol-worship.

Generals who believed that sensors and remotely operated machine guns could replace manpower saw the "smart fence" worth billions turned into a pile of useless metal within minutes. Hamas won not through force but through primitiveness. It turned out that a doctrine oriented toward "high-technology conflict management" was powerless against a drone costing 500 dollars. This was the moment of truth: when you castrate an army by stripping it of its spirit of aggression, no sensors will save you.

During the fighting, approximately 1,400 terrorists were eliminated, the majority as a result of air strikes, and another 200 were taken prisoner. The greatest number of terrorists who penetrated Israel came from the Nuseirat Battalion of Hamas's Central Camps Brigade. It was their terrorists who carried out the massacre at the Nova festival and in Kibbutz Be'eri, killing and wounding the maximum number of civilians in Israel.

The sea attack involved 40 terrorists in five fast motorboats, eight to a boat. Two boats were destroyed by the Israeli Navy; three managed to reach the beach at Zikim, where a massacre of unsuspecting vacationers was carried out. After the massacre on the beach, the terrorists attacked Kibbutz Zikim but were repelled by the local self-defense unit, and six terrorists were killed. Four more terrorists hid in the brush in the area until October 10, when they were discovered and eliminated by tankers of the 52nd Battalion, Maglan commandos, and infantry of the 17th Battalion.

As for the paragliders, there were eight of them, each carrying one terrorist, with one having fallen back inside the Gaza Strip after takeoff. A different matter were the paragliders that launched from northern Gaza. On them, three terrorists managed to penetrate Moshav Netiv HaAsara, where they killed 21 local residents, including four fighters of the local self-defense unit. Another Hamas air weapon was attack multicopters. Thirty of these were put into the air; their main targets were the towers with remote-controlled machine guns of the "Ro'eh Yore" ("See and Shoot") system. Only a few of these systems were not suppressed and were able to return fire.

The raid on the ground was led by the junior Hamas command, specifically 15 Nukhba company commanders and several battalion deputy commanders. Not a single battalion commander crossed the barrier, and the middle and senior command likewise remained inside Gaza and directed the terrorists from there.

Israel declared the war of "Iron Swords" on Gaza. On the side of Gaza stood the Hezbollah terrorists of Lebanon, the Arabs of the Palestinian Authority, the Houthis of Yemen, the Arabs of Syria and Iraq, and Iran. I write these lines in December 2025, when the war begun on October 7, 2023 is nearly concluded, all surviving hostages have been returned to their families, and Israel is striving for "complete" victory.

The Four Goals of the War as Defined by the Israeli Government:

1. The military defeat of Hamas: partially achieved.
2. The eradication of the Hamas political regime: achieved over half the territory of Gaza.
3. The return of all hostages: returned, with the exception of one who was killed.
4. The pacification of the Gaza Strip, guaranteeing that it will no longer represent a threat to Israel.

The shock of the tragedy of October 7, 2023 somewhat cooled the 'nuclear reactor' of internal conflict, but did not extinguish it: it remains active, though smoldering at a lower intensity.

The First Hours, Part Two

At 3:30 in the morning, residents of Gaza were at the fence. According to protocol, it was necessary in such a case to immediately place troops on alert and declare the "PARASH PALESTT" regime, meaning a Palestinian invasion. However, all warnings were ignored.

The supreme military leadership categorically forbade taking any action contrary to military protocols. The orders came from the Chief of the General Staff, who allowed the unfolding events to proceed without intervention.

At 4:30 in the morning, the Shin Bet dispatched the "Tequila" group and YAMAM special police to Kibbutz Kfar Aza in order to evacuate two senior Shin Bet employees. There was concern that they might be captured, and their knowledge represented extremely valuable information that could fall into the hands of Hamas. This fact proves that the Shin Bet anticipated an invasion of Israel. The question is: why did it not deploy forces to protect the communities?

The official explanation was: "We did not want to expose sources of information, so we gave the order not to take any action on the ground, not to place troops on alert, and not to sound the alarm." This version does not withstand scrutiny. If they did not believe that an invasion would occur, why at 4:30 in the morning did they send the special "Tequila" group to Kfar Aza to "save" two Shin Bet employees? Save them from what? Why was the "PARASH PALESTT" regime not declared at 3:30, as the instructions require, despite numerous emergency warnings from the field?

All combat applications, including the high-technology sensors, signals intelligence, the 'smart fence,' and the air force, in short everything, failed completely on October 7.

Where Was the Air Force on the Morning of October 7?

Channel 14 of Israeli television published materials from a secret internal investigation of the IDF Air Force's actions during the events of October 7, minute by minute. The material describes what was known in the air force on the night of October 7 before the massacre began, why steps were not taken to prevent the catastrophe, who was not informed, and from whom information was concealed.

The air force command, which for the past two years had claimed it was not aware of events and had been informed only shortly before the attack began, did in fact know what was happening. Commanders at both the upper and lower levels were informed, with one exception: Air Force Commander Tomer Bar.

What Was Happening at Air Force Headquarters on October 7:

2:50 a.m.: The first dramatic call arrives. The Chief of the Operations Department of the General Staff woke the head of air defense in the air force. Reports from the south were already causing concern. The operations officer warned that something unusual was happening in Gaza.

3:20 a.m.: The first briefing was held among senior officers. "This should be treated seriously," warned the Chief of the General Staff Operations Department, Shlomi Binder. "Expanded preparation is necessary," Binder told his counterpart in the air force, despite the Gaza Division and Southern Command asserting that there was no immediate threat. From this moment, the air force was fully involved in events, with an exchange of information continuing among senior officers, with one exception, a man who was asleep and received not a single call: Air Force Commander Tomer Bar.

3:30 to 4:00 a.m.: The air force commander's chief of staff sent him messages about unusual Hamas activity. The information was transmitted to the air force commander, but he did not read the messages. Even when a further message was sent indicating that the incident had been "closed" at the Southern Command level, with that command asserting there was no immediate threat, the message was not opened.

Around 4:00 a.m.: Binder in a WhatsApp message asks a senior air force officer to ensure that the air force commander is informed. The senior officer replied affirmatively, despite the fact that in reality Tomer Bar was still asleep, not responding to messages, and unaware of what was happening. No one attempted to wake him, despite the alarming activity in Gaza.

Approximately two hours before the massacre began, after 4:00 a.m.: a dramatic event occurred. Simultaneously with information updates arriving from army structures not connected to the air force, air force intelligence recorded unusual activity in the enclave multiple times, in more than one location. Aerial observations indicated heightened activity and the movement of Hamas attack drones. The data were recorded and collected in real time but were not transmitted further and remained within the department.

Approximately one hour before the massacre began, after 5:00 a.m.: two dramatic events occurred simultaneously. The air force commander woke up, and the first brief was held. The chief of staff informed Tomer Bar of the details and of the fact that a general operational meeting had been scheduled for 8:30 in the morning. Bar asked to be excused from participating, assigned the air force intelligence officer to substitute for him, and requested to be informed after the completion of his jog. At the same time, the head of the air force intelligence collection department woke two drone squadron commanders living near him at Palmachim base, told them something unusual was happening, and asked them to prepare personnel and equipment. However, this was not completed before the attack began.

At 6:30 in the morning, everything became history. The attack had begun, and the air force was in a state of minimal readiness, forced to respond to an unprecedented, sudden, and lethal attack in a completely unprepared state.

At the Nova Festival

The terrorists did not know about the Nova music festival near Kibbutz Re'im at all and arrived there by accident, having taken a wrong turn, and only an hour and a half after the attack had begun. The festival became the site of one of the most monstrous mass killings in the history of Israel, occurring in the first hours of the Hamas attack on October 7, 2023. On the night between October 6 and 7, several thousand people had gathered there.

At approximately 6:30 in the morning, when the festival was at its height, a massive rocket bombardment from the Gaza Strip began. The organizers urged people to leave the grounds; a "Red Alert" code sounded. Festival participants rushed to their cars to leave, but the roads quickly became blocked due to the influx of traffic and falling rockets.

Shortly after the beginning of the rocket bombardment, Hamas militants arrived at the festival grounds, using both ground transport and motorized paragliders. The militants took up positions on the only roads leading to and from the festival, blocking all escape routes. The terrorists methodically fired to kill at everyone they saw. People were shot directly on the dance floor and in their cars; the militants stopped vehicles, dragged people out, and killed them. Those who tried to shelter in roadside shelters called Mamads were often targeted, with grenades thrown into the shelters. In addition to the killings, the militants seized dozens of hostages, approximately 40 people, who were taken to Gaza. According to various estimates, 378 people were killed on the festival grounds and on the adjacent roads. Survivors described what they witnessed as "hell" and an "apocalyptic" sight: bodies of people everywhere, burned cars, and gunfire that lasted for hours. Many survivors hid for hours under cars or in bushes, hearing the conversations of the militants and the screams of the victims.

The army arrived at the festival only after the terrorists had shot 378 people and abducted 44.

The assault on the Nova festival became the largest mass killing of civilians in the history of Israel. The tragedy became a shocking symbol of how a peaceful gathering of young people was turned into a battlefield and an execution ground. The events at Nova formed the basis of the documentary film "We Will Dance Again," which received international recognition.

The Story of Libi Cohen-Meguri

Libi Cohen-Meguri was killed on October 7, just 22 years old. She was dancing at the Nova festival and was shot by terrorists when she tried to flee the party down Highway 232.

At 8:11, she called her parents and said: "I have been wounded in the stomach, I have been wounded in the arm, I am losing blood. I am dying." Calmly, with clarity, she understood that these were the last minutes of her life. She asked her parents to call Tomer, her twin brother, and Maya, her younger sister, and said: "I am dying; I simply want you to hear me. I love you, Yariv, you are the best father I could have wished for. Mama, stop crying; just listen to me. You are the best mother we could have had. Do not forget to be a good mother to Tomer and Maya after my death. Tomer, how lucky we were to have lived life together. I love you. My Maya, never forget that you are the treasure of my entire life."

Her parents asked her to get out of the car, lie down on the road, and play dead. She did so, but the terrorists noticed movement and approached to finish her off at close range.

"Mama, they are coming to shoot me again,"

Libi managed to say, and then in the telephone receiver the sounds of Arabic shouts were heard, followed by a long burst of gunfire until the connection was cut.

Such was the end of her life: alone, on the yellow center line of the highway, into which an entire Kalashnikov magazine was emptied. Libi was killed in cold blood. This terrible end was the complete opposite of her life, which was vivid and happy. One need only look at her photographs to see what light and beauty she radiated and how kind her heart was. Libi was a ray of joy, laughter, and generosity. She served as an infantry officer, knew how to enjoy life, and infected those around her with goodness and happiness. We will always remember you. (Yosef Hadad; post by Alex Lev Gold; Facebook; July 10)

Why Did the Shin Bet Not Warn?

The Israel General Security Service, the Shin Bet, failed to warn of the October 7 attack due to a combination of conceptual fixation, systemic shortcomings in the collection and assessment of data, and a misunderstanding of Hamas's intentions. Here are the primary reasons for the failure.

The main factor was the "misunderstanding" of Hamas's intentions. The dominant intelligence assessment was that Hamas was restrained and focused on the economic management of Gaza rather than on full-scale war. The Shin Bet knew about two Hamas invasion plans, including the "Jericho Wall" plan found years earlier, but these documents were "not properly processed" and were dismissed as unrealistic or fantastical because they did not fit the dominant conception.

Despite the presence of critical signals, they did not lead to the adoption of adequate measures. On the night of October 6 to 7, the Shin Bet was receiving specific signals about attack preparations but did not attribute sufficient significance to them, since similar activity had been observed earlier without serious consequences. Shin Bet head Ronen Bar made the wrong decision regarding whether to wake Prime Minister Benjamin Netanyahu that night, based on confidence in the existing intelligence assessments.

Systemic and Organizational Shortcomings

Israeli intelligence services lacked reliable agents both among the assault detachments and in the senior command of Hamas's military wing. The Shin Bet, like the IDF, had a "misunderstanding" regarding the strength of the technological barrier on the border with Gaza and the ability of the military to respond operationally to its breach.

Thus, the failure was systemic, rooted in a mentality and culture that allowed for the underestimation of the threat and the ignoring of data that contradicted an outdated conception.

The Hamas Narrative

The principal Hamas narrative in the war with Israel, which Hamas named "Al-Aqsa Flood," is deeply rooted in Islamist ideology and is directed toward achieving both internal and external propaganda goals. It represents a mixture of religious duty, a call to struggle for "liberation," and the exploitation of the humanitarian crisis for the mobilization of support.

The Hamas narrative is built around the following key themes. The fundamental thesis, based on the Hamas Charter, asserts that all the land of Palestine, meaning all of Israel, is sacred and not subject to alienation. Jihad, meaning armed struggle, is declared the only path for the "liberation" of all of Palestine and is a religious duty. The October 7 operation was named "Al-Aqsa Flood," which directly indicates the goal: the purported defense of the Al-Aqsa Mosque in Jerusalem against "Zionist encroachments." This religious slogan carries enormous mobilizing force in the Islamic world.

Hamas positions itself not as an antisemitic movement but as a movement conducting a struggle exclusively against the "aggressor, the Zionist occupier." This is an attempt to separate its struggle from accusations of antisemitism and to secure support in the international arena. Hamas claims that the attack was necessary to lift the Israeli blockade of the Gaza Strip. One of the declared goals was the liberation of Palestinian prisoners from Israeli jails. Hamas positions itself and its allies, Hezbollah and Iran, as "resistance forces" that alone are willing to engage in armed struggle for Palestinian rights.

Despite the subsequent destruction, Hamas and its supporters present the very fact of the border breach, the seizure of military bases and kibbutzim, which constituted the largest mass killing of Jews since the Holocaust, as an unprecedented success and a demonstration that Israel is vulnerable and its army is not invincible. Civilian losses in Gaza caused by Israel's response operation are actively used in propaganda to portray Israel as the aggressor and to mobilize international condemnation and pressure.

The Hamas narrative is aimed not only at the Palestinian population but also at radical circles in the Middle East and at international public opinion, where a portion of left-wing activists portray Hamas militants as "victims of colonialism" while ignoring the mass killings of peaceful Israeli residents.

Failure or Treason?

Was October 7 a case of negligence, systemic failure, or betrayal within the security service, the Shin Bet? The known facts are as follows. Hamas conducted a well-coordinated attack using drones, motorcycles, explosives, and paragliders. Israeli intelligence, the Shin Bet and AMAN, did not prevent the attack despite certain threat signals. The Shin Bet leadership took responsibility for the failure but declared the absence of malicious intent.

Was there treason?

Suspicions exist that the October 7 attack became possible not only because of negligence but also due to possible betrayal or deliberate ignoring of threats by a portion of the security system. These suspicions are based on the scale of the attack, the silence of intelligence, and the political context. There is no evidence.

The expert version is that of a systemic failure. The majority of military and intelligence experts assert that the cause of the catastrophe was not a conspiracy but a deep analytical error, an overestimation of control over Gaza, and an underestimation of Hamas's intentions.

At present, there is no direct evidence of treason within the Shin Bet, but trust in the service has been undermined. The truth most likely lies between negligence and deeply ingrained errors in elite thinking.

The Second Wave: When the Mask of the Peaceful Population Was Removed

The Collapse of the Humanist Illusion

These facts are among the most painful, as they destroy the last bastion of the "Conception": the belief that there exists a clear division between the terrorist organization and the population it controls. For years, the Israeli left-wing elite and the defense establishment promoted the thesis that "Hamas is a tyranny holding two million Gaza residents hostage." It was believed that if people were given work and humanitarian assistance, they would not want war. On October 7, this theory was trampled in the literal sense by the feet of thousands of "peaceful" Gaza residents.

8:30 to 11:00 a.m.: The Invasion of the Neighbors

After the elite Nukhba units had breached the defenses and seized the strongpoints, a "second wave" poured through the gaps in the fence. These were not soldiers in uniform. These were men in sandals, teenagers on bicycles, elderly people with sticks, and even women. They did not come to fight the IDF: they came to loot, rape, and kill.

Looting as celebration: video recordings from GoPro cameras and street recorders show crowds of Gaza residents removing everything from the homes of kibbutz members, from televisions to children's bicycles and agricultural equipment.

Complicity in kidnappings: it was precisely the "civilian" looters who were responsible for the chaos with the hostages. They seized wounded and frightened Israelis, including small children and elderly people, and dragged them into Gaza as "trophies" in order to later resell them to Hamas or use them for their own ransom.

"Civilian" sadism: evidence collected in 2024 and 2025 shocked even hardened investigators. It emerged that "peaceful" residents actively participated in the desecration of the bodies of the dead. A joyous crowd in Gaza met the trucks carrying the bodies of Israeli girls with jeering and the distribution of sweets. This was not "fear of Hamas": it was the ecstasy of complicity.

Informants among us: the most terrible discovery was that many of the looters of the "second wave" were the very workers who for years had been receiving work permits in Israel. They had maps of the houses. They knew who had a dog and who had small children. They knew where the safe rooms were. The system of "humanitarian gestures" so carefully protected by the legal deep state turned out to be the largest spy network in history.

UNRWA: The Humanitarian Facade of Terror

In this chapter, it is impossible to sidestep the role of international organizations. Investigations of 2024 confirmed that UNRWA employees not only celebrated the massacre but personally participated in it. UN teachers and doctors hid hostages in their homes. This became the final nail in the coffin of the idea of "uninvolved population."

The 'second wave' proved that the enemy of Israel on October 7 was not only Hamas but also a significant part of Gaza society, poisoned by decades of hatred.

The system's attempt to ignore this fact for the sake of "international legitimacy" led to Israel having itself opened the back door for its own killers, issuing them work permits and the status of "those in need."

No One Interfered

On October 7, 2023, at approximately 3:30 in the afternoon, Yasmin Porat emerged into the street from the home of Pesi Cohen in Kibbutz Be'eri, accompanied by several Hamas militants. Fourteen more hostages and several dozen militants remained in the house. The terrorists were not taking the hostages to Gaza, being confident that the routes to the border were cut off, since more than eight hours had passed since the capture of the kibbutz. They forced Yasmin to call the police and demand that they be given free passage to Gaza together with the hostages. The terrorists did not know that this was unnecessary and that they could still leave for the strip unimpeded. An hour later, the situation remained the same. Neither Yasmin nor the militants understood why the Israeli army had still not attempted to capture the kibbutz. The YAMAM police special forces arrived at Pesi Cohen's house only at 4:45 in the afternoon.

In Be'eri, the terrorists killed one in every ten residents.

101 residents of Kibbutz Be'eri were killed on October 7. Twenty-nine people were abducted to Gaza. One hundred and fifty homes were destroyed and burned. Of the fifteen hostages being held by the militants in Pesi Cohen's house, thirteen perished, including two children. Be'eri was not the only place where the IDF failed to protect the civilian population. The military came to the small Kibbutz Nir Oz on the border with the Gaza Strip only after the last Hamas militant had already left; in the end, one in every four residents was killed or abducted.

Where Was the IDF?

When the invasion began, the Israeli command was completely blind. The Gaza Division headquarters had been put out of action, but this was understood in the General Staff only much later. The Southern Command was unable to quickly take the defense upon itself. All border IDF bases and outposts whose task was defense were attacked simultaneously, and the fighters there tried to repel the assault. But there were too few of them: some fighters and commanders were on holiday leave because of the holidays, some had been sent to the West Bank where the threat was considered more serious. On the border there were three infantry battalions and one tank battalion, the minimum number of units required to be kept there in the absence of a threat. As a result, the enemy forces outnumbered the Israeli army by more than five to one.

One in every four residents of Nir Oz was killed or abducted to Gaza.

The air force was not prepared for defensive warfare at all. The helicopters scrambled in response to the alert could not fire at the terrorists from the air, because within the first minutes of the attack the militants had already intermingled with Israeli civilians and soldiers.

Highway 232, which connects the border areas with the north of the country, was under constant fire from terrorists, which greatly slowed the advance of units to the kibbutzim and other locations where their presence was needed. "And when the troops had already broken through to the border, neither the central command nor the local commanders could switch gears and understand that this was not a terrorist attack but a war."

Social schizophrenia encountered no resistance anywhere.

From 1990 onward, society was 'infected' by left-wing ideas of peace with the Palestinians, the 'peace process' of Oslo, and the 'disengagement' of 2005, hedonism and complacency blossomed, the media kept insisting that Israel was 'walking toward peace' with shields bearing this slogan filling the intersections. The paranoia of peace and wokism penetrated the IDF and filled the minds of officers and soldiers.

The atmosphere in the army increasingly resembled a "club of shared interests" with elements of the disorder characteristic of civil society. In such conditions, our generals, also processed through the Wexner Foundation (see Chapter 23), successfully "trimmed" the victorious IDF down to a "small and smart" army.

Hatred is hard to abandon: on September 13, 1993, the ruling elite of Israel renounced Zionism. On that very day, Prime Minister Yitzhak Rabin, standing in the Rose Garden of the White House, officially recognized the Palestine Liberation Organization to the enthusiastic applause of his supporters at home. Thus the Israeli elite collectively abandoned the interests of its nation.

The 'Kaplanist' protest groups formed in 2023 nearly paralyzed the country.

Worse still, by provoking a mutiny among IDF reservists, especially those serving in the air force and holding technical positions in the army, they created in Israel's enemies the impression that the country was already sufficiently weakened and divided and therefore would not be able to defend itself. And then October 7, 2023 came.

The leaders of the Israeli left continue to this day to blame Netanyahu rather than themselves. But the truth is that these groups not only stopped the judicial reform that the country needed but also created the conditions for the Catastrophe of October 7 and the war that followed it.

On that terrible day of October 7, 2023, two things occurred.

First, Arab terrorists with a sadistic thirst for blood shattered into pieces the myth that high technologies can free the bearers of advanced progressive views from the necessity of defending themselves together with those very brothers from whom the left had been so desperately trying to distance themselves. The only thing that worked that day was the crude and simple heroism and patriotism of Jews, both civilian and from the security forces, who without any orders rushed south to save the families and communities under attack.

Second, the world's elite discarded all distinctions between "good" and "bad" Jews. The photographs of the hostages from the kibbutzim of Be'eri and Kfar Aza were rejected with the same contempt and the same hatred that had previously been directed only at "aggressive settlers" or "identifiable Jews." Jew-haters on campuses no longer felt the need to pretend that some Israelis were acceptable to them.

Members of the post-Zionist stratum are desperately trying to make sense of the collapse of their delusions. Their leaders are attempting to double down. But their persistent assertions that all problems are connected exclusively with Prime Minister Benjamin Netanyahu, or with the ultra-Orthodox, or with settler-"messianists," or with "idiots" who weep at songs about the people of Israel are finding fewer and fewer supporters. Each successive left-wing protest fizzles out within a few days. The acute sensations are gone.

After the fig leaves of "peace" or "the startup nation," behind which the left had managed to hide until now, have fallen away, all that remains to the left is pure, unalloyed hatred. Thirty-one years have passed since the left, by recognizing the PLO, made hatred their standard. It is time to abandon it. For the survival of Israel now depends on this. (C. Glick; source in English: JNS)

The IDF Had No Plan

The key findings from the major investigation by The New York Times, published on December 30, 2023, under the headline "Where Was the Israeli Military on Oct. 7?" with authors including Adam Goldman, Ronen Bergman, and Mark Mazzetti, are as follows.

Absence of a plan for large-scale invasion: the IDF had no ready operational plan for the scenario of a massive breach of the border and the invasion of thousands of Hamas militants. The army was oriented toward scenarios of rocket fire and minor infiltrations, but not toward a full-scale ground attack. A quote from the article attributed to retired Brigadier General Amir Avivi, former deputy commander of the Gaza Division: "There was no plan for a surprise attack." One wonders why. What does an army normally do in the interval between wars if not prepare plans and the army for the next war?

Disorganization and a chaotic response: in the first hours of the attack, the command in Tel Aviv in the "Pit" bunker did not understand the scale. Units were sent south in small groups, often without coordination. Soldiers and officers relied on social media and WhatsApp for information about targets. Hamas quickly seized key roads, set up ambushes, and paralyzed the advance of reinforcements. Incomprehensible! Completely unclear, inexplicable, incredible: it goes beyond understanding.

Overestimation of technology and underestimation of the threat: the army excessively relied on the "smart fence," cameras, and intelligence, but Hamas neutralized all of this with drones and jammers. The Gaza Division base at Re'im was captured, which disconnected the regional command.

Delays in response: many units arrived late, by hours or even days, which allowed Hamas militants to operate unimpeded in the kibbutzim and at the Nova festival.

The investigation is based on interviews with officers and soldiers, analysis of video including from Hamas militants, and internal documents. The New York Times notes that this supplements Israeli media reporting but adds details about systemic failures. This material intensified the debate in Israel about the responsibility of Chief of the General Staff Herzi Halevi. Similar conclusions were later confirmed by internal IDF investigations in February 2025 and by independent commissions.

FROM A POLITICAL THRILLER: Dead Air

A Hypothetical Dialogue Based on Testimonies.

Setting*: The Central Command Post in Tel Aviv ('Kirya'). 8:30 a.m.*

Characters: Brigadier General Milo and the Duty Operations Officer.

Duty Officer: *"General Milo, we have lost contact with the Gaza Division. The last message was about the capture of the Re'im base. We are receiving hundreds of calls from civilians in the kibbutzim. They are pleading for help."*

General Milo: *(looking at blank monitors) "Where are the helicopters? Where is the Commando?"*

Duty Officer: *"The helicopters are waiting for orders. We do not understand the overall picture. The lawyers are asking whether targets have been confirmed so as to avoid 'collateral damage' among the hostages. Local commanders are afraid to take action without clear identification of the enemy."*

General Milo: *"What identification? We have thousands of militants in the rear!"*

Duty Officer: *"But according to the 'incident management' protocol, we must first deploy a coordination headquarters..."*

General Milo: *(erupting in a shout) "There is no headquarters anymore! There is no Division! While you are looking for the 'protocol,' they are killing our nation live on the air!"*

Duty Officer: *(quietly) "General Milo, we simply have no plan for this scenario. We never believed the fence would fall so quickly. We were prepared to 'mow the lawn,' not to save the country from our offices."*

The Failure of the IDF Doctrine

The IDF doctrine before October 7, 2023 was based on the so-called 'Conception,' a rigid strategic stance analogous to the error before the Yom Kippur War of 1973.

Hamas is restrained and not interested in a large war: following operations such as Guardian of the Walls in 2021, it was believed that Hamas was occupied with managing Gaza and that quiet could be "bought" through economic concessions, specifically work permits for Gazans in Israel and Qatari money.

Technological superiority is sufficient: reliance was placed on the "smart fence" with sensors, cameras, and underground barriers, the Iron Dome against rockets, and intelligence. Ground forces and preparation for a ground invasion were undervalued; the army focused on threats from Iran and Hezbollah.

No plan for a large-scale invasion: as retired General Amir Avivi noted, "there was no plan for a surprise attack." The army prepared for rocket fire and minor infiltrations, but not for the breach of thousands of militants.

This conception collapsed on October 7: Hamas breached the border in 114 places, neutralizing the technologies with drones and jammers. IDF investigations of 2025 confirmed the systemic failure: overestimation of technology, ignoring of warnings including those from Yitzhak Brick, and unpreparedness for a multi-front war.

The Principle of Ipcha Mistabra

The principle of "ipcha mistabra" is an Aramaic term from the Talmud, literally meaning "the opposite makes more sense." It is a principle of Israeli intelligence formulated after the failure of the Yom Kippur War of 1973. The phrase appears in the Babylonian Talmud, for instance in tractates Shabbat 69b and Bava Metzia 84a, and is used when obvious logic is being challenged: "The opposite is more reasonable."

After the 1973 failure, this principle was introduced in Military Intelligence AMAN as an official method. A special department was created, the mahleqet ha-baqarah, meaning the control department or "ipcha mistabra." The task of the department was to play the role of "devil's advocate" and deliberately propose counter-conceptions to the dominant threat assessments, even if they seemed unlikely. The goal was to avoid "groupthink" and cognitive distortions.

In November 2024, the Knesset approved the creation of an analogous structure in another intelligence service, also under the name "Ipcha Mistabra."

Many analysts and former intelligence officers have stated that the failure to prevent the Hamas attack occurred precisely because the principle of ipcha mistabra had been forgotten. The conception "Hamas is restrained and will not dare a full-scale invasion" dominated, while alternative scenarios were dismissed as "irrational." This was a repetition of the 1973 error. In the broader sense, "ipcha mistabra" is a Jewish approach to critical thinking: not to accept the obvious as truth but to turn it over and test it.

Operational Failures

On October 7, the IDF found itself in chaos. The Gaza Division was effectively defeated within several hours. The attack coincided with Shabbat and a holiday, which reduced readiness.

Troops in the southern sector were below full strength due to redeployment to the West Bank. Against 5,600 invading militants there were approximately 700 Israeli soldiers.

Slow response: the first hours involved small units without coordination. Command in Tel Aviv did not understand the scale. Reinforcements were delayed by hours and days due to road ambushes.

Soldiers communicated via WhatsApp and relied on social media. The majority of the killings occurred in the first six hours, when the southern division had been routed.

In 2025, Chief of the General Staff Eyal Zamir dismissed and sanctioned several generals, acknowledging a "flagrant systemic failure."

Hamas's Deception Tactics

Hamas successfully conducted a years-long campaign of strategic and tactical deception. It positioned itself as a "responsible administrator," requesting ceasefires, disciplining protesters at the border, and avoiding escalation with Islamic Jihad. It conducted exercises near the border openly, but these were interpreted as a "show." It avoided electronic communications and used couriers; it neutralized Israeli intelligence with Iranian support. Publicly, the focus was on Gaza's economy; secretly, preparations had been underway since 2016, with plans shifted due to COVID. It used non-military dress and motorcycles, pickup trucks, and paragliders for speed and surprise.

This allowed the achievement of complete surprise. Sources including the New York Times, Wall Street Journal, and BBC note that Hamas "lulled" Israel to sleep, repeating Egypt's 1973 tactics.

Why Was Hamas Underestimated?

The underestimation was the result of deep misconceptions: a refusal to consider Hamas's radical worldview and its long-term plans; Hamas was perceived as a weak, intimidated organization focused on economic management rather than jihad. The senior command including Gallant and Halevi demonstrated arrogance and overconfidence; these three points of the "conception" led to severe consequences on the ground and in the air. Netanyahu's policy of supporting a weak Hamas through Qatari financing in order to divide the Palestinians and prevent a unified state reinforced the underestimation and created a false sense of control.

The IDF Report

According to a Channel 7 publication, an independent investigative group composed of reserve Major Generals Sami Turjeman, Amikam Norkin, and David Sharvit, together with reserve Brigadier General Ofer Levy, conducted a review of the defense failure of October 7, 2023 and reached the following conclusions.

Former AMAN Military Intelligence chief Aharon Haliva refused to convene a meeting after Hamas terrorists activated Israeli SIM cards two days before the attack, saying that there was no need for one.

The senior intelligence officer of the Southern District was on maternity leave, and the then-commander of the district, Eliezer Toledo, claimed that the battalion commanders had not been mobilized due to a lack of information.

Chief of the General Staff Operations Department Shlomi Binder arrived at the Kirya only at 9 in the morning and for several hours did not document the decisions being made.

The IDF General Staff believed until late evening that several hundred terrorists had participated in the attack rather than the actual figure of 5,000.

As for the air force, an urgent request for bombardment of the fence through which the attackers were freely passing received a response only after two hours due to the absence of personnel and prioritized strikes on Hamas command centers.

As for the head of Military Intelligence AMAN, he did not consider these events worthy of his attention at all. Aharon Haliva was on vacation and, when awakened at around three in the morning, listened to his assistants and said that he should be awakened again only if the situation changed. Aharon Haliva acknowledged the failure in his work due to the Hamas attack.

The snobbery and amorality of the former Chief of the IDF General Staff Herzi Halevi break all records. What else can one call his "praise" of the terrorist organization Hamas: "I have no option but to praise Hamas for the deception it arranged for us"? *General Halevi also stated: "During all our discussions and exercises, we never admitted even the thought that even five percent of what happened could happen."*

Halevi noted: "I view responsibility as a matter of values, not as a legal matter. Values are above the law. I always felt my responsibility as the commander of the army, and especially in connection with the failure on Simchat Torah. This will remain with me forever." Halevi is mistaken: his failure is not a matter of his conscience and values; it is the most legal matter imaginable. I hope that the families of the thousands who perished will find lawyers and instruct them to bring the Halevi case to court.

Ten Key Tasks

1. Revision of the security conception. It is impermissible to allow the enemy to build up forces at the very border while relying only on deterrence and warning. A return of Hamas and Hezbollah to their former capabilities is unacceptable.
2. Abandonment of 'conflict management' with an enemy whose goal is your destruction. Buying quiet at the price of concessions means multiplying future problems.

3. Readiness for a sudden large-scale attack. A special strategic early warning center and a situational center are needed, capable of analyzing what is happening even under conditions of chaos.
4. Enlargement of the army. More forces on the borders, mobile intelligence, more ground firepower, and operational air assets.
5. Strengthening intelligence without blind faith in it. It is the most important tool but not an absolute truth. Even in the event of intelligence errors, the army must be ready at any moment to repel a blow.
6. Professional protection of civilian communities. Modernization of the armaments of local rapid reaction units and intensive training.
7. Basic combat skills in every soldier. Not only in elite units but also in regular formations.
8. More fortified positions on the border.
9. Creation of a Main Control Directorate.
10. Strengthening the army's combat traditions.

Monstrous Negligence

Preliminary IDF reports point to a systemic, multilayered incompetence and collective "conceptual blindness" rather than deliberate malicious intent. In this version there is no betrayal; there is overconfidence and the ignoring of the lessons of the past.

Conceptual blindness: the firm conviction, particularly in AMAN and the Shin Bet, that Hamas was restrained and interested in the economic management of Gaza rather than in full-scale war. Any warnings were dismissed as unrealistic.

Doctrinal collapse: excessive dependence on the technological barrier with minimal manpower support. This led to the reduction of reserves and unpreparedness for a scenario in which the barrier would be easily breached.

Culture of rejection of criticism: the ignoring of warnings from Yitzhak Brick and the female surveillance soldiers on the border. Senior command preferred "not to know" about problems in order not to disturb the "image of success" and to avoid responsibility.

Operational errors: unpreparedness of defense plans for a massive invasion; the coincidence of the attack with Shabbat and a holiday; slow response due to the disorganization of the command center at Re'im.

Political factor: the policy of dividing the Palestinians by maintaining Hamas in Gaza through Qatari financing created a false sense of a controlled threat.

Cognitive stagnation: many IDF officers and intelligence heads in AMAN and the Shin Bet became hostages of the dominant hypothesis, the "conception." Alternative opinions from below were not reported due to fear of not being heard.

HUMINT deficit: the emphasis on technical means and the neglect of agents in the political and military leadership of Hamas.

The "Yom Kippur War effect": a repetition of the 1973 failure, fixation on an erroneous conception and the ignoring of clear warnings.

Departure from Traditional Doctrine

Political decisions initiated by the left and the centrists led to a doctrinal shift for which the military ultimately paid the price.

The doctrine transitioned from offensive initiatives and fighting on enemy territory to an almost exclusively defensive posture. This reduced combat readiness at the border and led to insufficient forces at key positions.

Large-scale political disagreements within Israel, including the confrontation between the army leadership and the right-wing government over the judicial reform, distracted the attention of the supreme military command and affected the ability to concentrate on the primary threat.

Conceptual fixation is the mechanism through which the military and intelligence elite maintained the state of social schizophrenia in the country. They created and maintained the illusion of manageable security, which allowed the growing threat to be ignored until it broke through, causing a traumatic collision with reality. The human factor, arrogance, and an unwillingness to revise the dominant 'conception' became the direct catalyst of the catastrophe.

The main question that October 7 leaves behind is not who is to blame: answers to that will sooner or later be given. The question is whether Israel is capable of abandoning comforting illusions and accepting reality as it is, without cosmetic filters and 'humanistic' justifications.

As a physician with many years of practice, I have dealt with the medical errors of my colleagues, and have made errors myself.

A "medical error" is an unintentional action or inaction by a physician that has caused harm to a patient, arising from a good-faith mistake such as a wrong diagnosis, dosage, or procedure, or connected with the imperfection of medicine, the human factor, and organizational problems. A "medical error" does not carry the characteristics of a crime. A different matter is negligence and carelessness: these constitute intentional inaction or action subject to criminal liability.

Our generals suffered collapse due to intellectual blindness, snobbery, and prejudice toward "some terrorists or other." This does not resemble a good-faith mistake or a "medical error," and in the end it was not one patient but thousands who suffered. I cannot bring myself to call them professionals; rather, this resembles negligence and carelessness. However, it is not for me to judge: I hope that a just trial will take place.

Conclusion

"October 7 is the moment when the social contract between the state and its citizens was torn apart in the most brutal manner."

The catastrophe was the direct consequence of social schizophrenia: the heads of thousands and hundreds of thousands of citizens were occupied with fighting one another, but not with Hamas. While the elite in Tel Aviv was celebrating the supposed victory of 'democracy' over the government, the enemy was planning its victory over Israel.

The catastrophe of October 7, 2023 was the most lethal day in the history of Israel and the culmination of years of strategic and ideological drift. It was not merely an operational malfunction but a systemic collapse of a doctrine based on arrogance and the illusion of control. The failure was fundamental and multilayered. This description forms the basis of what future historians will likely call the "Collapse of Overconfidence."

The thesis of a "systemic collapse of the doctrine" can be broken down into three planes that confirm the depth of this catastrophe.

Intellectual arrogance: the 'dictatorship of the Conception.'

The illusion of control: the military elite believed it was reading Yahya Sinwar like an open book. This is a manifestation of intellectual arrogance, an inability to acknowledge that the ideology of religious destruction matters more to the enemy than work permits for Gaza residents. Intelligence and the senior command fell victim to "conceptual blindness" and the ignoring of Hamas's "Jericho Wall" plan. The supreme leadership and the General Staff consciously filtered out criticism and warnings. The collapse was the result of the left-wing shift in the army. Through ideological selection, the General Staff became part of the secular elite that promoted the doctrine of "conflict management" instead of decisive victory. The excessive influence of military lawyers constrained commanders, making the army less decisive and effective. Due to the absence of a plan and disorganization, the army could not respond adequately.

The 'wall in consciousness,' or the illusion of control, materialized in the form of the 'smart fence.'

Instead of active defense and the presence of troops, the emphasis was placed on sensors and algorithms. The system that cost billions proved to be "one-time use." The destruction of several communications nodes turned all the power of the Gaza Division into a pile of useless metal. This was the collapse of the belief that technological superiority can replace fighting spirit and the physical guarding of borders.

The political-legal drift: the 'split shield.'

The systemic collapse occurred against the background of what I call 'social schizophrenia.'

In 2023, the energy of the supreme command was directed toward internal debates about "reasonableness," reform, and relations with the political echelon. The army ceased to be an instrument of war and became a subject of domestic politics. The state for years had been assuring the residents of the border kibbutzim that they were safe. On October 7, that contract was torn apart in the most brutal manner.

In summary: the culmination of the drift was the transformation of the IDF from a 'people's army' aimed at victory into a 'high-technology corporation' aimed at conflict management and the maintenance of the status quo.

The crisis showed that the country needs unity of will and a fundamental revision of doctrine in order to restore the IDF's capacity for decisive victory rather than for "playing cat and mouse." The picture has clarified:

- the elite and the deep state paralyzed the political will;
- the left doctrine hollowed out the spirit of the army;
- the lawyers tied the hands of the soldiers;
- the "conception" blinded those who should have seen the real enemies;
- the hallucinations ended, and the country passed through a catastrophe.

The shock of October 7 deepened the social schizophrenia, showing that the status quo had been an illusion and that "conflict management" had been self-deception.

This chapter is not only about pain but also about the necessity of a total disinfection of the entire state system. We will need a 'prescription': what to do next? How to restore the 'Iron Wall' and how to heal the nation from the virus of self-destruction?

CHAPTER 26.
THE INTELLIGENCE FAILURES

Introduction

The failure of Israel's intelligence community on October 7, 2023, was not merely an error in data collection — **it was an intellectual catastrophe.**

The chief tragedy of October 7 lay in the fact that the intelligence services were led by highly intelligent people. But their intellect had become a closed ecosystem. In psychology this is called "intellectual incest" — when a narrow group of expert's stews in its own theories, encouraging only those conclusions that confirm their brilliance. They had constructed a primitive model of a "rational Hamas" that was flawless in every respect save one: it bore no relation to reality. The arrogance of the headquarters meant that the observation of a lookout girl on the border counted for less than a complex but erroneous analytical memorandum penned by a colonel in Tel Aviv.

In other words, by October 2023 Israeli intelligence — the IDF Military Intelligence Directorate (AMAN) and the Shin Bet (Shabak) — had fallen into a state of cognitive paralysis. In their offices, Hamas existed not as a terrorist army but as an economic actor. It was assumed that Sinwar had "something to lose." Every work permit issued to Gaza residents, every Qatari dollar brought into the strip, was perceived as a tranquilizer for the beast.

"Hamas Was Contained"?

When junior officers and lookout girls cried out: "They are training to seize our watchtowers and kidnap people!" the leadership responded: "This is merely a show for internal consumption. Hamas is contained." Possessing the world's most advanced electronic surveillance capabilities, the intelligence community turned out to be "functionally blind." The failure occurred against a backdrop of informational supersaturation. The testimonies of border observers and alarming reports about Hamas's unusual exercises did reach the offices of Shabak and AMAN. The true cause of the failure was the systematic refusal of the senior leadership to accept this data — a phenomenon one might call "conceptual fixation" (or cognitive stagnation). The conviction that Hamas was "contained" and interested solely in economic incentives became a mental filter that blocked out the truth.

On that fateful night, Shabak chief Ronen Bar made a decision grounded in this false doctrine: he focused on neutralizing a technical threat rather than preventing a strategic one. This error did not merely lead to an operational failure; it exposed the internal fracture and paralysis of will within the Israeli leadership.

The central problem lay in the interpretation of information. The intelligence community had formed a rigid concept: Hamas wants to govern, not to fight. Every enemy action was fitted to this model. If Hamas trained to capture kibbutzim, intelligence reported: "They are doing this to boost fighter morale, but will not dare to attack." The senior intelligence officers (including AMAN chief Aharon Haliva) created an environment in which critical thinking was suppressed. Junior analysts and lookout girls who observed actual preparations were regarded as "alarmists" obstructing the work of "serious strategists."

The night before the catastrophe: On the night before the catastrophe, the security system received a "golden signal." Technical means registered the activation of hundreds of Israeli SIM cards in the Gaza Strip — a classic prelude to an invasion: fighters were preparing communications for use on Israeli territory. Ronen Bar and Herzi Halevi held several nocturnal consultations. But instead of scrambling the air force and dispatching a division to the fence, they decided to wait until morning. Perhaps the virus of "legal caution" had taken hold — a fear of political noise. The system feared declaring a "false alarm" on the holiday of Simchat Torah, dreading criticism for "stoking panic" in an atmosphere already inflamed by protests.

"THE PRICE OF SILENCE"

Setting: *Encrypted video chat. 04:00 in the morning, October 7.*

Participants: General A. (Senior Headquarters officer, in pajamas thrown over his uniform). Colonel R. (Air Force duty officer). Legal Consultant B. (Representative of the military prosecutor's office, connected "for the record").

Colonel R.: (voice vibrating with tension) *Gentlemen, I repeat: Shabak has confirmed "red lights" on the SIM cards. The "Tequila" team has already moved out, but that is a drop in the ocean. I need authorization to scramble two flights of Apaches to patrol the perimeter. Just so they are in the air.*

General A.: (wiping his glasses) *Ron, do you understand what time it is? It is the morning of Simchat Torah. If we send aircraft over Gaza, in fifteen minutes Sinwar will begin launching rockets, deciding that we are beginning a preemptive strike. We will provoke a war that a "pragmatic Hamas" does not want right now.*

Colonel R.: *Sir, I would rather explain burned fuel than a breached fence! My boys in the south are reporting the sound of heavy machinery beyond the wall.*

Legal Consultant B.: (interrupting) *Colonel, allow me to remind you. According to the latest directives on "proportionality" and "friction reduction," the demonstrative presence of ground-attack aircraft near the borders of densely populated areas without an overt act of aggression may be interpreted by international courts as a violation of the status quo. If Hamas responds with a salvo, responsibility for the escalation will fall upon whoever gave the order to take off.*

Colonel R.: (in fury) *What "escalation"?! My sensors are going haywire! Counselor, will you be reading your directives to the terrorists when they cross the line?*

General A.: *Calm down. We have made a decision: we raise readiness by one level, but we do not scramble aircraft until dawn. Let Shabak verify the data. Most likely this is another round of their internal quarrels or an attempt to ruin our holiday. We will not give them that satisfaction.*

Colonel R.: *Sir, dawn is two hours away. In two hours a country can burn.*

General A.: (dryly) *By the regulations — we wait. Don't make a mountain out of a molehill, Colonel. We have the situation under control. And switch off your camera — there is too much noise behind you. Everyone get some rest.*

(The screen goes dark. Colonel R. remains in the darkness of his office. On his desk vibrates a personal mobile phone. A text message from the squad commander in the south: "Hearing explosions by the

fence. Requesting takeoff." The Colonel stares at the phone, then at the blank screen where the decision for "silence" was just made.)

"Through a Psychiatrist's Eyes": This dialogue lays bare three layers of catastrophe: The General fears "ruining the holiday" and provoking a war he does not believe in (political fear). The lawyer outranks the operator; his task is not victory but "procedural cleanliness" (legal paralysis). ***Hierarchical schizophrenia: The system is calibrated so that raising aircraft brings punishment, while inaction does not — because it is "within regulations."***

Technological Checkmate

Israeli intelligence fell victim to its own technological perfection. We relied so heavily on AI algorithms, wiretapping, and satellites that we forgot the simplest truth: war is the will of people, not the movement of digits.

The system was calibrated to find logic where fanatical hatred reigned. While AMAN analyzed the flow of Qatari money, Sinwar used paper maps and courier communications. We were building a digital fortress while the enemy came at us with a stone axe. October 7 was the day "Big Data" lost to primitive brutality.

When the invasion began, the "smart fence" that had cost 3.5 billion shekels turned into useless scrap metal within fifteen minutes. Hamas's cheap commercial drones destroyed the surveillance cameras and remotely operated machine guns. The command system was so centralized and technology-dependent that after the destruction of several key communication nodes, the headquarters of the Gaza Division went blind. Local commanders were dying in their beds, not even having time to understand that a war had begun rather than "another rocket barrage." An army that had spent decades preparing for the "high-technology war of the future" was defeated by a horde on motorcycles and paragliders. The failure was not technical but intellectual: the system was so convinced of its own superiority that it ceased to believe the enemy might simply climb over the fence.

Yahya Sinwar understood that Israel hears everything transmitted over networks. Hamas switched to "Stone Age" communications — couriers, handwritten notes, personal meetings in tunnels. When on October 7 Hamas used drones to destroy cameras and communication towers, intelligence was instantly deprived of ninety percent of its toolkit. It turned out that without "eyes" on the fence, headquarters had no idea what was happening one hundred meters away.

In 2023, intelligence was excessively politicized. The tragedy of Shabak in 2023 was that its leadership was too deeply involved in political discourse. Instead of tearing the teeth from terrorism, the security service began to occupy itself with "protest sociology." Analytical departments were spending resources evaluating how judicial reform affected "social resilience," instead of assessing how it affected Sinwar's resolve. When a security service starts playing at politics, it loses its scent. On the night of October 7, Shabak woke too late because its "warning lights" had been calibrated for internal threats to "democracy" rather than the external threat of genocide.

The events of the last night before the attack exposed the depth of the failure. At 22:00 on October 6, Shabak registered the activation of hundreds of Israeli SIM cards in Gaza — a "golden signal" signaling the launch of an operation. Instead of scrambling the air force and a division, the intelligence leadership decided this was "another exercise." The head of AMAN did not even interrupt his vacation in Eilat. The system feared declaring a false alarm lest it "look stupid" or ruin the holiday of Simchat Torah. In the end, legal and bureaucratic caution defeated the survival instinct.

Thus, intelligence missed an invasion army right under its nose.

The Appointment of Ronen Bar

The Shabak director is appointed by the prime minister, after which the appointment must be approved by the government and, when necessary, by the Advisory Committee on Senior Government Appointments (the Grunis Committee). The Shabak chief reports directly to the prime minister. In October 2021, then–Prime Minister Naftali Bennett proposed appointing Ronen Bar as Shabak chief. Bennett praised Bar as a "brave warrior and bold commander" who had risked his life for Israel's security and expressed confidence that he would lead the agency to "new heights of action and excellence."

Ronen Bar had been Shabak's deputy chief since 2018. Earlier he had headed the operations department (from 2011) and the resources development department (from 2016). He served in an elite IDF unit before transferring to Shabak as a field agent. He apparently had no political ambitions or public connections, which distinguished him from some other candidates. This was viewed positively — in theory he was supposed to be apolitical and focused solely on security. Since Bennett's government was weak and unstable at the time, any appointment was perceived in a politicized atmosphere: some saw Bar as a guarantor of professionalism, others questioned his ability to remain independent amid the constant political warfare.

Many people paid with their lives for his choices on October 7, 2023 — for his decisions and actions. The scandal surrounding Bar's failure to timely inform the country's leadership of operational intelligence concerning Hamas's preparations for "Black Saturday," his reliance on appeasing the terrorists, transformed Bar into one of the "bosses of the failure."

As for responsibility for the catastrophe of October 7, 2023 — it is borne not only by Bar but also by the IDF leadership, AMAN, the defense minister, and the government headed by Netanyahu; yet each person's responsibility is distinct, and it has not yet been fully determined.

Shabak's Role and the Protests

The General Security Service, charged with combating terrorism, found itself drawn into the epicenter of an internal political confrontation. The following is an analysis of how Shabak interacted with the protest movement and how this influenced the events of October 7.

Shabak as a "voice of warning": Throughout 2023, Ronen Bar played the role of a "prophet of catastrophe." In the context of the Kaplan protests, his position was as follows: Bar repeatedly sent letters and reports to Prime Minister Netanyahu, arguing that the "social rift over judicial reform is a gift to our enemies." He stated that Iran and Hamas saw weakness in Israel's protests and were preparing an attack. And in this he was right. But he went no further. Why?

In July 2023, approximately eight hundred former Shabak agents signed a letter warning that continuing the reform would lead to "immediate danger to state security." This reinforced the perception of Shabak as a structure sympathetic to the protesters.

Accusations of "Political Bias"

Shabak was accused of treating Kaplan protesters — who had been blocking the highway and blockading the airport — with kid gloves, while acting harshly against settlers or right-wing activists.

It was alleged that Ronen Bar used intelligence data not to prevent threats but to apply political pressure on the government in order to force it to halt the reform.

The 2023–2025 protests bore the character of a soft coup and were coordinated with external support. In this picture, Shabak under Ronen Bar appears not as a neutral guardian but as an active, if shadowy, participant. Below is a detailed analysis of what Shabak could have done but did not do, and how this fits the "coup" theory.

Foreign financing: One of the chief accusations against Ronen Bar is the ignoring of the financial flows that nourished the protest. What could he have done? Shabak has the authority to track foreign interference in domestic politics. If protests were being financed through NGOs (as US congressional investigations into State Department funding of opposition-linked groups allege), Shabak was obligated to produce a report on "subversive activities by foreign states." What did it not do? Instead of investigating the sources of funding, Shabak focused on monitoring "right-wing extremism." This created a situation in which millions of dollars for protest logistics (stages, screens, transport, media campaigns) passed outside the field of counterintelligence.

Suppression of "civil disobedience": The protests included elements that in any other country might have been classified as attempts at destabilization of the state order: the blockade of Ben Gurion Airport and key highways; and calls to refuse service. This was the most dangerous element of the "coup." Shabak, responsible for the resilience of state institutions, could have classified calls for reserve desertion as a threat to national security. Shabak not only failed to suppress these actions but also, in the view of critics, "legitimized" them by transmitting to the government the message that "the army is falling apart because of the reform" rather than because of those who incite refusal.

"SHABAK'S BLIND SPOT"

Setting: *A safe house in Tel Aviv. Evening. View of the lights of a protest bonfire.*

Characters: Senior Shabak Officer. Field Operative.

Operative: (placing a folder on the table) *Here is the data on financing. The money flows through three fronts from European foundations. The target: complete blockade of Ben Gurion Airport and paralysis of the transport system. This is a direct violation of the infrastructure protection law. Why are we not acting?*

Officer: (not looking at the folder) *Leave it. We have a directive: this is "civic expression of will." We do not engage in politics.*

Operative: *What politics?! They are calling on reservists to sabotage their service! This is the undermining of defense capability in a pre-war period. Iranian bot farms are pumping their slogans through social media. We should be arresting the organizers!*

Officer: (coldly) *We look for extremists, boy. But we look for them on the "right flank." Those on Kaplan — they are the "best people in the country." If we touch them, tomorrow the Supreme Court will destroy us ourselves. Our task is to see that the government does not "overstep" with suppression.*

Operative: *So while we watch the government, the enemy is staring at our crumbling fence?*

Officer: (turning to the window) *The enemy can wait. First we must deal with the "internal dictator." Those are the orders!*

Why Did Shabak Not Stabilize the Country?

There are three versions of why Shabak "allowed" the chaos of 2023. The Shabak leadership was flesh of the flesh of the same liberal elite as the protesters. For them, the reform was a greater threat than street disorder. Ronen Bar knew that any harsh action against the protesters would be immediately overruled by the Supreme Court, and he himself would become the target of legal prosecution. Shabak believed that its chief task was to force the government to halt the reform at any cost in order to "preserve unity," not understanding that this very process was destroying national security in the face of October 7.

Tragic paradox: blinding by Kaplan. The essence of the thriller lies in the fact that Shabak was so focused on the internal threat of civil war that it missed the real threat on the border. In 2023, the analytical departments of Shabak spent enormous resources monitoring "social resilience." In the end, the security service "could not see the forest (Hamas's army) for the trees (the protests)." In 2025, sworn testimony revealed that Bar had considered the actions of Netanyahu's government to be a "threat to democracy and security" — confirming that the head of counterintelligence was in a state of ideological conflict with the country's leadership.

The Night Before the Attack

On February 22, 2025, the "Mako" website published an article about what was happening in Shabak on the night of October 6–7, 2023. (https://oleggranovsky.livejournal.com /1473762.html). The timeline of events that night is as follows.

02:58 — Shabak transmits a warning to the IDF and the National Security Staff about unusual Hamas behavior that may indicate offensive activity. This unusual behavior includes: dozens of Israeli SIM cards activated in the Gaza Strip; the military wing leadership of Hamas descending into tunnels. "Mako" notes that, unlike the IDF, Shabak had no dismissive attitude toward Hamas and was not wedded to the concept that Hamas had been suppressed by the IDF's deterrent power. It was Shabak that sounded the alarm. However, this did not lead to a general raise in combat readiness. Why?

03:30 — Ronen Bar drives to the organization's headquarters (Tel Aviv) and summons several other senior Shabak officials. Simultaneously he rouses the IDF leadership (who begin their own telephone consultations).

04:00 — Shabak informs the IDF that Hamas is preparing for our active actions (???); this event will not happen immediately. Simultaneously, two "Tequila" teams in the vicinity of the Gaza Strip are put on alert. Reason: concern that a terrorist attack may occur during the night (with reference to a very limited scale of attack).

05:00 — Following the conclusion of the Shabak leadership consultation, two operational directives are prepared: a recommendation to postpone the security cabinet meeting scheduled for Sunday morning (reason: the assumption that Hamas mistakenly believes the meeting's purpose is to authorize a large-scale Israeli attack on Gaza, which in turn might cause Hamas to launch a preemptive strike); and a directive to immediately notify the prime minister's military secretary of the night's situation and the alarming warnings received.

06:13 — With a delay of more than one hour, the head of Ronen Bar's office wakes the prime minister's military secretary, Major General Avi Gil. He reports: "There are signs indicating a breach, but on the other hand, the phones of Sinwar and another senior Hamas official are in their apartments, not in the tunnels. I need you urgently on the Red Line."

06:29 — Hamas attack begins. At exactly this moment, Avi Gil calls Prime Minister Benjamin Netanyahu.

Investigations into what happened at Shabak have attempted to understand how, despite receiving important data and Ronen Bar's initially correct response, everything was reduced to the possibility of a small-scale attack and a corresponding response to that scenario. As one of the lessons of the 1973 Yom Kippur War, we know that one should not count on learning the enemy's intention — one must see his capabilities. This was known in Shabak. Therefore an analysis was conducted of what weapons Shabak believed would disrupt the balance of power with Hamas and must not be allowed.

The following points were identified: (1) possession of precision missiles; (2) acquisition of high-quality UAVs; (3) advanced naval special forces capabilities enabling surprise strikes on Israel's coast. At the same time, the strengthening of the "Nukhba Forces" (Hamas's special forces) was not identified as a strategic threat, since a full-scale mass raid on Israeli territory was considered impossible, as the threat of such an operation through tunnels had been largely neutralized by the construction of the barrier completed in 2021. Consequently, there was no general recommendation to strike Hamas preemptively.

Another cause of the failure is related to the use of intelligence materials by Shabak's Analytical Directorate: they focused primarily on attempts to influence Hamas and disrupt its plans, and to a much lesser extent on understanding original intentions. This created the illusion that it was possible to predict what Hamas would do. Moreover, the Analytical Directorate clearly had a problem of imagination. No one there — nor in Shabak as a whole — envisioned the scenario of a mass raid from Gaza. And here one recalls what was known as the "Jericho Wall" — the IDF's name for Hamas's plan for a massive attack.

There were the warnings of two women, Warrant Officers (analysts in AMAN), V. and S., who linked Hamas's exercises in the months before October 7 to the "Jericho Wall" plan. AMAN, after examining this plan, reached the erroneous conclusion that it was "merely a theoretical scenario for the construction of Hamas's military wing." Not a single meeting was convened on the subject. Moreover, both the plan and the reports of V. and S. were passed to Shabak, which likewise agreed with the IDF's assessment. On the night of October 7, at none of the consultations — either in the army or in Shabak — did anyone recall the "Jericho Wall" plan. Therefore no one spoke of the possibility of an invasion by thousands of terrorists; at most a few dozen were discussed.

The results of the consultations within Shabak's leadership, in essence, calmed Ronen Bar and made his position less paranoid (in a positive sense). For example: the argument of the activation of dozens of Israeli SIM cards — counter-argument: this had happened before; the argument of the Hamas military wing leadership descending into tunnels — counter-argument: the phones of Sinwar and another senior Hamas official are in their apartments.

One more interesting detail: at the beginning of September, Shabak and the IDF held a meeting on the subject of "Readiness for an Operation in Gaza." And the discussion concerned not a Hamas attack (as before, the "Jericho Wall" went unmentioned) but rather an IDF attack. At the end of the meeting, it was determined: the situation is unstable, we need to raise our readiness. In mid-September, at Ronen Bar's request, a meeting of service chiefs takes place. Besides Bar himself, those present include the prime minister, the Mossad chief, and a number of other senior officials. Ronen Bar speaks of the possibility of a multi-front war, but the scenario of a specific attack from Gaza as the starting point of such a war is not raised. Concerning Gaza, the principle of "quiet for quiet" is proclaimed.

Underestimation of the Threat

Shabak (Shin Bet) is considered one of the most professional domestic security services in the world, yet their failure before Hamas's October 7, 2023 attack became one of the most serious in Israel's history. This came about because of a combination of factors: underestimation of the threat, ignoring of signals, systemic intelligence errors, and the influence of political decisions. Here are the key reasons why the "professionals" failed to act, and precisely what "clouded the thinking" of Ronen Bar and his staff.

Within Shabak it was believed that Hamas had no interest in full-scale escalation, as this would threaten their power in Gaza. This led to the Hamas attack plan codenamed "Walls of Jericho" (from 2018 and 2022) being assessed as hypothetical rather than an actual threat. Ronen Bar later acknowledged that the agency did not connect the summer 2023 signals to attack preparations. This was "self-brainwashing" via their own doctrine: focusing on preventing attacks in Judea and Samaria, where the threat seemed greater, and not on Gaza, where Hamas had allegedly "quieted down" thanks to the "quiet for quiet" policy. Shabak's report states that this policy allowed Hamas to build up its forces, including rockets and tunnels, without firm deterrent measures.

On the night of October 6–7, Ronen Bar received multiple indicators: the activation of 45 Israeli SIM cards in Gaza (resembling operational preparation), unusual activity by Hamas brigades, and even a report about "emergency readiness." However, this was interpreted as Hamas's "unwillingness to escalate," and no serious measures were taken. Shabak had serious gaps in agent recruitment in Gaza, making them dependent on technical means (signals, intercepts) — but without context, these were useless. It was unclear who was responsible for "war warning" — Shin Bet (focused on terrorist attacks) or the IDF (military threats). Hamas had evolved from a terrorist group into an "army," but Shin Bet's methods had not adapted.

Ronen Bar assumed full responsibility: "Shabak did not prevent the massacre of October 7 ... I will carry this burden for the rest of my life." He resigned in June 2025, following a public scandal and accusations of politicizing the service. Despite the failure of October 7, Netanyahu managed to turn the situation around, transforming defense into offense. In his UN speech (September 2025) he said: "Israel is defending itself on seven fronts from barbarism" and emphasized that Israel stood "on the threshold of ending this war," having changed the balance of power in the region.

The Warnings of the Lookout Girls

For many years these units of young female conscripts were given a single task: to sit for hours at observation posts, watching for any signs of something suspicious. In the months before Hamas's October 7 attack, those signs appeared: training raids, staging of hostage seizures, strange behavior of farmers on the other side of the barrier separating Israel from Gaza.

The warnings coming from the lookout girls in the IDF field intelligence units, who monitored the Gaza border around the clock, constitute one of the most tragic and striking pieces of evidence of the conceptual fixation of the Israeli leadership before October 7. Their reports were systematically ignored by senior officers and intelligence command. The lookout girls working from cameras and sensors on the border saw direct signs of Hamas preparations for a large-scale attack. They repeatedly reported on unusually intensive and realistic exercises by Hamas fighters, who were rehearsing a breach of the barrier, seizure of military posts, and kidnapping simulations using mock Israeli military vehicles and concrete structures imitating IDF posts. The lookout girls recorded how fighters conducted detailed reconnaissance of the border fence, including weak points, and also studied the placement of cameras and sensors. In the weeks before the attack they noted actions that went beyond Hamas's usual routine and pointed toward preparations for a major operation.

These reports and warnings were rejected by the command at the division level and above. The reasons for ignoring them were as follows: Command was convinced that Hamas was contained and would not go ahead with a full-scale invasion. Any action contradicting this concept was considered either an exercise or "sabre-rattling." In some cases, the lookout girls may have been perceived as inexperienced or overly emotional — an example of organizational arrogance and bias toward the source of information. Several lookout girls claimed that their senior officers demanded they stop reporting on "meaningless" observations, since these contradicted the calm assessments of top leadership.

The tragedy of October 7 confirmed the lookout girls' rightness. They were among the first to understand what was happening, and many of those stationed at forward observation posts were killed or taken hostage in the first hours of the attack. Their testimonies and reports became a central element of all official investigations, emphasizing that the failure was caused not by a lack of information but by the top leadership's unwillingness to accept it.

***

Noa (name changed) says they transmitted information about what they observed to intelligence and to higher-ranking officers, but could do no more than that. "We were just eyes," she says. For some of them it was clear that Hamas was planning something big — in Noa's words, "a balloon about to burst." "The problem is that the military did not connect all the scattered facts," a former commander of one of the border units told the BBC. According to her, had they done so, they would have realized that Hamas was preparing something unprecedented.

Nineteen-year-old Shai Ashram was one of the women on duty on October 7. In a conversation with her family, with gunshots audible in the background, she said that terrorists were on the base and that "something very big" was happening. Shai and more than a dozen other lookout soldiers were killed. Others were taken hostage.

"DEATH LIVE"

Setting: *Analytical center of Unit 8200. A wall of monitors, soft light, the smell of expensive coffee.*

Time: *October 6, 2023, 22:00 (eight hours before the attack).*

Characters: Captain Daniel — lead analyst for the Gaza sector, 26 years old. Clean shirt, confident voice, two university degrees. Sergeant Maya — a lookout girl, 19 years old. Tired eyes, red from the monitors. She came from the border base to show the report in person.

Maya: *(pointing to the tablet screen) Captain, you don't understand. This is not "exercises." They have changed frequencies. They are using couriers. And look at these drone footage — yesterday they were practicing disabling precisely these types of cameras. Not cameras in general, but specifically ours, the 2022 models.*

Daniel: *(smiling) Maya, well done, your vigilance is excellent. But let's look at the "big picture." We have access to their leadership's bank accounts. We can see how Qatari money is entering the sector. Sinwar has just agreed to an increase of two thousand in the quota for workers in Israel. Why would he break the cash cow?*

Maya: *(raising her voice) He doesn't care about the workers! Yesterday on the fence, a Nukhba fighter approached the camera up close and smiled. He wasn't hiding. He looked straight into the lens and drew his finger across his throat. Have you entered that in the "big picture"?*

Daniel: *(irritated) That's psychological warfare, Maya. They are provoking us so that we scramble helicopters, burn millions of shekels on fuel, and ruin the holiday. If we declare an alert now, tomorrow I will be explaining to the legal adviser and the General Staff why we caused panic over a "terrorist's smile." Do you want* *the headlines to say that intelligence is again "frightening" the civilian population?*

Maya: *I want the people not to have their throats cut at my father's kibbutz tomorrow morning!*

Daniel: *(standing up, closing his laptop) Listen. We are the most technologically advanced intelligence service in the world. If something serious were being prepared, our algorithms would have issued a "red flag" a week ago. Your "feelings" are noise. My data is signal. Go back to base, get some sleep. Tomorrow is a holiday, it will be quiet. That is the rational forecast.*

Maya: *(quietly, leaving) Rational... You have simply fallen in love with your own algorithms more than with the lives of those they are supposed to protect.*

(The camera lingers on Daniel's monitor: an article open about "Female Tank Crew Members as a Symbol of Progress," while in the corner blinks a small, unidentified message about a communications failure at one section of the fence. Daniel swipes it away without reading it.)

***

At the end of September, one of the lookout girls at "Nahal Oz" writes in a WhatsApp group to her unit friends: "What, another incident?" In response, a voice message quickly follows: "Where have you been? We've had an incident every day for two weeks." The lookout girls we spoke with told of incidents they observed in real time in the months before October 7. Some feared the attack was imminent. "We saw them rehearsing the future raid every day," Noa, who is still serving in the army, tells the BBC. "They even had a mock-up of a tank and were practicing capturing it." "They also had a mock-up of barrier armaments and were demonstrating how they would blow them up and coordinating the capture of soldiers, killings, and abductions," she says. Several women also report that bombs were being laid and detonated near the barrier (called the "Iron Wall" in Israel), apparently to test its strength. In footage taken on October 7, powerful explosions were also shown, after which Hamas fighters on motorcycles immediately rushed through the gaps that had opened.

The tragedy of the lookout girls from Nahal Oz became a symbol of the failure: fifteen of them were killed in the first hours of the attack, seven taken hostage. Their warnings about Hamas's training to capture posts and disable cameras were dismissed as "panic" or "immaterial." As investigations have noted (including IDF internal reports of 2024–2025), this was not sexism in the pure sense but organizational arrogance: junior personnel (often women) were perceived as less authoritative than the "strategic" male analysts.

***

As reported in a New York Times article, Israeli officials had a detailed document describing Hamas's plans in their hands more than a year before the October 7 attack. However, it was considered unrealistic and reflecting the group's ambitions rather than its capabilities. Three months before the attack, a veteran analyst from Israel's Intelligence Unit 8200 warned that Hamas had conducted intensive exercises resembling those described in the document, but her concerns were also dismissed, the newspaper reports. "The signs were there," says retired Major General Eitan Dangot. "If gathered together, a decision could have been made earlier and something done to stop it. Unfortunately, this was not done." He says that although a full investigation has yet to be conducted, it is clear that the observers' reports "did not receive proper attention." Brigadier General Amir Avivi, former deputy commander of the Gaza division, does not believe it was sexism, but agrees that more should have been done to take the observers' concerns into account. In his view, "the biggest failure" was the conclusion that Israel was successfully deterring Hamas — that "yes, they are training, yes, they have a plan, but they are not going to carry it out."

The "Jericho Wall" Plan

"Jericho Wall" is the code name that Israeli intelligence (AMAN) gave to a 40-page Hamas document captured more than a year before the October 7, 2023 attack. The document was written in Arabic and described the scenario that Hamas implemented with striking accuracy. Israeli intelligence considered the plan unrealizable, overestimating its own forces and underestimating Hamas. The full text of the document has never been publicly released (it remains classified), but its contents are described in detail in the New York Times investigation (November 2023), internal IDF reports (2024–2025), and other sources. Below are the key elements of the plan.

Massive rocket barrage at the start of the attack: thousands of rockets and mortar shells across southern Israel. Goal: to distract IDF soldiers, force them to take shelter in bunkers, paralyze the response. Use of drones to neutralize the border: commercial and homemade drones (including quadcopters with explosives) to destroy surveillance cameras, automatic machine guns, communication antennas, and observation towers along the "smart fence." This was to blind and deafen the Israeli border protection system. Fence breach in dozens of points: breach in 60+ locations (according to some versions — up to 65) using explosives, bulldozers, and hand tools. Simultaneous breaches to prevent the IDF from plugging the gaps.

Ground force invasion: thousands of fighters from the elite "Nukhba" unit and regular Hamas fighters. Methods of penetration: foot groups, motorcycles and pickup trucks (for speed), motorized paragliders, boats from the sea. Numbers: the plan assumed up to 3,000–4,000 fighters in the first wave (in reality ~3,000–6,000). Seizure of targets inside Israel: capture and destruction of military bases, primarily Base Reim (headquarters of the Gaza Division) and other Southern Command bases. Seizure of kibbutzim and towns (Sderot, Ofakim, Netivot, etc.) up to 20–30 km deep into Israeli territory. Killings and mass capture of hostages (civilian and military) for subsequent exchange.

Additional details from the plan: increase in Hamas fighter numbers to 27,000–40,000 (actually achieved). Precise data on the disposition of Israeli forces, communications nodes, and weak points in the fence (this raised questions about possible leaks). The plan did not specify an exact date but emphasized surprise and simultaneity.

Why Was the Plan Underestimated?

AMAN and the General Staff believed Hamas had neither the resources nor the desire for such an operation (the concept of "deterrence": Hamas was supposedly interested only in money from Qatar and work in Israel). In July 2023, a Unit 8200 analyst (a woman from signals intelligence) warned that Hamas had conducted exercises precisely according to the "Jericho Wall" scenario — she was ignored, the scenario labeled "imaginary." The document circulated among the senior command but did not reach the political level (Netanyahu denies having seen it).

Implementation on October 7, 2023: Hamas executed the plan almost 1:1 — approximately 5,000–7,000 rockets in the first hours; drones destroyed 100+ cameras and towers; breach in approximately 100 locations; paragliders, motorcycles, pickups; seizure of bases, kibbutzim, approximately 250 hostages. This became one of the chief charges in the failure of AMAN and the IDF — worse than in 1973. Investigations of 2024–2025 confirmed: the plan was known, but the "concept" blinded intelligence.

The Network of Double Agents

According to a senior representative of Hamas's military wing, on the eve of the October 7 massacre, double agents were activated who were passing disinformation to Shabak with the goal of creating a false impression of "stability" in Gaza. According to the terrorist, this information influenced the Israeli intelligence assessment and allowed preparations for the attack to be concealed. Hamas's security service succeeded in 2017 in exposing a large espionage network working in Israel's interests. Some of the exposed agents, it is alleged, became double agents and were re-recruited by the Izz ad-Din al-Qassam Brigades, Hamas's military wing, to collect information.

According to Mahmoud Mardawi and Jaser Barghouti — senior Hamas representatives, in an interview published in February 2025 — one of the main steps of this operation was the detention of 45 Palestinians whom Hamas had identified as Israeli agents, following the elimination of Mazen Fuqaha in 2017. Mardawi claimed that these arrests "paralyzed the enemy's ability to collect intelligence" and made it difficult for Israel to receive timely warnings before the attack. Jaser Barghouti stated that as a result of the wide-scale arrests and dismantling of the spy network, Hamas managed to understand the working patterns of Israeli intelligence

— and in this way double agents were activated who passed targeted or false information to Israel. According to him, these agents distorted intelligence assessments and became part of the "Al-Aqsa Flood" plan.

New Accusations

Channel 14 journalist Yara Zered, in her report, leveled serious accusations against Shabak chief Ronen Bar.

(https://mignews.com/news/politic/smi-v-133-710-vse-mozhno-bylo-predotvratit-esli-by-ronen-bar-dejstvoval.html)

She emphasized the significance of a moment first heard in official Shabak chief testimony. According to her, only now — a year and a half later — is it becoming known that at 01:33 at night, the Southern Command commander received a message about Shabak units and YAMAM special forces moving south. According to her information, events occurring at that critical moment had far-reaching consequences for the entire country. She noted that this was not some secondary technical detail — on the contrary, it was a key turning point upon which many people's lives depended. To ignore it, the journalist believes, is unacceptable.

"Ronen Bar knew. He understood. He had the data. But the most basic thing he did not do: he did not wake the soldiers in the field. Not the army. Not the state. Not the prime minister. At 01:33 it was still possible to block the road to the Nova festival. Stop the cars. Set up checkpoints. Protect the kibbutzim, save the lookout girls' lives, direct forces to Sderot and Ofakim. Wake people up. Save lives. But Ronen Bar did not act," declared Zered.

The strategic surprise achieved by Hamas revealed a whole range of errors made by Israeli intelligence services, as

well as the inadequacy of the entire Israeli strategy in countering terrorist threats.

***

Bar convened a meeting at 4:30 in the morning but did not wake Netanyahu and did not raise the alarm at the highest level. It is alleged that by 4:30 in the morning Bar already understood the probability of a Hamas attack but did not wake the prime minister and did not warn residents of border areas. Netanyahu declared "a loss of trust" and justifiably accused him of concealing information. The situation around Shabak chief Ronen Bar's decision not to wake Prime Minister Benjamin Netanyahu on the night of October 7, 2023, is the subject of fierce political disputes in Israel. Bar and Halevi (the IDF Chief of Staff) "looked at" the signals but did not "see" the actual threat. They received indicators (unusual Hamas activity, Egyptian warnings about "something big"), but interpreted them as "exercises" or a "bluff."

Bar convened a meeting at 4:30 in the morning but did not wake Netanyahu and did not raise the alarm at the highest level. The Shabak internal investigation (March 2025) acknowledged: had the signals been assessed differently, the attack could have been prevented or mitigated. He failed precisely in "seeing" the immediate danger, despite previous strategic warnings. Some commentators (for example, Gadi Taub) argue that Bar did not wake Netanyahu due to bias: he allegedly wanted to "contain" the right-wing government in order to prevent escalation. This allegedly led to an underestimation of the threat and the decision not to raise the alarm, leaving soldiers and civilians unprepared. Other posts speculate that Bar "concealed threats" from Netanyahu, relying on "deceptive" Egyptian intelligence, and that this cost lives. There are accusations of Bar's "leftism" (for his criticism of "Jewish terror"), which allegedly made him "independent" of his political superior. I do not endorse these ideas.

No direct, officially confirmed "personal" reasons for the breach of subordination have been named. However, it is widely discussed that this was the result of a deep crisis of trust and a functional breakdown against the backdrop of strained political relations. The core version, following from the initial reports: Conceptual error — at 3:00 in the morning on October 7, when Ronen Bar arrived at Shabak headquarters, intelligence could not unambiguously determine whether what they were seeing was an actual attack or another round of Hamas military exercises. The conviction dominated that Hamas had no interest in a full-scale war. It was believed that even unusual activity was no more than exercises or provocation not requiring the immediate waking of the prime minister. Bar evidently decided that the threat level had not reached the critical threshold requiring immediate notification of the head of government, remaining within the bounds of standard night-time protocols.

The Shabak Law designates the prime minister as the sole superior of the service chief. Bar's decision not to wake Netanyahu (and the defense minister) was interpreted by the prime minister's office as a direct violation of subordination and trust. It is widely discussed in the media that between Netanyahu and Bar there existed an acute crisis of personal and professional trust even before October 7. This crisis was exacerbated by the internal Israeli conflict over judicial reform, in which Shabak was accused by the government of insufficient containment of the protests or even of "incitement" against the political leadership. Reports indicated that the prime minister's office accused Bar of "failure to prevent the launching of signal flares" by protesters toward the prime minister's

Caesarea residence, pointing to deep antagonism and mutual recriminations. The political and personal backstory between him and Netanyahu lays the groundwork for a version involving "personal" motives. Bar may have believed that given the existing distrust, Netanyahu would be unlikely to make quick and adequate decisions in the night, or that waking him would be politicized. Reluctance to engage political leadership before the situation had been fully clarified may have been Bar's attempt to shield the service from immediate political criticism in the event of a false alarm.

Thus, while the official reason likely lies in erroneous intelligence assessment, the crisis of trust and political antagonism between the Shabak chief and the prime minister undoubtedly played a role in the decision not to fulfill the obligation of immediate notification.

"THE KEYS TO THE STATE"

Setting: *Office of the Shabak Chief. 04:15 in the morning, October 7.*

Characters: Head of Shabak. Senior Operational Officer.

Officer: *Sir, the data on the SIM cards is confirmed. Breaching groups in Gaza are on the move. Per the "Red Folder" regulations we are obligated to immediately wake the Prime Minister. This is code "Peak." The system must wake up.*

Head of Shabak: *(without turning around) Wait with "Peak." Do you understand what will happen if we wake him?*

Officer: *Mobilization, sir. The country switches to combat mode. Every minute means lives on the border.*

Head of Shabak: *(with a bitter smirk) No. What begins is chaos and politics. Bibi will turn this into his show, and if the alert turns out to* *be false — he will make us look like idiots who ruined the holiday and undermined the economy. We have "special" relations with him, as you know. He doesn't trust us, and we don't trust him.*

Officer: *But sir, it is the law! He is the head of government! We cannot decide such things in a narrow circle.*

Head of Shabak: *(coldly) Tonight — we can. We are professionals. We have sent out "Tequila." That is enough to check the situation. We will "steer" the situation ourselves until dawn. The prime minister only gets in the way of operational work. We will report to him in the morning when we have facts, not assumptions. Let him sleep. There is already too much noise from politicians in this country. That is my order.*

Assistant: *But what if this is it? What if it is a big attack?*

Head of Shabak: *(quietly) Then we will be the first to meet the blow. Without his "advice." We will not wake the system. We will handle it ourselves.*

(The officer freezes. At this moment, Ronen Bar effectively detaches the elected authority from the management of the country. He leaves Netanyahu — and thus the entire military machine waiting for orders from above — in artificial suspension. The price of this "self-steering" will become clear in two hours.)

"Psychiatric Analysis"

This involves making decisions in a narrow circle of "our own" (from the military and intelligence echelons), bypassing the legitimate hierarchical center. This is a voluntary isolation of "the hand" from "the brain." The state enters a state of "functional coma." The sense organs (intelligence) function, the muscles (special forces) contract, but the consciousness (political will) is switched off. On October 7, Israel was dying not because it was weak but because its "head" and "hands" had decided to ignore each other's existence.

Without Oversight of the Head of Government

A coup d'état is a seizure of power, usually carried out by the military, police, or other state structures. This most radical interpretation may be applied on the basis of the following arguments: *The head of a security service with enormous power and being a key element of national security deliberately excludes his only lawful superior (the prime minister) from the decision-making process at the moment of the highest national danger.* This is perceived as an attempt to de facto usurp executive power in the security sphere. If one assumes that personal animosity and political antagonism were motives, then Bar's decision appears as a sabotage of political control aimed at undermining the prime minister's authority. By excluding Netanyahu, Bar and his colleagues created an artificial "vacuum" of political control over the supreme security forces during the critical hours.

"THE SHADOW LABORATORY"

Setting: *Operational hall of the security service. 04:30 in the morning.*

Characters: Head of the service. Senior Analyst.

Analyst: *Sir, we are obligated to pass the data to the Prime Minister's office. Per all regulations — that is their level of decision-making.*

Head of service: *(not looking at him) Their level? Do you want to wake up now the people who are calling us "traitors" in the Knesset?*

Do you want them to start dictating to us how to conduct sector clearing operations? They do not understand the nuances. They politicize our every move.

Analyst: *But if we stay silent and the situation gets out of hand ... it will look like a conspiracy.*

Head of service: *It will look like professional autonomy. We are the wall. A wall does not ask the house's residents how to stand. We will deal with this "noise" from Gaza ourselves. Inform the district headquarters: we operate by "quiet verification" protocol. The government will learn of the results in the morning. If there is anything to report at all.*

"Through a Psychiatrist's Eyes": The accusation of a "coup" is the most radical political assessment of the October 7 failure. It allows one to accuse specific individuals of deliberate sabotage based on their political views (Bar's conflict with the right-wing government). Actual assessment: the evidence presented to date — including Bar's own testimony and IDF reports — points to a massive operational and intelligence failure caused by conceptual fixation, weak analytical thinking, and arrogance, rather than by an intention to overthrow authority. However one describes it, what occurred bears the hallmarks of illegality on the part of the security leadership vis-à-vis the elected head of government. It reflects the fracture and mistrust that reigned between Israel's political and military echelons on the eve of October 7.

The Prime Minister accused Bar of failing to prevent the Palestinian attack on October 7, 2023. "He did not wake the system; he completely put it to sleep... Bar's blindness is the greatest intelligence failure in the history of the State of Israel," he declared. Ronen Bar departed following a public scandal with Netanyahu.

Analysis of Type I and Type II Errors

The intelligence community did not deploy critical thinking and did not properly consider alternative scenarios. Any alarming data (for example, Hamas exercises simulating breaches of the border) were rejected or fitted to the existing concept that Hamas was merely conducting exercises or would not cross the "red line" of full-scale invasion. Let me briefly remind the reader of the chronology of events on that unhappy night.

At approximately one o'clock in the morning, the Shabak chief was summoned to headquarters after being informed that several dozen Israeli SIM cards had become active in Gaza — cards used for communication in the event of a border crossing attempt. Shortly afterward, other signs of unusual Hamas activity appeared. Shabak and military intelligence continued receiving alarming signals without taking the necessary defensive measures. The Shabak chief understood that something was happening, but saw no clear signs of a large-scale attack and did not warn of the mortal danger to the music festival near Kibbutz Re'im. Shabak allowed for the possibility that Hamas might make isolated attack attempts and dispatched the "Tequila" special forces unit to the border. At 6:29 in the morning Netanyahu was informed of what was happening. At 6:30 in the morning a massive rocket barrage hit central and southern Israel.

The described situation is characteristic of many cases of medical diagnosis well known to me from forty years of clinical work, when there are unclear signs — symptoms "for" and "against" the diagnosis of a number of conditions, a state of uncertainty, and limited time for decision-making and necessary measures. The IDF and Shabak found themselves in an analogous situation. The best algorithm for decision-making, which we teach medical students and young doctors, is based on the concepts of Type I and Type II errors from mathematical statistics. The errors concern the acceptance or rejection of the so-called null hypothesis (H0) — the assumption of the absence of disease (attack, war, etc.).

Type I Error (False Positive Result)

The situation in which a test rejects a true null hypothesis (that is, asserts that the disease is present), although in reality the patient is healthy. False Positive (FP). Example — breast cancer screening (mammography). Type I error: The patient is healthy (no cancer), but the mammogram shows a suspicious area and the test result is declared positive. The patient experiences intense stress and may be prescribed an unnecessary biopsy (an invasive procedure) that does not detect cancer.

Type II Error (False Negative Result)

The situation in which a test does not reject an incorrect null hypothesis (that is, asserts that the disease is absent), although in reality the patient is ill. False Negative (FN). Example — breast cancer screening (mammography). Type II error: The patient has a small tumor (she is ill), but the mammogram failed to detect it, and the test result is declared negative. The patient receives false reassurance, and critically important treatment is delayed, allowing the cancer to grow. A Type II error — the false negative result — is considered the more dangerous type of error in medicine, particularly in the diagnosis of serious diseases.

Error Type	Name	Test Result	Actual Condition	Consequences
Type I Error (α-error)	*False Positive result* ***(False Positive)***	Positive (disease present)	Negative (no disease)	Unnecessary treatment, anxiety, additional procedures, unnecessary expense.
Type II Error (β-error)	*False Negative result* ***(False Negative)***	Negative (no disease)	Positive (disease present)	Delay in treatment, disease progression, worsening prognosis, missing a critical condition.

Type I and Type II errors are two types of false results arising in the conduct of any test or screening. It was precisely this error that Shabak made, concluding there was no real danger of a terrorist attack, when in reality a catastrophic attack had already been launched. Therefore, no adequate measures were taken against the attack — for which the country and thousands of citizens paid beyond all measure.

The failure of October 7 was a failure in information analysis and interpretation of intentions. Israel completely ignored the existential, ideological goal of Hamas — to inflict maximum damage on Israel.

The Crisis Between the Military and Politicians

Examples of military insubordination to the political leadership of a country in Israel and the United States, although rare, are key moments in history, since they threaten the principle of civilian control over the armed forces. In Israel, examples of direct disobedience to orders are extremely rare, but there have been cases of public disagreement and overstepping of authority on strategic questions, which effectively amounted to undermining the political line.

The Sharon–Eitan Crisis

During the First Lebanon War (1982), Defense Minister Ariel Sharon (who was the architect of the war) constantly expanded the initial military objectives that had been approved by the political cabinet. Chief of General Staff Rafael ("Raful") Eitan and Northern Command Commander Amir Drori did not disobey direct orders, but at some point the senior generals — including military intelligence chief Yehoshua Saguy — began expressing sharp disagreement with Sharon. The generals believed that Sharon was deceptively expanding the scope of the war and deepening the invasion beyond the mandate approved by the government. The conflict between Sharon and the IDF senior command contributed to the generals becoming more cautious about political control over military operations. While this was not a coup, it was a deep crisis of trust and a public challenge to the political line by the military leadership.

Reservist Threats (2023 Protests)

In 2023, on the eve of October 7, thousands of IDF reservists — including Air Force pilots and senior intelligence officers — publicly threatened to cease voluntary service (miluim) in protest against the judicial reform of Netanyahu's government. This was an unprecedented collective insubordination, though it concerned voluntary rather than mandatory service. It was assessed as interference in civil politics and damage to the army's combat readiness. Defense Minister Yoav Gallant publicly opposed continuation of the reform, stating that it was undermining the army — a statement that led to his temporary dismissal. These actions constituted direct military pressure on the political leadership with the goal of changing domestic policy.

USA: Conflict in Strategic Planning

In the USA, the principle of civilian control over the military is a cornerstone. The most famous and instructive case of a general's direct insubordination to a president occurred during the Korean War. During the Korean War (1950–1953), President Harry Truman pursued a policy of limited war, seeking to prevent escalation of the conflict with the Soviet Union and China. The Supreme Commander of UN forces in Korea, General Douglas MacArthur, was categorically opposed. He publicly called for expanding the war to the People's Republic of China, including calls for the use of nuclear weapons and support for Chiang Kai-shek's forces on Taiwan. MacArthur violated direct orders from Truman not to make public statcmcnts contradicting official administration policy. On April 11, 1951, President Truman relieved General MacArthur of all his command posts. This event became the classic example establishing the principle that the US President as Commander-in-Chief has absolute and unquestionable authority over the military leadership.

The Bar–Netanyahu Conflict

This is a deep, multilayered crisis that went far beyond professional disagreements and became one of the main symbols of the internal split in Israel, sharpened after October 7. The conflict has two main components. The official line of the conflict focused on responsibility for the catastrophe: Shabak failed to provide timely and adequate warning; the Prime Minister declared "growing distrust" of the security service chief; his circle accused Bar of inadequate preparation and incorrect threat assessment. (https://www.bbc.com/russian/articles/c4g2054xdeyo)

A much deeper and more scandalous aspect of the conflict concerns the alleged attempts by Netanyahu to use Shabak for political purposes — something Bar interpreted as a direct threat to democracy: Ronen Bar claimed that Netanyahu demanded personal loyalty and subordination directly to the prime minister (as defined by law, not to the Supreme Court or democratic principles). Bar stated that Netanyahu demanded from Shabak the passing of information about the organizers and participants of the protest movement against judicial reform. Bar refused to do this, considering the use of the security service for surveillance of civil protests to be unlawful and anti-democratic.

Netanyahu accused Bar of "obstructing reforms" in the agency after October 7 and of political bias. Breach of protocol: the crudest violation of subordination and the "rules of the game" was the decision not to inform the prime minister and minister of defense when signals arrived about a potential attack. This was an impermissible violation of the high-readiness protocol, based on overconfidence in his threat assessment, which deprived the prime minister of the ability to make a political decision about full-scale force deployment before the massacre began.

In April, Bar announced a voluntary resignation, which took effect on June 15, 2025. He emphasized personal responsibility for the October 7 failure, but accused Netanyahu of pressuring the

service for personal ends. This episode became a symbol of the deep crisis between the political leadership and the security services. Netanyahu, as a strategic leader, made a number of critical decisions that reversed the situation after the failure: rapid transition to the offensive in Gaza, strikes against Hezbollah and Iran, and management of the "war on seven fronts" (Gaza, Lebanon, Yemen, etc.). By October 2025, this had led to the weakening of Hamas and Hezbollah, demonstrating his "long-range vision."
(https://www.trtrussian.com/article/d5a704d13551)

"Personal Responsibility Without Consequences"

Ronen Bar was the first to assume responsibility but did so in a manner specific to a senior official. In his letter to subordinates he wrote: "Responsibility rests with me as the service chief ... We failed to create adequate warning." While acknowledging guilt, Bar simultaneously emphasized that Shabak was a heroic institution now "engaged in war." Fearing a "wrong signal," Shabak recommended lowering combat readiness, not informing the government and army, in order to exclude possible escalation. This led to no mobilization order being issued and no local defensive preparations being made. This error, which became a key factor in the October 7 catastrophe, recalls the failures at the start of the Yom Kippur War (1973) and June 22, 1941 (USSR), when excessive caution before "partners" led to a surprise blow.

Conclusion

We have come to the final act of this drama — to the moment when the shock of the first weeks gave way to the cold survival instinct of the bureaucratic machine. The initial statements of Ronen Bar and Aharon Haliva ("Responsibility rests with me") were at first perceived by many as an act of courage. By acknowledging a "professional failure," the security service chiefs were foreclosing the possibility of a systemic investigation. They said: "We made an error of judgment," but not "Our ideology is flawed." The main slogan became: "One cannot investigate during wartime." This gave the system precious months in which to prepare archives, align narratives, and wait for public anger to burn out or shift to the politicians.

The government's legal adviser occupied a key position in the defense of the system. Her task was to direct the fire of future commissions in one direction only — toward the political echelon (Netanyahu). Any attempt by the government to create a supervisory body to examine the actions of the prosecution or the army ran into a "legal veto." Baharav-Miara insisted that only a "State Commission" headed by a Supreme Court justice had the right to investigate October 7. Why? Because the judges are part of the same caste that created the "Concept." They speak the same language as the generals and will judge "political irrationality," not the "legal paralysis" of the army.

By 2024–2025, troubling facts had begun to emerge about what was happening inside headquarters in the first weeks after the tragedy. It became known that some records of operational meetings on the night of October 7 had been "improperly preserved" or deleted. Junior officers who tried to testify about how their warnings were ignored were subjected to pressure. The system squeezed out "troublemakers," replacing them with those willing to maintain the official version of the "unpredictability" of the attack.

The media, closely tied to the defense establishment, launched an aggressive campaign of heroization of the senior leadership despite the failure. Instead of asking "How did you allow this to happen?", the emphasis shifted to "How heroically they are managing the war now." The October 7 failure began to be presented as an "inevitable price for decades of right-wing rule," although it was precisely the liberal-left establishment (the army and the courts) that had for decades imposed the doctrine of containing Hamas.

The system's self-defense succeeded. The deep state managed to turn a national-scale catastrophe into an instrument of struggle against political opponents. Instead of a deep reform of the intelligence services and the courts, Israel received a "cosmetic renovation" and an attempt to preserve the old elite at the helm, despite its complete intellectual and professional failure.

The intelligence failure of October 7 proved that professionalism does not substitute for strategic thinking and political will. A highly professional service like Shabak was paralyzed by its own "concept," failing to apply even the basic principle of "Ifcha Mistabra" (the opposite may become reality). The principle of "Ifcha Mistabra" in intelligence had degraded to the level of formality. In the corridors of AMAN, an atmosphere had formed in which doubting the Concept meant writing off one's career. We witnessed induced blindness: when the senior leadership literally silenced those who saw signs of the invasion. October 7 is not a failure of intelligence as an instrument; it is a failure of intelligence as a hierarchy. We created a system in which loyalty to the Concept was more important than fidelity to facts. The inability to accept the warnings of lookout girls and foreign partners was a direct consequence of this intellectual inertia.

The actions of the Shabak chief that night — including ignoring the worst-case scenario — had nothing to do with a "coup," but reflected tragic complacency and self-righteous certainty against the backdrop of a political conflict with the prime minister. This internal conflict and the struggle for loyalty only deepened the external blindness.

The intellectual catastrophe of October 7 is the natural result of a year spent on internal squabbles. Intelligence was too occupied analyzing the "social resilience" of Israelis in response to the reform to notice the enemy picking the lock of their own house. This was the collapse of faith in the idea that "smart" technology could replace vigilance and the readiness to kill the enemy at the border.

Responsibility for the catastrophe rests not only with those who ignored the facts but also with those who created a culture in which those facts could be ignored. The profound failure of intelligence demands not only a change of faces but a fundamental revision of doctrine — a departure from the paralyzing concept of "containment" and a restoration of the principle of zero tolerance for threat, regardless of its source. The security services must once again become guardians of reality, not instruments for maintaining a desired political illusion.

October 7 intelligence resembled a sleeping giant who had surrounded himself with the most expensive motion sensors but forgot to open his eyes. This failure must enter the textbooks not as an error of communication or technology, but as the moral bankruptcy of an elite that decided it knew the enemy better than the enemy knew himself.

The end of 2025. We are still clearing the rubble of this self-confidence. And the lesson is simple and terrible: when intelligence services begin to believe in their own myths, they become accomplices in catastrophe. For this not to be repeated, we need more honest doubt and readiness for the worst.

CHAPTER 27.
THE MEDIA MONOPOLY OF THE HEADQUARTERS

Introduction

In this chapter we encounter the most sophisticated form of manipulation — the exploitation of collective trauma. Hamas seized hostages, but the "Hostage Families Headquarters" (guided by the political technologists of the Kaplan protests) seized the mind of a nation. ***The tragedy of the hostages was elevated out of the humanitarian category and transformed into an ultimatum political weapon:*** *Hamas presses the "hostages" button, and Israeli media and the "Headquarters" transmit this impulse, paralyzing the government's will.* The death and suffering of people became the currency with which they attempted to purchase Israeli sovereignty. This is a form of media masochism: the country watched its own wounds around the clock while the enemy savored the effect.

"A Bleeding Wound"

The tragedy of October 7, 2023, inflicted on Israel not only a physical but a deep moral blow, embodied in the capture of more than 350 civilian and military hostages. ***Among them were the elderly, men, women, and children; the sick and the wounded; civilians and soldiers.*** They were bound, abused, and driven off to the Gaza Strip to the jeering of a jubilant crowd. From that day, for two years, the country lived with the tragedy of the hostages and their families. Acts of abduction accompanied by abuse turned this issue into a genuine "bleeding wound" on the body of the nation. This "bleeding wound" became not merely a humanitarian catastrophe but the most powerful instrument of psychological terror, which Hamas methodically used to destabilize the foundations of Israeli statehood. The taking of hostages became a strategic lever with which the enemy forced the entire society to plunge into a state of collective trauma and political paralysis.

From that day Israel has lived under conditions of political and ethical dissonance: two key values on which the state had traditionally been built — the saving of life (Pikuach Nefesh) and national security — have entered into irreconcilable conflict. Hamas understood that in the Israeli code, the "value of human life" is simultaneously the highest virtue and the Achilles' heel. Publication of videos with hostages, deathbed recordings, and dosed information about the condition of the captives became part of a sophisticated psychological war. The goal was not only pressure on the government but the creation of a deep rift within society: between those demanding "a deal at any price" and those insisting on "victory at any price."

For Israelis, safety in their own home is a foundational condition of the social contract. On October 7 that contract failed. The sight of children and elderly people dragged through the streets of Gaza became tangible proof of the helplessness of those very structures that for years had convinced the nation of their infallibility. This engendered a sense of defenselessness that cannot be healed by military successes alone.

The hostages became the object of political speculation. The tragedy quickly spilled beyond the bounds of national mourning and became an arena for the resumption of internal strife. Protest movements that had quieted in the first weeks of the war found their voice again, using the slogan of the return of hostages as the chief instrument of pressure on the political leadership. The system once again found itself in a state of social schizophrenia: hostage families, driven by unbearable pain, often became tools in the hands of political forces pursuing their own ends. The hostage problem posed impossible dilemmas for Israel. The legal system and military command found themselves caught between the need to continue the fierce offensive to destroy Hamas and the risk to the lives of hostages in the tunnels. Every decision was weighed not only on the scales of military expediency but also under the watchful, often condemnatory gaze of the world community and legal advisers — limiting the army's freedom of maneuver.

A nation already exhausted and divided was shattered by an act of savage cruelty embodied in the capture of hundreds of hostages — elderly people, children, women, and soldiers. These innocent people, driven off to the jeering of a triumphant crowd, transformed the tragedy into a "bleeding wound" that has not healed for two years. From that day, the internal political fracture was transformed into an unresolvable moral and ethical dilemma. Society split into two camps.

The "Deal Now!" camp, represented by family activists who demand immediate capitulation, a ceasefire, and the release of all terrorists. Their motto is "the religion of hostages," which places saving life above any military goals.

The "Victory Only!" camp, supporters of Israel's historical ethos who insist: one does not surrender to terrorists. They argue that victory must be achieved so that the soldiers' sacrifices are not in vain, and so that the state retains the ability to defend itself.

Two years later, the echo of October 7 continues to sound in every home. The hostages became a symbol of the fact that this war is not merely a battle for territory but a struggle for Israel's very right to be a refuge for the Jewish people. Until the last of them returns, the wound remains open, a reminder of the price of the "era of blindness" and strategic arrogance that allowed peaceful citizens to be turned into human shields for terrorists. This chapter is devoted to the analysis of this fundamental fracture, its historical roots (the refusal to submit to blackmail at Entebbe), and its influence on the government's strategic decisions — determining what precisely became the true goal of the war: the return of people or the preservation of national dignity and security.

I turn to one of the darkest and psychologically most complex chapters of this analysis. Here "social schizophrenia" reaches its peak, when the nation's natural compassion for its kidnapped citizens collides with the cold calculation of terrorists and political players. The tragedy of the hostages became a psychological noose around the nation's neck — and the hostages a strategic weapon of Hamas. For Yahya Sinwar, the 250 (at that time) hostages were not merely "bargaining chips." They were a remote control for Israeli society. Hamas quickly understood that Israeli democracy is extremely sensitive to the suffering of the individual. The publication of hostage videos was mathematically calibrated. They were released precisely when Israel was on the verge of another round of political disputes — to pour fuel on the fire. Hamas used false information about the condition of the captives to keep the families in a state of constant emotional swings — from hope to despair. This exhausted the psychic resources of the entire country.

Hostage Forums

In response to the catastrophe, Israeli society, reflecting its deep schizophrenization, fractured into several associations of hostage families, each of which took diametrically opposed positions. At one pole — those who demand "capitulation at any price" and an immediate ceasefire for the lives of their loved ones, even if this makes "the soldiers' sacrifices meaningless." At the other — supporters of the traditional Zionist ethos, whose position was formulated by one commentator: "How long will we be slaves to the religion of hostages?"

Hostage Families Headquarters — 1

The "Headquarters," or forum of the abducted, is the largest, most public, and most aggressive group, which dominates world and national media. It has successfully transformed its tragedy into a national protest. Its chief strength is moral blackmail of the government, based on the Israeli ethical code. Its weakness is that it is politicized and raises the price demanded by Hamas. The "Headquarters" adheres to a strict humanitarian priority based on the Jewish principle of **"Pikuach Nefesh"** (saving life above all). Its main headquarters is located in Tel Aviv, on the square now unofficially called "Hostage Square." It demands a deal at any price and immediately. It is prepared for a complete cessation of the war and mass prisoner exchange (including convicted terrorists) for the return of every hostage.

The Merger of the "Headquarters" and "Kaplan": The tragedy of the hostages did not remain a purely humanitarian question. Very quickly the leadership of the "Hostage Families Headquarters" came under the influence of the same political consultants and sponsors as the reform protests. *Radicalization of slogans: Instead of the unifying "Bring them home," the political slogan "Deal now, government resign" rang out in the streets.* This created a false dilemma: allegedly only the fall of the government can save their loved ones. Split among the families: It is important to note that not all families went down this path. Groups holding right-wing views (the "Tikvah" forum) argued that only military pressure would save their children. However, the media gave ninety percent of airtime precisely to those demanding capitulation before Hamas for the sake of a deal — effectively isolating other voices.

The Headquarters' key tactic is the deliberate creation of chaos. They regularly organize blockades of main transport arteries (Ayalon highway) as well as mass demonstrations at government buildings. The goal: to attract attention and create a sense of a national crisis incompatible with the continuation of normal life. The group's rhetoric is the sharpest and includes personal, aggressive accusations against Prime Minister Netanyahu of "deliberate abandonment" or "murder" of the hostages. **This emotional blackmail serves as the main political driving force of the protest.**

The Headquarters members organized something like a "concentration camp" in Tel Aviv. They demand capitulation at any price. To do everything to make the soldiers' sacrifices meaningless. To do everything so that two years of the people's suffering prove to have been in vain. To do everything so that Israel loses this war. "We appeal to the Israeli government and the US administration: the time has come to conclude a comprehensive agreement and end the war. No more delays. End this nightmare and bring them out of the tunnels and home," reads their statement. *This is how, by hook or by crook, the country's arm was twisted at the time of the Gilad Shalit deal. Then Sinwar was released, and this led to the catastrophe of October 7. Will there be a new catastrophe if one capitulates to the "Headquarters?" Do not doubt it for a moment.*

"THE STAGING OF PAIN"

Setting: *The makeup room of one of the central television channels. Evening prime time.*

Characters: News Producer (cynical professional). Talk show host. Activist of the "Families Headquarters" (with traces of weariness on his face).

Producer: *(to the host) Listen carefully. In this segment we don't need military experts with their maps of Gaza. The viewer is tired of that. We need emotion. The activist will talk about "a deal at any price." When he starts to cry, camera — close-up.*

Host: *But we have in the second part of the broadcast a report on how a ceasefire will allow Hamas to regroup and kill even more soldiers. Maybe we give them a chance to speak?*

Producer: *(irritated) Do you want to tank the ratings? "Any price" — that's what sells. If we start discussing "strategic risks," we'll be accused of heartlessness. Tonight we work from the script: "Bibi left them to die." That's the main line.*

Activist: *(quietly) But my brother is there, in the tunnels ... I don't want politics; I just want to bring him back.*

Producer: *(putting his hand on the activist's shoulder) We all do, dear. But to bring him back, we need to pressure the government. And for that you have to say on air that the war is lost and the hostages are the only thing that matters. Understand? The only thing. Army, victory, the country's future — those are all words. Your brother is reality. Go and say that.*

(The host walks out to the studio. The red camera lights switch on. All evening the country will watch the tears, not knowing that backstage these tears have already been packaged into a political slogan that deprives the army of any chance of victory.)

Psychiatric Analysis and Metaphor

Diagnosis: *Hypertrophy of compassion as a method of suppressing reason.*

Description: The media monopoly created conditions in which any attempt at rational military analysis was equated with betrayal. *Social schizophrenia manifested in that society was forced to choose between "love for one's neighbor" (return the hostages) and the "survival instinct" (destroy the enemy).*

Mechanism: Emotional blackmail was used as a blocker of strategic thinking. When "any price" becomes the official slogan, the enemy ceases to fear the army, because he knows that the media inside Israel will do all the work of compelling the government to capitulate.

Forum "Gevura"

The "Gevura" (heroism, strength) group is the direct antipode of the main Headquarters and represents the voice of families who support the government's military course.

It is founded on the principles of National Security and heroism. Its members believe that the soldiers' sacrifices must not be in vain, and that concessions to terror represent a strategic defeat. It includes the families not only of hostages but also of fallen soldiers. It demands that the war not be halted until all goals have been fully achieved, first and foremost the destruction of Hamas. A deal should be achieved only from a position of strength and maximum military pressure. *It is pro-government. The group provides moral cover and support for Prime Minister Netanyahu's tough line, rejecting the moral blackmail from the Headquarters.*

The "Gevura" group takes the opposite position: its activity is directed toward supporting the government. The group does not engage in street protests or disturb public order. Its rhetoric is focused on moral support for the IDF and on the patriotic imperative of achieving full military victory. Its main public activity consists of press conferences and non-public meetings with ministers, where they call for not halting the war.

Forum "Tikvah"

"Tikvah" (Hope) occupies an intermediate, conservatively centrist position, criticizing the government but avoiding extreme demands. *It seeks to find a balance between the need to return the hostages and the achievement of military goals, but leans toward the right-wing political camp.* It opposes the demand for an immediate cessation of the war. It is a critically inclined right-wing opposition. It applies pressure on the Likud government with the goal of more effective action, but without calls for revolution. *This group's activity is moderate and focused on lobbying.* They avoid street protests and do not seek to create collapse. "Tikvah" criticizes the government for ineffectiveness and a lack of a clear strategy for returning the hostages, but their tone is more restrained than that of the main Headquarters.

Forum "Law and Justice"

This group concentrates its efforts on questions of accountability for the October 7 catastrophe rather than solely on the war itself. *It demands the immediate creation of an independent commission to investigate all aspects of the failure (intelligence, military command, political leadership).* Its chief priority is establishing blame and bringing those responsible for the tragedy to accountability. This group is less concerned with the urgency of a deal. The group's activity is concentrated exclusively in the legal sphere. They do not affect the daily lives of citizens. Their confrontation is legal and political in character. They apply uncompromising pressure through the Supreme Court and public demands for the creation of an independent State Investigative Commission. This pressure is aimed at the immediate resignation of guilty officials and generals.

Forum "October Council"

This forum views the crisis from the perspective of Israel's long-term political and social future. Its members believe that the October 7 failure is rooted in the country's deep political and social fracture. *They demand a fundamental rethinking of the security systems, a change in the political discourse, and the establishment of a new ethics of leadership.* Their goal is systemic change to prevent future catastrophes, raising questions about the state's future above tactical political disputes. **This group focuses on ideological and systemic reform of the state.** Its activity consists of holding conferences, publishing manifestos, and collaborating with civil organizations. The rhetoric is systemic and constructive. They criticize the deep problems of Israeli political culture and governance rather than individuals, striving to create a reform plan for the post-conflict period.

Morality Against Strategy

The conflict between the desire to free the hostages without capitulating to the enemy is the key, agonizing dilemma of this war, having no simple solution. This conflict sets the moral imperative (saving lives) against the strategic imperative (national security). The activity of certain hostage families affected the consolidation of society. Their actions — with all the human right to pain — harmed social unity. The mentioned dilemma can be reduced to two incompatible goals.

Freeing the hostages ("Leave no one behind"): From the families' point of view, any price is justified for saving living citizens. This means a deal including a full ceasefire, troop withdrawal, and the release of thousands of Palestinian prisoners (including those convicted of murder). The success of such a deal for Hamas is tantamount to a political victory. It will allow Hamas to preserve its power, restore its military potential, and, in essence, entrench terrorism as an effective instrument for obtaining concessions from Israel.

Not capitulating ("Victory over terror"): This strategic imperative demands from the government the fulfillment of two declared goals: destruction of Hamas and assurance of long-term security. It requires the continuation of military pressure until Hamas is destroyed, and a deal, if one takes place, will not look like complete surrender. The tough position endangers the lives of the remaining hostages. Time works against them, and military actions increase the risk of their death both at the hands of Hamas and as a result of Israeli strikes. This also deepens the fracture within the country.

In Judaism, the conflict of "morality against strategy" is resolved through one of the highest moral imperatives. The prevailing view inclines toward maximum effort to save life, but the strategic risk (strengthening the enemy) is also taken into account. The hostage families became a symbol of human tragedy and the state's moral obligation. However, over time, their movement — originally unifying — divided along political lines, and part of its activity became a tool of political pressure on the government. The prime minister and his coalition, as well as the "Gevura" group, view the demand for an immediate ceasefire as a strategic capitulation to Hamas. They argue that if Hamas survives, the war was lost, and the threat of October 7 will repeat in the future. Ultimately, the dilemma reduces to a choice between immediate moral victory (saving lives) and long-term strategic victory (ensuring security), with each decision carrying an unacceptable risk from the point of view of the other side.

But Whom to Fight?

The Hostage Families Headquarters began acting in the interests of the abducted with the aim of organizing a public struggle for their return. ***But whom to fight? By the logic of things, one should fight Hamas. Well, that is the healthy logic! The "schizophrenic" left-wing logic works differently.***

The Hostage Families Headquarters was not left to itself for long. In the media, a single image of "hostage families" quickly emerged, as if only one position existed. This image formed around the Headquarters group closely tied to the Kaplanist protest movement, as well as to the PR teams that had previously serviced the 2023 anti-government actions. The editorial offices of major television channels — primarily channels 12 and 13 — actively built communications precisely with this part of the families, providing them with priority access to the airwaves.

Israel's media conglomerates in this war appeared not as informers but as retransmitters of Hamas's psychological terror. Every video of Sinwar with hostages immediately entered prime time, accompanied by the hysteria of studio experts. This was an ideal synergy: Hamas supplied the content, and Israeli media ensured its delivery to every home. The monopoly on "proper compassion" led to any attempt to speak of national security being declared sacrilege. The media created a situation in which military victory began to be perceived as an "obstacle" to the return of people. In this way a media monopoly on suffering took shape. Activists from the Headquarters of the Abducted and Missing began to actively participate in demonstrations, using slogans directly accusing the government and the army — "Free all hostages and now!" — immortal, against ... the government and Netanyahu.

The Kaplanist movement recognized in the hostage theme colossal emotional potential. *PR specialists proposed combining family rallies with government protests, creating the effect that personal grief became a political argument. A layer of regular experts consolidated — former generals, ex-officials, and commentators connected with academic and left-wing centers.* Their positions almost always coincide: acknowledge the political responsibility of the government, stop the war for the sake of a deal, open a "diplomatic window" with US participation. Why did precisely these people become the voice? First, former generals inspire trust. Second, think tanks (such as INSS, Reichman University, Molad, IDI) collaborate with media, offering "ready-made commentators." Third, editorial offices are accustomed to these faces: they speak clearly, without pauses, creating the drama of the broadcast. Finally, some experts in the past were active participants in the party center and the left wing; returning to the media field is a way to preserve influence.

The media monopoly operates through several mechanisms: substitution of scale — tragedy is transformed from national to personally political; emotional accompaniment — relatives alongside experts; displacement of alternative positions; and the effect of a single narrative — the viewer sees a multitude of voices but the meaning does not change: the government is not saving them, the war is a mistake, an exchange is needed and new power.

This transformed a national tragedy into a matter of political choice: "for Bibi or against." Statements by some families, resonating in the media ("the government abandoned our people," "the army is interested in image, not in saving lives") undermined public trust in the IDF and Shabak. This was felt especially acutely against the backdrop of reservist mobilization — creating a sense of "internal accusation" during wartime. As a result, part of society ceased to see in the families a symbol of pain, and began to see — a political instrument.

The consequences are obvious: intensification of schizophrenization, fracture and erosion of national unity, decline of sympathy, politicization of suffering, informational dependence, demotivation of fighters, weakening of the moral effect of unity, and decline of trust in the media.

The tragedy of the hostages became a mirror of the Israeli media landscape: pain is concentrated, packaged, and directed into the political stream. Neither the families nor society are to blame — but the mechanisms of media, PR, and expert dependence made personal grief into a systemic instrument of influence.

The boundless financial "oxygen supply" revived the protests, despite the grief of many and the joy of Hamas. *The slogan "Free all hostages and now!" called for Israel's capitulation and Hamas's victory.* A choice that is morally unbearable and, from the standpoint of state survival strategy, impossible.

Hostage Families Headquarters — 2

The Hostage Families Headquarters created a propaganda machine modeled on the Gilad Shalit campaign. *The Kaplanists used them to bring down the government. They are not insane, not blind, and not stupid. They use grief for political ends.* Where, then, should one categorize them? I will venture a suggestion: in the category of social schizophrenia. This was explained on the state television channel Kan by Eliyahu Libman, whose own son is among the hostages.

"It is important that the public knows: when people speak on behalf of the Headquarters of Families, on behalf of the families of the abducted, about policy and negotiations — it is not on behalf of the families of the abducted!" said Libman. "They speak on behalf of ten, twenty, thirty, forty families who, with all due respect to them, are nothing like the families of the two hundred and forty hostages. If you want to make statements on behalf of all families, then all families must sign. If you want to speak on behalf of families, then say precisely which families. Name the hostage and the close relative on whose behalf Ronen Tzur is now speaking. For over forty days already they have been confusing everyone's minds and undermining government policy."

Libman noted that the humanitarian activity of the Headquarters in providing genuine assistance to the families of the abducted deserves every praise, but that it also has a political component that is "completely false and not coordinated with the families." "The organizers do not express the general opinion of all families. Instead, the portion that has a specific political agenda enlists the support of families who share that agenda, and then this is presented as the 'position of the hostage families.'"

The families are in a state of extreme trauma and despair. Their rhetoric reflects their pain and the conviction that the prime minister, who should be responsible for their security, is actively obstructing the return of their loved ones, placing military success above their lives. Although the families' goal is to return their loved ones and the Kaplanists' goal is to change power, their interests coincided: strong public pressure on the government that would compel it to accept an unpopular decision or resign.

Although the Hostage Families Headquarters is a volunteer non-profit organization (NGO), many of its volunteers and key organizers were active participants in the mass protests against judicial reform before October 7. The forum uses the same effective methods of street mobilization and PR pressure that were honed during the protests. The families' demand to conclude a "deal at any price" with Hamas intensified pressure on the government, which weakened Israel's negotiating position: the enemy saw the internal stratification and sought to exploit it. In Hamas and Qatar, reports in the media indicate, the family protests were directly assessed as "a useful internal instrument of pressure on Bibi."

Thus, the hostage families encouraged Hamas to raise the price for the hostages, since public opinion in Israel was on their side. Critics accused the Headquarters of being an "extension" of the protest movement, and that its true goal was the overthrow of Netanyahu rather than solely the return of the hostages.

The statements of leaders and family members often went beyond ordinary criticism, becoming emotional accusations and threats: the sharpest statements concern the direct accusation of the government — "the blood of every hostage killed in Gaza is on the hands of the prime minister and his cabinet"; forum activists constantly called for the immediate fall of the government as the only guarantee of the hostages' lives; threats to intensify street protests to the point of paralyzing the country and forcing the government either to conclude a deal or resign; and threats of unprecedented international lobbying and lawsuits that might damage Israel's reputation on the world stage. The families regularly met with heads of state, applying external pressure on Israel.

When part of the families declared that the government was obligated to halt the war "at any price," this entered into direct contradiction with the values of other families of the fallen and soldiers at the front. A conflict arose between "save at any price" and "do not surrender to terror" — two moral principles collided at the center of the national psyche. The result was moral disorientation and undermining of the shared national narrative.

Israeli media, especially Kan, Channel 13, and Haaretz, amplified one side — turning hostage families into a moral flag for the opposition. Other voices — the families of fallen soldiers, residents of the south — remained less audible. *This created the perception that one group of suffering people had gained a monopoly on morality, which provoked irritation and counter-polarization, with growing bitterness and mistrust between social strata.*

For all the harm, the hostage family groups also played a positive role — they kept the hostage issue in the public's focus and prevented indifference. But the absence of coordination and a neutral moral center (rabbis, military figures, national leaders outside parties) transformed the movement from a unifying force into a divisive one.

Thus, the Hostage Families Headquarters functions as a moral and political battering ram that uses grief and tragedy as a lever to achieve its chief goal — the return of the hostages — even if this contradicts Israel's strategic military objectives.

A History of Shameful Deals

Israel, in the course of its history, has conducted dozens of prisoner and body exchanges for living terrorists. Every such deal was subsequently assessed as "shameful" or "catastrophic," because many of the released terrorists returned to terrorism, and the human price turned out to be enormous. Below are the most significant ones, which still provoke fury in Israeli society (in chronological order).

First exchange: January 21, 1968. In this first deal, two Israeli soldiers — Aharon Aaronson and Israel Kastner — who had been kidnapped by Arab terrorists, were released in exchange for imprisoned terrorists. This set the precedent for Israel's participation in hostage exchanges, creating a template for future negotiations.

The Avraham Amram deal: January 11, 1979. After Israeli soldier Avraham Amram was kidnapped in Lebanon and held for more than a year, he was released in exchange for 76 terrorists, including several convicted murderers. The Lubavitcher Rebbe sharply criticized this deal, arguing that such exchanges are illogical and dangerous.

The Jibril deal: May 21, 1985. Under this deal, 1,151 security prisoners were released in exchange for three IDF soldiers captured in combat at Sultan Yaaqub. Among those freed was Sheikh Ahmed Yassin, who subsequently founded Hamas. This deal played a direct role in triggering the First Intifada. The deal shocked society because of the disproportionate price. Many of the released prisoners returned to terrorist activity, which critics argue directly led to the surge of violence in subsequent years.

The Oslo Accords: September 13, 1993. As a gesture of goodwill, approximately 9,200 Arab prisoners were released. This deal paved the way for the Second Intifada (Al-Aqsa Intifada) in 2000, one of the most traumatic and violent periods in recent history.

The Tannenbaum–Har Dov deal: January 27, 2004. Four hundred Arab terrorists and 35 foreign terrorists were released, including those implicated in the kidnapping of Israeli officer Elhanan Tannenbaum and the Har Dov captives. Hamas and Hezbollah came to understand better that kidnappings could produce successful outcomes.

The Goldwasser–Regev deal: August 16, 2008. Israel's release of 10 prisoners and 199 bodies of Hezbollah terrorists in exchange for the return of soldiers Eldad Regev and Ehud Goldwasser only further inflamed Hamas's desire to engage in new kidnappings.

The Shalit deal: November 18, 2011. This cursed deal, in which the underperforming soldier Gilad Shalit was exchanged for 1,027 terrorists. Gilad Shalit was captured in 2006 by Palestinian militants who had tunneled through the Gaza–Israel border. Given the absence of a military option for freeing Shalit, the defense minister opted for secret negotiations with Hamas. Israeli publicist and director of the Palestine-Israel Research Center Gershon Baskin initiated negotiations with Hamas that in October 2011 led to the exchange of soldier Gilad Shalit for 1,027 Palestinians. The devastating attack from Gaza on Israel during Simchat Torah on October 7, 2023, is the obvious consequence of this deal. The experience of protests against the government was put to use after the October 7 failure.

I remember the hysterical media publications and sophisticated posts, demands and protests applying pressure in favor of exchanging a poor soldier "immediately and at any price." With Netanyahu's consent, the exchange took place — and thus the clock was set for the October 7, 2023 attack. This is an unforgivable mistake by Benjamin Netanyahu.

How It Was Done

Formation of pressure on the government: After Gilad Shalit's kidnapping in 2006, spontaneous and then organized protests began. They grew into a mass public movement demanding a deal with Hamas at any price and applying pressure on the Israeli government.

The Shalit Headquarters became the center of pressure: his family founded a tent camp near the prime minister's residence in Jerusalem. It became the hub of actions and a symbol of the struggle. Mass marches were conducted, including the "March for Shalit" in the summer of 2010, in which tens of thousands of Israelis participated.

Activists skillfully used the media and visual images — school desks with Gilad's name, flash mobs, letters. Israeli media actively supported the campaign, amplifying the public resonance. Despite internal disputes and the resistance of part of the cabinet, mass pressure became the decisive factor in approving the deal.

It is clear to all that consenting to exchange a captured soldier for a significant number of terrorists is direct encouragement of further captures, encouragement of terror, and a means of replenishing terrorist ranks with old and experienced personnel.

Israel had not experienced such nationwide jubilation as the return from captivity of soldier Gilad Shalit. Crowds of people who had come from all parts of the country besieged the small settlement of Mitzpe Hila, where Gilad's parents live, filled the approach roads, strewing them with flowers, and filled the entire space with joyful shouts.

Never mind a thousand murderous terrorists for one hostage! Journalists on all television channels clumsily explained why it had been necessary. There was the Jewish tradition of ransoming captives at any price, and assurances that the freed cannibals would not be able to do much harm since they would be vigilantly watched and neutralized if necessary. The emotional climate at such moments is off the charts and the answers are rarely rational. But this is precisely what happened on October 7, 2023.

Let Us Free Ourselves from the "Religion of Hostages"

In an interview with a correspondent of the newspaper Maariv, **Brigadier General (res.) Erez Wiener said: "How long will we be slaves to the religion of hostages?"** He reminded his audience that "the State of Israel was built on the ethos that one does not give in to terrorists. Already at Entebbe we refused to release a small number of terrorists for the sake of dozens of kidnapped citizens and sent out four Hercules aircraft to save them. We acted the same way in other operations as well. No one asked who made the decision and why we fought rather than negotiating." (https://moshiach.ru/view/actualia/26075.html)

Wiener is convinced that there is no connection between those who have been leading the discussion on hostages — disseminating their messages on every poster and from every screen — and the genuine desire to return the hostages: "I believe this was a sponsored and coordinated campaign whose goal was to attack the government." According to him, "if they truly wanted to return the hostages, they could have taken a quarter of the campaign budget and held a demonstration in front of Qatar. The State of Israel has acted from day one to return the hostages, but as soon as the headquarters campaign appeared, its efforts were blunted. Even the term 'Headquarters of Families' is incorrect, because we know that a significant portion of the families does not agree with the headquarters' actions, and some of them have even been silenced."

In the brigadier general's reserve officer's opinion, such actions lead to a situation where Hamas will not return the hostages at any price. "In negotiations, if the other side knows that you want the 'goods' at any price, it will keep raising the price. Hamas will never return all of them: they are the sole reason the terrorists still exist. Hamas is prepared to release them in portions. Initially it had many hostages and holding them was difficult. Now the situation has changed," noted Erez Wiener.

"How long will we be slaves to the religion of hostages?" reflects the criticism of the Hostage Families Headquarters and that portion of Israeli society and political establishment that places the saving of hostages above all other strategic and national goals. Wiener criticizes the moral imperative of society, which in his view has become dogmatic, irrational, and harmful to the state. By agreeing to Hamas's maximum demands, Israel itself becomes a hostage not only of the captives themselves but of the terrorist mechanism. An excessive readiness to pay the price causes Israel to capitulate before blackmail, thereby forfeiting sovereignty in making decisions about its own security. Every costly deal concluded under this "religion" reinforces terrorism as an effective instrument, guaranteeing that kidnappings will continue in the future.

Israel must be guided by reason and strategy, not solely by emotions and moral blackmail, in order to ensure the long-term survival of the state — even if this means making the painful decision that not all lives can be saved immediately without threatening the future.

"Hostages — at Any Price"

Rock musician **Andrei Makarevich** expressed sharp opinions about demonstrators who regularly gather near the Kirya complex in the center of Tel Aviv. The occasion was his visit to a concert by friends — Alexei Kortnev and Maxim Leonidov. In social media, Makarevich shared his impressions of the performance, emphasizing that, like the other spectators, he had received a charge of positivity. However, according to him, this event was "somewhat marred by yet another demonstration in the very center of Tel Aviv." The musician was outraged by the protesters' actions, calling them "a hundred blissful people with burning eyes" because of whom, in his words, "they again stopped the life of the whole city" and "tens of thousands of citizens could not get where they needed to be on time." He also criticized the slogan "Hostages — at any price!" under which the protests take place. After this Makarevich posed a rhetorical question to the demonstrators:

"I want to ask these fighters with their little placards: what is your 'any price'? Our soldiers who die every day defending us (and you!), trying to free the hostages with weapons in their hands rather than waving ribbons — what price is that? And the animals released by the hundreds from prisons who will tomorrow start blowing things up and killing us (and you!) — what price is that? Are we not trampling on the memory of our soldiers by setting them free? And your children — what price is that? Any price? Do you want to give them in exchange?" He concluded his message briefly and sharply: "Enough already."

"The broad campaign and intensive public discussion in Israel is communicating to the enemy how sensitive this issue is, and as a result the price for the hostages' release is rising" — so argues **Professor Israel Aumann, Nobel Prize laureate in economics.** According to him, this is killing the hostages. We are convincing the enemy that their release is important to us, and so he does not want to compromise. This campaign is also a direct incentive for Hamas to continue taking people hostage in the future. We have proved that this is very painful for us, so they understand clearly that it will pay off again.

Useful Idiots

"Useful idiot" means an easily manipulated, naive person who is cynically used in someone else's interests, often to their own detriment — for example, in a war on the side of the enemy.

In recent days in the country a campaign of "useful idiots" has taken place, having signed a petition with a similar demand for "the immediate return of hostages and cessation of war": the first were Air Force reservists, followed by naval officers, doctors, intelligence officers, scientists, and university professors. They call the war "politically motivated," and the refusal to return the hostages at the price of capitulation "a violation of the state's obligations to ensure the security of its citizens."

Air Force reservists: out of 38,000 Air Force personnel and 55,000 reservists, approximately 950 people signed the

petition. But the majority of them have long since ceased serving in the reserves. More than 900 Israeli artists and people in creative professions signed a petition and declared that the war has lost its meaning, serves political interests, and brings suffering on both sides of the border. The signatories called, with a cry from the depths of their hearts, for the sake of Israeli society and in the name of the human spirit, to break the circle of horror, immediately return the hostages, and stop the war. Israel has already freed thousands of killers who will take hostages again, and we will free killers again, and they will kill us again. Any price means the lives of our citizens and future hostages. They need to be made to understand, once and for all, that we will conduct no negotiations with terrorists. Then there will be no reason for them to take hostages.

Not wishing to lag behind, more than 7,000 conscript and reserve soldiers signed a petition in which they stated that they impose no conditions on their military service. Unlike various pilots engaged in blackmail, the overwhelming majority of Israel's defenders have no intention of imposing any conditions on the country or government. "We are Zionists who love Israel and serve in the military service (regular or reserve) in the Israel Defense Forces and do not make our military service conditional on anything," the petition of 7,000 soldiers reads.

Israel has approximately 45,000 doctors; the petition was signed by about 200 — less than half a percent of all Israeli doctors. Representatives of academic circles gathered about 1,900 signatures. Given that universities and colleges are branches of left-wing parties, that is not very many. Of all the signatories of yet another letter from Unit 8200 alumni, only five actually serve in reserve duty in that unit. The rest either do not serve at all, or are in other units, or signed the letter anonymously — making it impossible to determine who they are or whether they even exist. A similar proportion is observed in other such letters.

The "Bitahonistim" movement (former security service employees), numbering approximately 40,000 participants — including retired generals, former senior Shabak and Mossad officials — issued a statement against the letters and calls for a cessation of hostilities. In their words, "these calls only harden Hamas's position. While Hamas controls the Gaza Strip, there will be neither liberation of hostages nor security for Israel." The movement's statement reads: "Calls and letters demanding that combat operations be stopped, even if they originate from pain and the desire to free the hostages, only harden Hamas's position in the current negotiations and distance the liberation of the hostages. There will be no return of hostages and no security for Israeli citizens as long as Hamas remains in power in Gaza." They also added: "Those who call for stopping the war before achieving its goals are in effect wishing to return to the reality that existed before October 7."

Former senior security officials emphasized: "We support the continuation of the war as a necessary means for returning the hostages, eliminating Hamas, and achieving the three goals of the war defined by the political and military leadership — all of them are critically important for ensuring our security and existence." They also noted: "We oppose a unilateral ceasefire or agreements that would leave Hamas in power." And they concluded with a call to the government: "To continue to act decisively until Hamas is completely destroyed and conditions are created under which there will no longer be a terrorist army in the Gaza Strip."

"I, Warrant Officer Suren Karapetov— IDF reservist, light infantry. I am 53 years old. I completed mandatory reserve duty 13

years ago. Since 2012 I have been called up for service voluntarily. From October 7, 2023, I have been in the army continuously, for more than 18 months. I have no intention of signing calls to refuse service for any reason, and I am prepared to continue fulfilling my duty to the people and the Land of Israel for as long as necessary. I have a family and a small business that has stopped operating because of the war. However, I consider it necessary, for the security of the people and the country, to do everything necessary for the defeat of the enemy. Together — we will win!"

Professor of Law Yuval Elbashan, dean of the law faculty of the Ono Academic Center, published an article on the Ynet portal in which he called a series of "reservist letters" calling for the freeing of hostages at the price of stopping the war in Gaza "Potemkin villages." Having explained to readers the meaning of the term he used, Elbashan reported that, being himself a reservist in military intelligence Unit 8200, he examined the list of signatories of the letter issued in the name of that unit. According to him, many of the signatories have long had no connection to the unit, and the bases at which they served closed back in the 1980s, while some have even been living abroad for many years. Elbashan argues that the same applies to other letters as well, the majority of whose signatories have long since ceased serving in the reserves, and that "they understand this perfectly themselves, which is why they hide behind Potemkin village headlines about former and current reservists."

Hamas is monitoring the scandal over the refusal letters, seeing in this an excellent opportunity to harden its positions. The Palestinians welcome the notorious "pilot letters," letters from intelligence officials, and from other groups protesting against the continuation of the war and declaring it to be of a "political character." Itamar Marcus, chairman of the Palestinian Media Watch organization: "There is great interest in this matter in Palestinian society," he said, pointing to hundreds of Telegram channels engaged with this subject. "Some were simply passing on the information, but some saw it as grounds for encouragement and optimism about the collapse of Israel," Marcus added. He then cited a quotation from one such Telegram channel: "The 'pilots' war' is the fuse that will ignite the gunpowder planted within the fracture" — after which he pointed to two hashtags as further evidence of the Palestinian interpretation, which regards the protest letters as a factor capable of tearing Israeli society apart from within.

Yonatan Was Killed Because of Oslo

Aggai Luber — actor, playwright, theatrical director, head of a theater and acting school. Father of Yehonatan, who was killed in Gaza, leaving behind a pregnant wife and a small son.

"To all those who blithely signed letters against the continuation of the war! Do not wave your military past and your professions before us. You are no more worthy than anyone else in Israel. Your past is irrelevant, and your profession is irrelevant. You are contemptible. And you have become insufferable. 'Who are you to call my son a war criminal? Your morality erases the boundary between good and evil, between those who thirst for killing and those who are forced to fight killers.'"

"We have seen enough former 'emeriti' who, in the name of their military record, pushed us into the blood-soaked, glaring **catastrophe of Oslo;** we have seen the 'intelligentsia' and the 'wise experts' who forced us to leave **Gush Katif,** promising that not a single rocket would be fired from there and that calm would reign on our southern border. Everything turned out the exact opposite.

My dear son Yonatan was killed because of the adventure with the Oslo Agreement and the Disengagement — plans that most of you supported. The spirit of those catastrophes pervades every line of your letters. Despite this, I do not accuse you of not valuing my son's life and the lives of many others. I do not accuse you of 'personal and political interests' that caused you to promote the vision of the vaunted 'New Middle East' that came crashing down on us."

"Do not dare accuse me. You have no right to blacken my reputation and that of millions of others who think differently. You have no right to say that we want the war to continue because of a 'desire for revenge' — that is an odious lie. You have no right to say that we are prepared to abandon the hostages because of 'political and personal interests.' That too is an odious lie. And do not dare lecture me about the 'sanctity of life.' Stop saying that all truth and morality is in your hands. That insults me. Get used to listening to dissenters with respect, even on critical matters, and learn to heed other opinions. Leave your echo chamber." (https://dandorfman.livejournal.com/4283020.html)

What can one say? Again, a fracture, again schizophrenization. No, no, I am not against different opinions *— freedom of speech above all! What is not visible in any of these petitions, written as if from a single template, is responsibility toward the state that was awaited and desired for more than 2,000 years after a similar fracture. No one has thought about what will happen after Hamas's victory. This is somehow diasporic thinking — even from those who were born here. I have also heard sober,* *rational voices, which gives reason for hope. Capitulation will not pass!*

I Choose War

Dr. Ze'ev Itzhak, Major (res.), co-founder of the Forum for Civic Solidarity: *"Yesterday evening I was returning to Tel Aviv from the north of the country, having left behind towns and villages devastated by war and looking like ghosts, which not long ago had been flourishing. We were driving along the sixth highway. To our left, just a couple of dozen kilometers away, was the sea — into which we are planned to be thrown. To our right, very close, just a few kilometers away, one could see Arab villages of the Palestinian Authority, which all of 'liberal and progressive humanity' led by America and Europe sees as the future Palestinian State, where, in the event of free and democratic elections, all polls indicate Hamas would rule.* A detour became necessary due to a mass anti-government demonstration under the slogan 'A Deal at Any (!) Price.' The news reported the deaths in Gaza of two more soldiers. The journey took just under 3 hours. That is the scale of our distances. At the entrance to Tel Aviv, I was greeted by an enormous billboard: **DEAL or VERDICT.** 'For whom?' I asked. 'Naturally, for the HOSTAGES,' replied my companion. 'I think it's for the STATE OF ISRAEL,' ***I answered grimly, and quoted Churchill's well-known expression: 'AN EMPIRE THAT CHOOSES SHAME OVER WAR WILL GET BOTH SHAME AND WAR.'"***

"'Saving the hostages' lives is the highest priority,' my interlocutor objected. Moreover, if we don't agree to a deal, the whole world will be against us: an arms embargo, economic sanctions, arrest warrants for state and army leaders... and we will perish. We cannot fight. The world is against us. And look what is happening in the country: raging crowds of protesters, a weak, conflict-torn government, rabbis calling for refusal to serve in the army and claiming that their prayers are stronger than air defense. Madness! We must agree to this terrible 'deal,' and afterward...' 'Afterward there will be nothing,' I answered grimly. 'Perhaps a temporary calm will be achieved and we will embrace the few surviving hostages. Shame and defeat will be sold to the people as an act of statecraft, but afterward political and social decay will begin in the country, mass emigration — especially of the young generation, which has understood that it has no future, that it and its fallen friends have been betrayed by their own people. Because THE BLOOD OF THE HOSTAGES IS NO REDDER THAN THE BLOOD OF OUR FALLEN HEROES. No — this is not cynicism. This is cruel reality.'"

"I cannot know what future Israeli courts will decide about the 'Kastners' of our day, if Israel even exists at that point — but I know firmly that if our country's leaders show weakness, the tragedy of October 7 will repeat itself, and the Jewish state will disappear amid the triumph of Islamic fascism and aggressive liberalism. And those of us who remain alive will continue arguing in the diaspora about who was to blame and what should have been done. BUT WHILE WE STILL HAVE STRENGTH AND THE PEOPLE'S SPIRIT IS NOT YET BROKEN, FULLY AWARE OF ALL THE RISKS, I CHOOSE WAR. But who am I...?"

"Don't Let Yourself Be Fooled!"

Tank commander **Kfir Zar** attempted to bring striking Israelis to their senses in August 2025, addressing them with an emotional video message in which he emphasized that while they were striking and protesting, he had been fighting for them, and their strikes were happening "at his expense," disrupting the functioning of the country. He called on them to come to their senses and not harm the rear while soldiers risked their lives at the front.

Zar addressed them with this message: *"About a year and a half ago I was very severely wounded in combat in the Gaza Strip. For four months I lay unconscious, cut off from the world. My body was fighting for survival. Since then I have been going through a long, complex, and difficult rehabilitation process that daily pushes me to the limit of my physical and mental strength."* (https://www.7kanal.co.il/news/278709)

"Citizens of Israel and families of all hostages — don't let yourselves be fooled! Millions of dollars every second are being used to distract your gaze from the real enemy, who is on the other side of the fence. I remember well the previous strike that left-wing organizations organized supposedly for the sake of the hostages. In those days I was hospitalized and dependent on constant medical care. Because of the strike, many wounded people, including me, did not receive the necessary treatment. Look into the eyes of the fighters — those who gave their bodies and souls for you, for the hostages, and for our country. Come and spit in these fighters' faces — because that is what you are doing when you choose to strike at the expense of those who were on the line of fire at the front."

"Your protest will not return the hostages. It does not intensify combat operations; it does not contribute to security. It radiates weakness, confusion, and above all reveals disunity. If you truly believe your way is the right one, then stand before the fighters and say to them aloud: your blood, your wounds and scars that will never heal, mean nothing to us. Tell them that their efforts were in vain. Tell them that the country they fought for does not support them. When you block roads and paralyze the country, the last thing you are doing is returning the hostages. You are only deepening the fracture, distancing unity, and weakening the front. To the grieving families I wish to say — we are with you. We embrace you, we salute you, we remember. You are not alone. As the prophet Jeremiah said: 'Thus saith the Lord: Refrain thy voice from weeping, and thine eyes from tears: for thy work shall be rewarded, and they shall come again from the land of the enemy. And there is hope in thine end, that thy children shall come again to their own border.'"

Schizophrenism for the Hostages

Schizophrenism in the context of protests is the inability to reconcile the national ideal with military reality. This phenomenon consists in the fact that the state and society simultaneously adhere to two mutually exclusive ideas, creating a state of deep internal conflict — or, in scientific terms, cognitive dissonance.

1. **The logic of hostage families:** The existential motive — the life of a loved one. All the state's strategic goals fade into the background. Distrust of the state: two years of war have brought no liberation, so the families are convinced that without pressure on the authorities their loved ones will be forgotten. Historical memory: precedents of deals (for example, Shalit) reinforced the belief that protests can compel the state to make concessions.

2. **How these plays into Hamas's hands:** Delegitimization of the war — protests create a picture as if the government is sacrificing citizens for abstract goals. Destruction of unity — internal fracture is Hamas's strategic asset. Elevation of the hostages' value — the louder the families' pressure, the more expensive the hostages become in Hamas's eyes.

3. **Why the families continue:** Cognitive dissonance — the enemy is Hamas, but the greater evil is the government. Media schizophrenization — the media amplifies their voice, making the

protests a factor in domestic politics. Social dynamics: severe social schizophrenia in the country. The Headquarters and the hostage family protests became an independent political force on the left-wing spectrum under the Kaplanists' leadership.

4. **Split consciousness:** The hostage family protests make this dissonance public, painful, and unbearable. The war cabinet and Prime Minister Netanyahu are forced to speak in two languages: directed inward (to the families): "We will do everything to bring them home" (fulfilling the "moral imperative"); directed outward (toward Hamas and Iran): "We will fight until complete victory, Hamas will be destroyed" (fulfilling the "strategic imperative"). Schizophrenia of action: any step toward one imperative immediately sabotages the other. If Netanyahu speaks of a deal, he is accused of betraying victory (by Gevura critics). If he speaks of victory, he is accused of betraying the hostages (by Headquarters critics). The citizen who supports both the army and the hostage families falls into a moral trap. He must either agree to the return of the future security threat in order to save the hostages (violating national security), or agree to the potential death of hostages (violating Pikuach Nefesh) in order to ensure long-term security.

Blackmail Through Compassion

The legal establishment and the senior military command used the hostage issue as a lever of pressure on the cabinet. Ronen Bar and Herzi Halevi repeatedly stated at sessions that "the army has done everything it could" and now "the ball is in the politicians' court." This was a way of removing responsibility from themselves for the inability to destroy Hamas quickly and transferring it to Netanyahu.

Baharav-Miara and her apparatus carefully monitored that the conditions of Hamas terrorists' detention in Israeli prisons "met standards," while Israelis rotted in tunnels. This asymmetry drove society to distraction.

Sinwar, through intermediaries (Qatar and Egypt), impressed upon the Israeli negotiating team: "I want a deal, but Netanyahu is blocking it." Part of the Israeli media and opinion leaders repeated this Hamas thesis as truth. As a result, tires were being burned and roads blocked in Tel Aviv not against Sinwar but against Israel's own government. Hamas saw that Israeli society was doing its work itself, destroying discipline and unity. This allowed the terrorists to harden the conditions of each deal, understanding that internal pressure on the Israeli government would only intensify.

The tragedy of the hostages became the ideal instrument for deepening "social schizophrenia." The families' pain was cynically privatized by political forces striving to bring down the government. In the end, the nation found itself in a paradoxical situation: the struggle to save the lives of the kidnapped citizens became the main obstacle to the destruction of those who had kidnapped them.

The hostage family protests are a powerful psychological weapon that sharpens the schizophrenization of Israeli society. They do not merely request an exchange — they force the state to choose between its moral soul and its strategic survival, thereby placing the entire nation in a state of chronic, unresolvable conflict.

Stop Using the Hostages

Eli Shtivi, father of Idan who was kidnapped from the Nova festival, calls on people to stop using the hostage issue for political ends. In doing so he emphasizes that he is addressing not the families of hostages but other people who are turning the families' pain into an instrument of political struggle. According to him, the protest methods not only cause harm to citizens and disturb the normal course of life, but send the enemy a signal of our general weakness, of hatred and fracture within us. "Those who genuinely want the return of the hostages home should stand for unity, for the State of the People of Israel."

The forces in the intelligence operation found Idan's body. He was killed on October 7, 2023. Idan is coming home. May his blood be avenged.

(https://www.instagram.com/reel/DOA2hlZCmeI/)

Protests Multiply Chaos

The "Kaplan Intifada," sheltering behind the hostage families, is committing genuine terror on the roads. Blockades, arson, chaos — all this has already become a familiar picture. But not all families support the terrorizing of Israelis. For example, the mother of hostage Ran Gvili — Talik Gvili — is categorically against these measures. "We are dealing with monsters who want to undermine our unity." She spoke of this in an interview with Ynet, emphasizing that the pain of loss and waiting must not be turned into a club for political pressure. She stated that such actions do not help but only raise the price of the hostages and serve the terrorists' interests. Gvili emphasized that life in Israel must not be paralyzed for the sake of freeing the hostages. "I am certain that 100% of citizens want the war to end and the abducted to return. We are dealing with monsters who seek to sow fracture."

"'Rage Day,' or whatever it is called, serves Hamas's interests and only distances us from a deal," she noted. "Every action that disturbs the normal rhythm of life is perceived by the terrorists as a victory." Talik Gvili's position differs sharply from part of the families of the abducted, who continue to demand active pressure actions against the government. She believes that such steps in the current circumstances are ineffective and even harmful. The chief priority, in her words, is concentrating on victory over Hamas and the liberation of all the hostages without exception. Protests only multiply chaos and obstruct the achievement of the goal. In her words one hears both a mother's despair and a political message: the unity of society is the chief resource in the struggle against terrorists.

"THE ORCHESTRA OF ANGER"

(Hypothetical dialogue)

Setting: *A tent of the protest headquarters on Kaplan Street. Night. On the table: scattered leaflets, black flags, and megaphones.*

Characters: Political technologist (one of the overseers of the protest against the reform, now switched to the hostage issue). Hellen Raz (mother of a hostage, the face of the protest).

Political technologist: *(softly but insistently) Hellen, have you seen the polls? Your speech yesterday exploded the internet. When you curse Bibi personally — it works better than any of our slogans. People sympathize with a mother.*

Hellen: *(wearily) I don't want to "explode the internet." I want Matan. I got a call from intelligence, they said that the pressure on Sinwar must be military, otherwise he will never give them back...*

Political technologist: *(interrupting) Intelligence is part of Bibi's system. They are lying. The only way to get your son back is to force the government to capitulate. You must go out and say: "Victory is not important, the blood of my son is on Netanyahu's hands."*

Hellen: *But if we stop the war now, Hamas will win. My son will return to a country that will not exist tomorrow?*

Political technologist: *(leaning closer) Hellen, dear. The country is an abstraction. Your son is flesh and blood. We will give you prime time, we will bring hundreds of thousands into the streets. We will make it so that Bibi cannot leave his house until he signs the deal. Don't think about strategy — that is what we are here for. Your role is to be the embodiment of anger. You must become the force that brings down this cabinet of ministers.*

Hellen: *(looking at the poster with her son's photo) Sometimes it seems to me that you use his photo as a shield to punch through the door to the prime minister's office...*

Political technologist: *(coldly) We use everything we have to bring down this regime. And your son is our strongest argument. Go — it is time to charge the megaphones. The crowd is waiting for a "mother-heroine," not a military analyst.*

Diagnosis: Political Exploitation of Grief

Description: The process of transforming individual trauma into mass psychosis. Social schizophrenia reaches its peak when the natural slogan "Bring them home" is replaced by the political slogan "Topple the power at any price."

Mechanism: Hellen Raz and other families become hostages a second time — now within the Israeli media machine. They are made to transmit theses that are advantageous to Hamas (ceasefire, withdrawal from Gaza), being convinced that this is the only path to salvation. This creates a cognitive trap: society begins to believe that the enemy is in Jerusalem, not in the tunnels of Gaza.

The New York Times published a lengthy article about Hellen Raz under the headline: *"How an Exhausted Mother Became Netanyahu's Fiercest Enemy."* Netanyahu and his government must be overthrown, since they place personal and political interests above the lives of the hostages. Style of statements: emotional, direct, often using accusatory and extremely harsh rhetoric directed personally against Benjamin Netanyahu and his wife Sara. Her statements focus on accusing the prime minister of personal disregard for the lives of the hostages: *"Netanyahu is a murderer! He killed the hostages. I will not let him kill my Matan!" "The only thing Benjamin Netanyahu cares about is his seat. His seat matters more than my son's life." "Our government, this failed cabinet, must resign immediately. They are incapable of returning our children. No deal, no victory!" "Bibi! You will burn in hell if you don't return my son!" (The use of such phrases as "burn in hell" or "blood on your hands" became typical for the most radical members of the Forum).*

On October 13, 2025, Matan Raz returned home alive. If anyone thinks she apologized — forget it!

Ceasefire — October 9, 2025

US President Donald Trump announced on the night of Thursday, October 9, 2025, that Israel and Hamas had signed a first-phase ceasefire agreement in the Gaza Strip and for the release of all hostages. On Truth Social, Trump wrote: "I am very proud to announce: Israel and Hamas have signed an agreement for the implementation of the first phase of our peace plan. This means that all hostages will be released very soon, and Israel will withdraw its forces to an agreed line — as a first step on the path to a durable, stable, and eternal peace. All sides will receive fair treatment! This is a great day for the Arab and Muslim world, for Israel, for all neighboring countries, and for the United States of America. We thank the mediators from Qatar, Egypt, and Turkey who worked with us to make this historic and unprecedented event possible. Blessed are the peacemakers!"

The Associated Press reported that the release of 20 living hostages was expected by Sunday, October 12. Prime Minister Benjamin Netanyahu confirmed the agreement with Hamas and announced that on October 9 he would convene the government to ratify the agreement.

"THE FINAL CREDITS"

(Hypothetical dialogue)

Setting: *Studio of the central television channel, one minute before the end of broadcast. October 9, 2025. On the screens: footage of the signing of yet another "ceasefire agreement."*

Characters: Host — prime-time hero who has been stoking the fires of protest for two years. Old Analyst — a former

intelligence officer invited "for balance" but not given a chance to get a word in edgewise.

Host: *(to the camera, solemnly) So — this is a victory of the spirit! Under pressure from the families, under pressure from Kaplan, the government has finally surrendered. We pay "any price." The hostages are returning. This is the end of the war. We have won.*

Old Analyst: *(quietly, not to the camera) You have just read out the obituary for Israel and you call it victory.*

Host: *(switching off microphone while footage rolls, in a whisper) Listen, old man, don't ruin the moment. The country wants to cry for joy. Have you seen the ratings? We have united the nation around this pain.*

Old Analyst: *You have not united the nation — you have castrated it. You have taught the enemy that they can slash, rape, and steal from us, and then make us pay for it and beg their pardon. You have turned the army into a ransom delivery service. Sinwar is sitting in his bunker laughing because your television has done more for him than all his rockets.*

Host: *(adjusting his tie) People wanted the hostages. We gave them hope. That is humane.*

Old Analyst: *(standing up) Humane? You used Hellen and the others to bring down Bibi, and in the end you brought down the very idea of security. Tomorrow, when they come again — and they will come, because they saw our weakness — whom will you blame? The government again? Or yourselves, for having traded the country's survival for beautiful footage in the evening news?*

Host: *(director's voice in earpiece: "5 seconds to the end") Smile, old man. Now we will show the family reunions. This is the best finale one could imagine.*

Old Analyst: *(leaving the studio) This is not the finale. This is only the beginning of the end. You have just watched the first episode, and the most terrible part is still ahead.*

(The host puts on his mask of empathy again. The camera takes a close-up of his face. Caption on screen: "WE HAVE WON. THEY ARE COMING BACK." In the background, on a small monitor, footage is visible from Gaza where Hamas fighters emerge from tunnels with victory signs — but the cameraman quickly switches the picture to embraces at the airport.)

"CATAMNESIS"

(Catamnesis is medical information about a patient collected after discharge from the hospital, completion of treatment or initial examination.)

Condition: Deep decompensation.

Cause: Social schizophrenia. The organism chose "immediate pain relief" (return of some) at the price of "lethal infection" (loss of deterrence and strategic collapse).

Prognosis: Unfavorable unless radical therapy is undertaken — complete cleansing of power and media structures from carriers of the "any price" virus.

Final words: October 7 was an intelligence catastrophe. October 9 (the date of the "deal") became a catastrophe of spirit. We became a society that pays any price for blackmail.

The Hostages' Return Home

A total of approximately 251 people were captured (including foreigners). Key deals:

- **Deal — November 2023 (November 24–30, 2023):**

  Freed: 105–110 hostages (mainly women, children, elderly + 23 Thais and 1 Filipino outside the quota). Freed by Israel: approximately 240 Palestinian prisoners (mainly women and minors). This was the only successful deal throughout all of 2024.

- **Deal — January–March 2025: Announced January 15, 2025,** launched approximately January 19–20. First phase: Hamas committed to freeing 33–34 hostages (humanitarian category: children, women, elderly, sick men). Actually freed alive: approximately 30–33 Israelis + several Thais (in stages: January 25 — 4 women soldiers; February — Ofer Kalderon, Keith Siegel, Yarden Bibas and others). Bodies: approximately 8 bodies of deceased hostages. Freed by Israel: more than 1,000–2,000 Palestinian prisoners (including serious terrorists). The deal collapsed in March 2025: Hamas accused Israel of a violation (non-withdrawal from the Philadelphi Corridor), Israel accused Hamas of delays. The truce was broken, the war resumed.

- **Deal — October 2025 ("Trump plan"):** Announced beginning of October 2025, ceasefire from October 10–13. Freed alive: All remaining approximately 20 living hostages (October 13 — the main wave, including the last ones). Bodies: Approximately 23–28 bodies of the deceased are being gradually returned (process continuing in November). Freed by Israel: approximately 2,000 Palestinian prisoners (including serious offenders).

Current status (January 26, 2026):

Living hostages in Gaza: 0 (all returned in October).

Remaining bodies: 0 (January 26, 2026).

Conclusion

In a normal state, discussion of national policy is built on rational, strategic, and substantive grounds. But in Israel in recent years — especially since the beginning of the "Iron Swords" war — any attempt to raise a complex dilemma is immediately rejected as "immoral," "cruel," or even "demonic," without delving into the substance. When the left encounters an argument they cannot refute, instead of asking: "Is the freeing of hostages at the price of renouncing victory justified?" they shout: "How dare you even pose such a question?!"... This is an emotional, irrational, and in significant measure anti-democratic reflex.

The conflict that unfolded in Israeli society after the taking of hostages is a battle for the national ethos. The demand for capitulation at any price, advanced by part of the families and their headquarters staff, calls into question the very principle of the existence of the State of Israel, which, as Wiener reminded us, was founded on refusing to submit to blackmail in the most critical situations (for example, Operation Entebbe). If Israel surrenders to return the hostages, it will not only render the soldiers' sacrifices meaningless but will guarantee the repetition of similar attacks in the future, providing terrorists with an infinite lever of pressure.

On the other hand, it is impossible to ignore the families' pain and the universal moral imperative of saving life. The hostage tragedy became a tactical weapon in Hamas's hands, aimed at destroying Israeli society from within. The government did not engage in full capitulation and in practice returned virtually all living hostages and almost all the killed ones (except three) — which means an ideological victory in a war whose scale will surpass any military achievement. Thus, the outcome of this internal conflict determined not only the fate of the hostages but also Israel's future political doctrine: will it remain a state that fights for its security, or will it be transformed into a society always forced to pay any price for blackmail.

Despite the unprecedented pressure from the "Headquarters" and the media monopoly, Israel in 2024–2025 proved that it can return its people not through capitulation but through the crushing of the enemy. This became an ideological turning point. We began to emerge from the condition of "a society that always pays any price," returning to the status of a nation that dictates its own terms. We received a lesson in how important it is not to allow our feelings to become weapons in the hands of killers.

CHAPTER 28.
THE IRANIAN ATOM AND MISSILES

"...It is not so important what the Gentiles will say, what matters is what the Jews will do."

Ben-Gurion

Introduction

Iranian expansion is not only rockets and proxy groups at the borders — it is also a precision game on the internal fault lines of Israeli society. In the context of the analysis of "social schizophrenia," the connection between Tehran's strategy and the intra-Israeli crisis of 2023 looks like a perfect symbiosis of external aggressor and internal self-destruction. Tehran studied Israeli society for years as a laboratory subject. Iran's strategy of the "ring of fire" would have been incomplete without a "ring of internal chaos." In 2023, the ayatollahs watched with delight as Israeli elites dismantled their own security system. For Iran, our internal fracture was as much a strategic asset as the centrifuges at Natanz. They understood: to strike Israel, it is not necessary to penetrate a "Hetz" (Arrow) missile — it is enough to wait for Israel to paralyze its own will.

Iran is often called the "Head of the Snake" — a description of Iran's fundamental role in conflicts in the Middle East. It is Iran that is the primary source of financing, weaponry, and ideological guidance for the entire network of groups hostile to Israel. Iran provides Hezbollah (Lebanon), Hamas (Gaza), Shia militias (Iraq/Syria), and Houthis (Yemen) with everything necessary for the conduct of war. Annual money flows (for example, Hezbollah receives up to $700 million per year), supply of rockets, drones, technologies for the production of precision weapons, and training. Iran is the command post that coordinates the actions of its satellites. Its goal: to surround Israel with a "ring of fire" and destroy it. Therefore, it is necessary to strike Iran directly (its nuclear program, drone production, IRGC leadership) in order to deprive the "snake" of the ability to poison the region.

The reason Iran became a "malevolent enemy" of Israel is rooted not in historical or territorial disputes but in a fundamental ideological and geopolitical shift that took place in Iran in 1979. Before 1979, under the reign of Shah Mohammed Reza Pahlavi, Iran and Israel were allies. They were bound together by common opposition to Arab states in the region, and actively cooperated in the spheres of economics, security, intelligence, and even nuclear technology. Everything changed with Ayatollah Ruhollah Khomeini's rise to power as a result of the Islamic Revolution. The new leadership proclaimed a radical Islamist ideology founded on the necessity of fighting the "Great Satan" (the United States) and the "Small Satan" (Israel). The Islamic Republic of Iran refused to recognize Israel's right to exist, calling it a "Zionist regime" and a "cancerous tumor" in the Islamic world.

According to the concept of "Decapitating the Snake," in the night of June 13, 2025, Israel struck military and nuclear facilities in Iran. Before 2025, Israeli strategy resembled fighting weeds: we trimmed the leaves (Hamas, Hezbollah), but the root remained untouched in Tehran. The night of June 13, 2025 entered history not simply as a brilliant military operation but as an act of national liberation from fear. For decades, the deep state and the international community had impressed on us that a strike on Iran would lead to an apocalypse. This was a form of collective hypnosis. The strike on Iran was a strategic antibiotic. We ceased to be hostages of the Iranian threat and became its liquidators. When Israeli planes were erasing nuclear facilities and missile factories from the face of the earth, the world did not collapse — it changed. We proved that Jabotinsky's "Iron Wall" can be not only defensive but preemptive. ***This is the ultimate medicine for schizophrenia: the transition from the illusions of appeasement to the reality of crushing victory.***

The Strategy of "Waiting for Collapse"

Everything changed with Ayatollah Ruhollah Khomeini's rise to power as a result of the Islamic Revolution. The new leadership proclaimed a radical Islamist ideology whose foundation was the necessity of combating **the "Great Satan" (USA) and the "Small Satan" (Israel).** The Islamic Republic of Iran refused to recognize Israel's right to exist, calling it a "Zionist regime" and a "cancerous tumor" in the Islamic world. Anti-Israeli rhetoric became an instrument of Iranian foreign policy aimed at achieving regional supremacy. Having proclaimed itself the defender of the Palestinian cause and a fighter against Israel, **Iran created a broad network of proxy forces (the "Axis of Resistance") for projecting its influence over the Middle East, surrounding Israel with hostile forces.**

From Israel's side, the conflict is conditioned by the perception of Iran as an existential threat. Iran's development of a nuclear program is viewed by Israel as a direct threat to its existence, since Iranian leaders openly call for its destruction. Iran develops long-range ballistic missiles capable of carrying nuclear warheads and reaching Israeli territory — a key factor in Israeli concern.

Iranian operations also affect the diaspora: attacks on Jewish targets abroad (for example, in Argentina in the 1990s) intensify global anxiety among Jews. Iran conducts influence operations aimed at stoking internal disagreements in Israel. *In general, Iran's influence intensifies internal fractures and stress, making the Iranian issue central in the national discourse.*

"ARCHITECTS OF FEAR"

(How Israeli elites "fed" Iran for years with their unwillingness to act)

Setting: *An elite restaurant in Tel Aviv. 2022.*

Participants: ***High-ranking retired general and liberal journalist.***

Journalist: *(writing) So you believe that a nuclear Iran is something we will have to live with?*

General: *(cutting a steak) Let's be realistic. A strike on Iran means the end of Tel Aviv. Hezbollah will hurl 150,000 rockets at us in the first hour. Bibi is simply using this "threat" to hold on to power. In reality, Iran is a rational player. They want the regime's survival, not war. We need to negotiate, not shake our fists.*

Journalist: *But they openly say they will wipe us off the map...*

General: *(smiling condescendingly) That is rhetoric for domestic consumption. We in the General Staff call this "risk management." The real danger is not Iran but the "messianic right" inside Israel, which could drag us into an unnecessary adventure. We will do everything to ensure the army does not allow this to happen.*

(Transition to 2025. The same general in a news studio after the strike on Natanz. He looks confused. His "rational forecast" has

crumbled, and Iran failed to deliver the "apocalypse" with which the general had been frightening the country for ten years.)

Iran shifted from plans for direct military destruction of Israel to the doctrine of "Collapse from Within." Iran's Supreme Leader Ali Khamenei repeatedly declared in 2023 that Israel would "collapse under its own weight" due to internal dysfunction. For Iran, the Kaplan protests, the calls to refuse military service, and the legal war against the government were signs that the "Zionist entity" had reached the stage of biological decay. While Israeli elites (the army and the judiciary) were busy "saving democracy" from their own government, Iran saw in this the long-awaited window of opportunity for the October 7 attack. Here is how Iran's "ring of fire" strategy became intertwined with Israel's systemic crisis.

Use of protests as "informational noise": Iranian cyber units actively participated in the Israeli digital space in 2023–2025. Through bots and fake accounts, Iran fanned the flames of hatred on both sides — both supporters of the reform and the protesters. The goal was to turn a political dispute into a civil war. Israel's intelligence (AMAN), overloaded with the analysis of "internal threats" and "social resilience," began to perceive the internal conflict as the chief danger, thereby missing the physical preparations of Hamas and the IRGC for the "Al-Aqsa Storm."

"Ring of fire" and legal paralysis: Iranian expansion in Lebanon, Syria, and Gaza was built on the use of civilian infrastructure (schools, hospitals, residential buildings). Here the "diseases of political leftism" and legal activism served Iran's purposes. The Israeli army, shackled by the strict framework of "humanitarian law" imposed by Baharav-Miara's legal system, often refused preemptive strikes on Iran's proxies, fearing international condemnation and domestic courts.

Direct confrontation against the backdrop of fracture: The events of June 2025 (Israel's direct war with Iran) showed that Tehran decided to attack, believing that Israel had finally been paralyzed by internal protests over the hostages and the judicial system. While the Israeli government was fighting for the country's physical survival, part of the media elite continued to blame "escalation" on the "messianic government," effectively echoing the theses of Iranian propaganda.

Conclusion from the analysis: Tehran was not simply waiting for a moment of weakness — it methodically fed the Israeli demons of internal discord, understanding that the "judicial seizure" of power and the ideological blinding of the elites would do the job better than thousands of rockets. October 7 and the subsequent war proved: when a nation loses internal unity, its external borders become merely a backdrop for the enemy.

"Decapitating the Snake"

This is a complex and multifaceted process that Israel has been conducting for many years, using a combination of technological superiority, intelligence, and diplomacy. Below are the main methods Israel uses to weaken, slow, and ultimately "decapitate" the Iranian threat. Technological sabotage — this is the main method Israel uses to directly slow Iran's development without starting a full-scale war: cyber warfare through the use of sophisticated cyberattacks (for example, the Stuxnet virus) to physically damage or disrupt Iranian uranium enrichment centrifuges at facilities such as Natanz; sabotage and explosions through covert operations aimed at destroying or damaging key equipment at Iranian sites; and liquidation of scientists — suspicion that the Mossad systematically conducts targeted elimination of leading Iranian nuclear scientists and managers, such as Mohsen

Fakhrizadeh, to deprive the program of key personnel and set it back by years.

Destruction of "tentacles": This is the "war between wars" (MABAM) strategy aimed at preventing Iran from arming its satellites. The main focus is on intercepting deliveries of precision rockets and drones from Iran to Syria and Lebanon. The IDF regularly strikes warehouses, convoys, and airports in Syria and Iraq. The goal is to preserve Israel's qualitative military edge and prevent Israel from being surrounded by an arsenal of precision rockets. Striking key Islamic Revolutionary Guard Corps (IRGC) officers who coordinate, train, and supply proxy forces in Syria and Lebanon — disrupting Iran's chain of command and hampering its overseas operations. These methods show that Israel is conducting a comprehensive war against Iran that encompasses cyberspace, the territories of neighboring countries, and the diplomatic arena, in order to contain its chief enemy.

Iranian Operations in Israel

Iranian operations have evolved into three main phases, adapting to Israeli developments. They began with a focus on social disagreements, shifted to political ones, and now exploit the war with Hamas.

Stoking social disagreements (2021–2022): The campaign targeted the conflict between ultra-Orthodox Jews (Haredim) and the LGBT+ community. Fake accounts imitated rabbis and activists, spreading hateful content. For example, posts were created claiming that "rifts in Israeli society cannot be bridged" and proposing a geographic separation of secular and Orthodox groups. A network of dozens of fake profiles on Facebook, Telegram, and other platforms created fake businesses (for example, a bakery in an ultra-

Orthodox city) and stole the identities of real people, including a deceased Jew from Russia. Impersonation of well-known rabbis was used to spread disinformation.

Political polarization (2022–2023): Focus on the left and right political spectrums, especially during the protests against judicial reform in 2023. Accounts supported both sides in order to worsen the discourse and undermine trust in the government. During mass protests (hundreds of thousands in the streets), the Emerald Divide network used Telegram accounts to spread anti-government messages, including calls for anarchy. The network included email campaigns on crowdfunding platforms and geomapping for targeting. Fake Reporter identified dozens of fake groups on WhatsApp and TikTok spreading lies and hatred to deepen the divide.

Anatomy of Betrayal

Iran's recruitment strategy in 2024 became a mirror of our internal disintegration. This was not spy aesthetics from the Cold War — it was a cheap and cynical "marketplace of betrayal." Iran used social depression and fracture, buying Israelis with cryptocurrency.

Iran's recruitment successes ("Virus Within"): Iranian intelligence in 2023–2024 shifted from seeking "spies" to seeking "social outsiders." They exploited Israel's deepest internal fracture. Recruitment proceeded through social media, where Iranian handlers posed as "fighters for democracy" or, conversely, as "defenders of tradition." Their success lay in exploiting "social depression." People disappointed in the state, paralyzed by hatred for political opponents, became easy prey. Posting flyers, setting cars on fire, and then collecting data about military installations —

Iran was creating a "fifth column" not from convinced traitors but from victims of social schizophrenia who no longer understood where protest ended and state treason began.

The success of Iranian recruitment in 2024 was based on the shocking cheapness and accessibility of betrayal. Shabak uncovered dozens of cases where the "entry ticket" to state treason consisted of ordinary assignments on social media.

The Vladmir Varkhovskiy case (September 2024): An ordinary resident of Petah Tikva agreed for $100 to post flyers, and just a month later agreed for a few thousand dollars to liquidate an Israeli scientist.

The Rami Habib-Ullah case: A resident of Reina (Arab sector) who not only collected data about secret installations for Iranian intelligence but also attempted to recruit others, using religious and political subtext.

The Ramat Gan couple case (October 2024): Vladislav Viktoson and his partner Anna Bernstein. The Iranian handler under the pseudonym "Mari" hired them for graffiti and arson of cars, gradually pushing them toward purchasing weapons for the assassination of a senior Israeli.

These were not professional spies. These were people whose moral compass had been demagnetized by social schizophrenia. Iran paid them in cryptocurrency, turning them into "disposable agents."

"THE PRICE OF YOUR HOUSE — $500"

Setting: *A cheap apartment in the center of the country. Night. Blue light of a monitor.*

Character: "Ordinary citizen" (let us call him A.).

A.: *(typing in Telegram) "Photo of the facility taken. No guards at the gate. Waiting for payment confirmation."*

Handler *("Mari"): "Good work. $500 credited. Next assignment: a package needs to be left at the entrance to a research institute in Rehovot. You don't need to know what's inside. It's just a check of their alertness."*

A.: *(hesitating, looking at the photo of his family on the wall) "Is this dangerous? I don't want trouble with the police."*

Handler: *"What trouble? You're just a courier. The police are busy with the demonstrations on Kaplan — they have no time for you. You are helping 'justice.' Soon you will be able to leave, as we agreed."*

A.: *(closes the laptop. He has convinced himself that this is just "a little extra income." He does not see how at the other end of the line in Tehran, a Quds Force officer checks off his name in a list of targets for elimination once the assignment has been completed. A traitor is needed alive by neither those he has betrayed nor those who bought him.)*

"Through a Psychiatrist's Eyes": Moral Sepsis

Symptoms: Citizens' readiness to cooperate with the enemy for negligible sums.

Mechanism of disease: Social schizophrenia has driven society to a condition where the "state" is perceived as something alien or even hostile. Iranian intelligence services acted as an opportunistic infection: they did not break down the wall — they simply entered the rotted sections of the social fabric.

Verdict: The fact that less was being asked for the elimination of an Israeli general or scientist than a used car costs speaks of the complete loss of the value of life itself within the framework of Israeli "selfhood." Victory over Iran in the sky would have been meaningless if Shabak had not begun "chemotherapy" within the country.

"Laughing at Cassandra"

(On how Netanyahu's prophecies were mocked until they came true)

For a long time the media elite entertained itself by calling Netanyahu's warnings about the Iranian bomb or the threat from Gaza "scaremongering" and "paranoia." **The irony of fate: in psychiatry there is a condition in which a patient laughs at the doctor warning him about gangrene.** Today, when October 7 has become reality, this laughter sounds like an echo in a morgue. Those who called him "Mr. Security" in quotation marks now demand responsibility from him for the catastrophe that they themselves had been preparing for years, tying his hands with legal suits and army protests.

Chronology of the 12-Day War with Iran

The war between Israel and Iran, known as the "Twelve-Day War," took place from June 13 to June 24, 2025. The conflict began with Israel's preemptive strikes on Iran's nuclear and military facilities and escalated into an exchange of rocket strikes, with US involvement in the later stages. We found ourselves in a unique situation: military titans but diplomatic pariahs. The West applauded us in the sky over Isfahan but condemned us at UN podiums. This is the price of sovereignty. Israel finally adopted Ben-Gurion's concept: "It is not so important what the Gentiles say, what matters is what the Jews do." We evacuated the north, we lost tempo in normalization with the Arabs, but we preserved the most important thing — the right to life. In the Middle East, strength is respected, not sympathy. The strike on Iran restored to us that respect which had been almost lost in the dust of Kaplan. *The war ended with a ceasefire declared by US President Donald Trump.*

"THE RED BUTTON IN THE KIRYA"

Scene in "The Pit" (underground command post) in June 2025.

Setting: *General Staff command post. Night. On the screens: satellite images of facilities at Natanz and Parchin.*

Participants: Benjamin Netanyahu (Prime Minister), Air Force Commander, Mossad Chief.

Air Force Commander: *(pointing to the screen) Our F-35s have already entered the "zone of silence." Iranian air defense didn't even realize that the sky was no longer theirs. We are waiting for your confirmation to enter Iranian airspace.*

Mossad Chief: *(quietly) Sir, we have received the latest data from our network in Tehran. There is panic there. They didn't expect us to decide to strike the "head" while the proxies are still shooting in the north. They thought we would play by the old rules.*

Netanyahu: *(looking at his watch) For ten years we waited while the world "negotiated" with them. For ten years we were told that a strike on Iran would be a regional apocalypse. (Pause) It turns out the apocalypse is what happens when we allow them to prepare the noose around our necks.*

Air Force Commander: *Sir, in three minutes they will pass the point of no return.*

Netanyahu: *(calmly) Go ahead. Today the "snake" will learn that it no longer has a body behind which to hide. From this moment on, the proxies in Lebanon and Gaza are just a tail that will thrash in convulsions without a head.*

(On the screens the first indicators of hits flash up. Silence falls in the room. This is not merely a military operation — this is the moment when Israel finally cured itself of the fear of "escalation.")

***General balance**: Iran launched approximately 550 ballistic missiles and 1,000 drones, the majority of which (80–99%) were intercepted; Israel struck more than 150 targets in 27 Iranian provinces. Casualties: 28 killed in Israel, at least 610 civilians in Iran. Below is a chronology of key events based on available sources.*

June 13 (Day 1: Start of War): Israel launches Operation "Rising Lion" ("Am ke-Lavi") — massive airstrikes on Iran's nuclear facilities (including Natanz and Fordow), military bases, and radar systems in Tehran and other regions. Key Iranian nuclear scientists and military commanders are killed. Explosions in Tehran, Babol Sar, and other cities.

June 14 (Day 2): Iran responds with the first wave of rocket strikes on Israel (Operation "True Promise III"). Several dozen ballistic missiles and drones are launched, targeting Tel Aviv and Haifa. Israeli air defense (including "Iron Dome") intercepts the majority (approximately 90%). Residential buildings in Israel are damaged; first civilian casualties. Israel conducts additional strikes on Iranian radar systems and IRGC bases.

June 15 (Day 3): Escalation: Iran intensifies its attacks, launching hundreds of rockets and drones. Israel reports intercepting 99% of threats. Strikes on Iranian oil facilities and military airfields.

First signs of proxy group involvement: Houthis in Yemen and Shia militias in Iraq attack Israeli targets. Israeli hackers steal $90 million from an Iranian cryptocurrency exchange and destroy data at Sepah Bank.

June 16 (Day 4): Israel strikes Iranian uranium storage facilities. Iran responds with strikes on Israeli cities; apartments in Tel Aviv are damaged. Israeli residents spend time in shelters. French forces in the region intercept Iranian drones.

June 17 (Day 5): Iranian militias in Iraq attack American and Israeli targets with drones. Israel bombs Iranian airfields and radar systems. Casualties are growing: dozens killed in Iran from Israeli strikes.

June 18 (Day 6): Massive Iranian strikes on Tel Aviv; smoke over the city. Israel responds with attacks on Tehran and other provinces. The Israeli death toll reaches 10–15. The US warns Iran of possible intervention.

June 19 (Day 7): Israel declares the degradation of Iran's military capabilities. Iran launches additional rockets; Houthis attack Israeli ships.

"DEADLY CHAOS"

(How intelligence was working inside Iran, creating chaos.)

Setting: *An apartment in northern Tehran. Windows curtained. On the table: an Iranian passport and several smartphones.*

Character: Sara, Mossad agent (looks like a Tehran University student).

Voice in earpiece: *(in Hebrew) Target "Phoenix" has left the office. You have five minutes to upload the virus to his home network.*

Sara: *(calmly, in flawless Farsi, into the phone) Mama, I'll be late at the lecture. (disconnects the call, quickly inserts a flash drive into the router) Done. The network is under control. Now they will see "ghost targets" on their air defense consoles every half hour.*

Voice: *Pull back. What is the mood in the city?*

Sara: *They are frightened. They don't know who among them is their own and who is not. Yesterday three colonels were arrested at the defense ministry — purely on the basis of paranoia. We didn't even do anything — they started eating each other themselves. This is more beautiful than any explosion. We are not just breaking their centrifuges. We are breaking their faith in their ability to hide.*

June 20 (Day 8): The exchange of strikes continues. Israel bombs Iranian nuclear facilities; Iran focuses on precision strikes on Israel.

June 21 (Day 9: US Entry): The US under Trump's leadership strikes three Iranian nuclear facilities. This is the first direct American strike on Iran. Iran accuses the US of aggression. Iranian casualties exceed 500.

June 22 (Day 10): Iran responds to American strikes; Trump threatens further sanctions. Israel bombs Iran's mountains (presumed uranium storage). Ceasefire negotiations begin through Qatar.

June 23 (Day 11): Trump announces a ceasefire on social media, calling the conflict the "12-Day War." Israel reports a shortage of interceptors; the US helps with supplies. Iran agrees to a ceasefire.

June 24 (Day 12: Ceasefire): The ceasefire takes effect. Both sides accuse each other of violations, but the strikes stop. Netanyahu calls it a "historic victory"; Iran's Supreme Leader Ali Khamenei declares that "the US achieved nothing." Total casualties: 1,054 killed in Iran (per NGOs), 28 in Israel. Israel declares that Iran's nuclear program has been set back by years.

Aftermath

"Operation 'Am ke-Lavi' became an outstanding historical success. Israel achieved its strategic goals and joined the ranks of world powers," the official statement concludes. Israel eliminated the dual immediate existential threat — both in the nuclear and ballistic missile spheres. In addition, the IDF achieved full control of Tehran's airspace, inflicted serious damage on the military leadership, and destroyed dozens of central Iranian government facilities. The war led to a significant weakening of Iranian proxies (Hezbollah, Houthis were not fully employed) but intensified regional tensions. Israel expanded its THAAD missile defense system. The ceasefire is fragile; analysts note the risk of new escalation. Trump positioned himself as a "peacemaker," but critics see the war as a spectacle to distract from domestic problems.

Results of the War with Iran (June 2025)

Israel conducted Operation "Rising Lion," striking more than 150 targets in 27 Iranian provinces, including nuclear facilities (Natanz, Fordow), missile factories, IRGC bases, and energy infrastructure. Approximately 30 Iranian military leaders and 11 nuclear scientists were killed. The US joined on Day 9, striking three nuclear facilities. Iran's nuclear program has been set back 1–2 years but not completely destroyed — part of the uranium was moved beforehand.

Iran launched approximately 550 ballistic missiles and 1,000 drones. The majority (80–99%) were intercepted by Israeli air defenses with allied support (USA, France). Strikes damaged residential areas in Israel but did not achieve strategic goals. Proxy groups (Houthis, Shia militias) conducted limited attacks but did not change the course of the war. In Israel — 28 killed (civilian and military), in Iran — at least 1,054 including 610 civilians. Iran arrested 21,000 suspects and executed 6 on espionage charges. Cyber attacks: Israel stole $90 million from an Iranian cryptocurrency exchange and destroyed data at Sepah Bank.

For Israel and the US: The cost of the war — more than $40 billion (direct defense costs $15 billion, damage and reconstruction $6–8 billion, missile production $12 billion). Israel's GDP contracted by $6 billion in the second quarter of 2025, but long-term costs may exceed $50 billion.

The Tel Aviv Stock Exchange rose 67% from October 2023, the shekel strengthened 12% against the dollar, GDP per capita — $57,000 (higher than Germany). For Iran: Strikes damaged oil facilities, nuclear storage, and infrastructure. The economy weakened by sanctions; Iran's GDP (with a population 9 times larger than Israel's) is only 80% of Israel's. Internet shutdowns, arrests, and executions intensified the internal crisis. Iran continues selling oil to China, but recovery will take years. Regional consequences: Weakening of Iran's proxies (Lebanon, Syria, Iraq, Yemen) exacerbated their poverty. Israel strengthened its position but risks isolation.

Ceasefire: Announced by Trump on June 23; took effect June 24 after 12-hour pauses by each side. Iran canceled negotiations with the US on a nuclear deal. Netanyahu called the war a historic victory, Khamenei — "a slap to the US." The war changed the balance of power — Israel strengthened its dominance, Iran was weakened. Syria: Assad left in December 2024, Turkey expanded its influence. In Iran, the strikes united the population against Israel but intensified protests (youth rejecting the regime). In Israel, Netanyahu strengthened his position, but critics accuse him of politicization. In the US, Congress is divided: some support Israel, others fear escalation.

Opposition Channels in Iran

The Islamic Republic will never return to its former state. The temporary cessation of conflict is the beginning of the regime's struggle with a flood of endless questions from its support base. The self-confidence of the Islamic Republic's supporters has collapsed, the people's fear has disappeared, and the regime's seemingly absolute power has crumbled. Israel will not agree to anything less than "unconditional surrender," as Trump declared. Such surrender by the Islamic Republic was impossible while the war was ongoing; Ali Khamenei and IRGC commanders would need to be provided the opportunity to emerge from their basements and sign a surrender agreement. Starting tomorrow, the Islamic Republic again faces IAEA decisions, referral to the Security Council, activation of the trigger mechanism, and — most terrifying of all — resumption of negotiations with the US.

Israel Rewrote the Rules

The war between Israel and Iran in June 2025 became the most large-scale and unprecedented conflict in the history of the Middle East involving two states without a direct land border. In just 12 days, decades of diplomacy, intelligence dogmas, and defensive templates were destroyed. *Israel demonstrated five things: It is capable of striking at the heart of Iran — from Tehran to Fordow — while maintaining the internal rear and civilian resilience.*

The IDF applied the full arsenal — from drones and cyberattacks to F-35s and commandos — demonstrating full synchronization of the armed services branches. The defensive concept of multilayer missile defense was replaced by an offensive strategy oriented toward the proactive destruction of the enemy's military and infrastructure centers. The alliance with the US proved to be situational: Israel acted autonomously, often without notification — a certain litmus test in the alliance. Israel successfully exported psychological superiority: strikes on key facilities, including in Tehran, dealt a blow not only to military potential but also to Iranian national pride.

At the same time, Iran showed that it is prepared for an asymmetric but large-scale response, launching more than 500 rockets and drones at Israeli territory and its allies. However, the effectiveness of this strike was minimized thanks to the coordinated operation of the missile defense system and the Home Front Command. Iran, despite its powerful arsenal, proved incapable of either paralyzing Israeli infrastructure or creating internal instability.

The Deadly Beauty of the Mossad

On September 17, 2024, in Lebanon, hundreds of explosions thundered almost simultaneously. Charges that had been secretly embedded in the latest model pagers used by members of the pro-Iranian armed group Hezbollah, some politicians, and Iranian diplomats were detonated. The pagers were manufactured in Taiwan and, as Reuters alleges, Israeli Mossad agents had planted explosives in them that were to be activated after the device received a certain code. On September 18, the situation repeated: on that day it was not the pagers but radios and portable radio stations used by Hezbollah that detonated simultaneously.

THE DOMINO EFFECT

(The Dismantling of Hezbollah's Leadership)

The elimination of Hezbollah's military leadership in 2024–2025 entered the textbooks of intelligence services as a cascading collapse of a system. Israel successively eliminated those considered to be the "brain" of the organization: Fuad Shukr (Sayyid Mohsen) — Nasrallah's "right hand," responsible for the rocket program. His elimination in the heart of Beirut showed that Hezbollah's air defense is a myth. Ibrahim Aqil — commander of the "Radwan" special forces. His elimination along with the entire staff during a meeting was a shock: Israel knew not only the building but the specific underground room. Hassan Nasrallah (September 27, 2024): The final chord. A strike with 80 tons of bunker-busting bombs on a bunker 30 meters deep not only killed the leader — it destroyed the Arab street's very faith in Iran's "divine protection." This was not merely the killing of leaders — it was the deconstruction of fear. Israel proved: in the Middle East there is no bunker that can protect against the truth backed by technology.

September 2024 changed the rules of war forever. The pager operation and the subsequent elimination of the entire Hezbollah leadership — from Fuad Shukr and Ibrahim Aqil to Hassan Nasrallah himself — became an act of technological castration of the enemy. Israel proved that 30 meters of concrete and thousands of rockets offer no protection if your own communications have been turned into your death sentence. The elimination of Nasrallah on September 27 with 80 tons of bombs is not merely a military success — it is the destruction of the theological myth of the "Axis of Resistance." It turned out that divine protection is powerless before Israeli intelligence, which sees through walls.

"THE LAST BREATH IN BEIRUT"

Setting: *Bunker beneath a residential district of Dahiya. Minutes before the strike.*

Characters: Nasrallah and an advisor from the IRGC.

Advisor: *(nervously) Hassan, we must change location. The pagers were only the beginning. The Zionists have cracked our closed communication lines. They know everything.*

Nasrallah: *(calmly, but with a shadow of doubt) We are under thirty meters of concrete. No rocket will penetrate this. The Ayatollah assured us that their air force would not dare a direct incursion into Beirut. They fear escalation...*

Advisor: *(looking at the monitor, which is starting to go dark) They no longer fear anything, Hassan. They have stopped playing by your rules.*

Communications officer *(to Advisor): Hassan said the pagers are safe — whispered the communications officer, looking at the blinking device. A short beep sounded. He brought the screen to his eyes.*

In the next second *the silence of Beirut exploded with thousands of small pops. It was the sound of a collapsed empire of fear. The system built over decades self-liquidated in 15 seconds.*

*(**At this moment the floor beneath them begins to vibrate**. It is not an explosion — it is the sound of approaching death: the first bomb pierces the upper layers, clearing the path for the second, the third, the tenth... Nasrallah manages only to raise his eyes to the ceiling before the "impregnable" bunker turns into a concrete mass grave.)*

"Through a Psychiatrist's Eyes": Desacralization of Evil

Symptoms: Shock and apathy among supporters of the "Axis of Resistance."

Mechanism of treatment: The elimination of Nasrallah acted on the region like an exorcism. For decades, Israeli society (and the army) had been in a state of "social schizophrenia," believing in the mystical power of Nasrallah and his rockets. The strike on the bunker destroyed this enchantment.

Verdict: Healing came through the physical destruction of the source of hallucination. Israel regained "clarity of vision": the enemy is not a myth but a target. And any target can be destroyed, if one stops fearing its "sacred" status.

The pager operation (September 2024) became the triumph of the concept of "informational dominance." Israel showed that it can penetrate not only headquarters but also the pocket of every terrorist.

The elimination of Hassan Nasrallah in his underground bunker put an end to the myth of the "invulnerability of proxies." This was not merely a military action — it was an act of desacralization of evil. When thousands of Hezbollah commanders simultaneously went out of action due to explosions of their communication devices, and then their leader was destroyed in his "impregnable" refuge, Iran's strategy of the "ring of fire" disintegrated. It turned out that the "snake's head" cannot protect its tentacles when Israel shifts from "mowing the grass" to full disinfection.

"SIGNAL IN THE POCKET"

Setting: *South Beirut, Dahiya. A meeting of Hezbollah middle management.*

Character: Mahmoud, communications officer.

Mahmoud: *(irritated) Why has headquarters banned smartphones? These old pagers can't even receive a message properly.*

Commander: *Nasrallah's order. The Zionists crack any camera, any GPS. A pager is safe. The old school.*

(At this moment, an insistent signal sounds on the pagers of all present. *Mahmoud raises the device to his face to read the message. A moment of silence. And then — a series of pops resembling an explosion of firecrackers, but with horrifying consequences. A minute later the entire district is transformed into hell: people who considered themselves "invisible" turned out to have been marked and punished by their own communications. The system created for protection became a detonator.)*

"Through a Psychiatrist's Eyes": Collapse of the Illusion of Control

Symptoms: Complete disorientation of Iranian proxies after the "Pagers" and "Bunker" operations. A condition in which the enemy fears its own shadow and any electronic device.

Mechanism of treatment: Israel applied the method of "shock destruction of identity." When the leader (father/god figure) is destroyed and communications (the nervous system) are turned into a weapon, a terrorist organization falls into a state of collective psychosis.

Verdict: These operations became medicine for Israel itself. They proved that the "invincible" axis of Iran is a colossus with rotten insides. The social schizophrenia within Israel began to recede, giving way to pride in the power of the state that was finally applied for its intended purpose.

"VIRUS WITHIN THE SYSTEM"

Setting: *Iranian air defense command post, a facility near Tehran. June 13, 2025, 02:10 at night.*

Characters: Duty officer and young radar operator.

Operator: *(rubbing his eyes) Captain, the outer perimeter is all clear. Israeli aircraft have not even crossed the border of Iraq. Why are we on highest alert?*

Officer: *(lighting a cigarette) Quiet down. It's an order from Tehran. They fear shadows. Sit and watch the screen. Not a bird will fly past unnoticed. Our S-400s will cover them before they even get close.*

(At this moment, in the civilian car park just a couple of hundred meters from the air defense radar, the tarpaulin on an ordinary dusty pickup slides back. From the truck bed, silently, a launcher extends.)

Operator: *Captain... I have a failure on the near-field radius. The sensor shows a launch... but the sky is empty! The signal source is right here, in sector 4, at our gate!*

Officer: *What nonsense? Who could...*

(A muffled clap. A second later the radar screen floods with white noise. The building shudders from a direct hit by a precision missile fired from that very pickup. From the sky, from what seemed empty clouds, dozens of kamikaze drones drop down, having taken off from a secret Mossad base in the neighboring forest.)

Officer: *(grabbing the radio) We are under attack! We are under attack from within! It's not planes! It's... they are already here!*

(The radio hisses. A calm voice sounds on the air in Farsi with a slight accent: "Good night, Captain. You can switch off the lights. Your sky belongs to us now.")

"Through the Psychiatrist's Eyes": Invasive Shock

Symptomatology: Complete paralysis of the Iranian air defense system in the first minutes of the war. The condition was caused by the threat arriving not from outside (exogenously) but from within the organism (endogenously).

Mechanics of defeat: The Mossad acted like a virus that had been dormant in the body's tissues for years, embedding itself into its daily routine (automobiles, drone bases, logistics). At the moment of activation, the "immune system" (the Iranian army) experienced shock: it had been preparing to repel an airstrike but received a bullet in the back of the head in its own bedroom.

Result: Internal paranoia in Iran reached the level of "social schizophrenia." Now every Iranian officer looks at his car, his neighbor, and his equipment as potential weapons of Israel.

Verdict: Trust within the Iranian elite has been destroyed. This is not merely a military defeat — it is the psychological castration of the regime.

"THE INTERVIEW ON THE COGNITIVE BREAKTHROUGH"

Setting: *The studio of one of the "old" channels. Live broadcast.*

Characters: Alon (the host): Well-groomed, liberal, a representative of the "Oslo elite." Tomer Ben-Ami (former adviser to the prime minister): Sharp, laconic, with the cold gaze of a man who has seen classified files.

Alon: *(with poorly concealed indignation) Tomer, let us be honest. The strike on Iran in June was pure Netanyahu adventurism. We were one step away from a world war. The international community is in shock; our allies in Washington learned about it from the news! Do you really believe that this "cowboy raid" was worth destroying our relations with the West?*

Tomer: *(leaning forward, his voice sounding like the creak of steel) You know what your problem is, Alon? You live in a world of "relations," while we live in a world of "survival." You are afraid that someone in the State Department will raise an eyebrow disapprovingly, while I am afraid that in a year a nuclear mushroom cloud will rise over Tel Aviv.*

Alon: *But there is diplomacy! There were sanctions!*

Tomer: *(laughing) Diplomacy? We spent ten years watching your "rational Iranians" build a noose around our necks. Hezbollah to the north, Hamas to the south, the Houthis in the south — these were all tentacles. In June we simply took an axe and struck at the head.*

And what did we see? That the "great and terrible" Iran is a house of cards. Where was their "crushing retribution"? There was none, because they respect only force. As for your "world community"... it always condemns living Jews and is very sympathetic to dead ones. We decided to break with that tradition.

Alon: *You speak like a radical rightist. You have destroyed the status quo!*

Tomer: *The status quo — is it when we are being slaughtered while we ask permission for a retaliatory strike from the legal adviser? That status quo burned on October 7th. We are treating the country for schizophrenia. We have stopped believing that the enemy can be "bought" or "appeased." We have restored to Israel its primal instinct — to destroy those who come to kill us, right in their lairs. If you do not like this new Israel — well, get used to it. We have no other one for you.*

Alon: *(at a loss, staring into the camera) But the cost... the cost of this victory...*

Tomer: *The cost of freedom is always high. But the cost of slavery and waiting for a slaughter is far higher. We chose life. And if for that it was necessary to burn the Iranian centrifuges along with your illusions — it was the best deal of my life.*

"Through the Psychiatrist's Eyes": Fracture of the Cognitive Model

Symptomatology: The host (Alon) demonstrates a classic refusal of reality. He prefers "the beautiful lie" (diplomacy, status quo) to "the terrible truth" (the necessity of war). His fear of "the world's condemnation" is stronger than his fear of the enemy's nuclear bomb.

Mechanics of healing: Tomer Ben-Ami plays the role of "shock therapy." He forcibly returns his interlocutor from the world of fantasy to the world of physical facts. The strike on Iran is an act of the supreme psychological health of a nation that has decided to break the cycle of self-destruction.

Verdict: The interview did not "work" for the media elite, because it destroyed their monopoly on truth. But it "worked" brilliantly for history, capturing the moment of death of the old, weak Israel.

Real Interview with Zvi Hauser

June 20, 2025. Former Secretary of the Netanyahu Government and former chairman of the Knesset Committee on Foreign Affairs and Defense, Zvi Hauser, gave an interview to Newsru.co.il. Interviewed by Gaby Wolfson.

— Mr. Hauser, the first week of the war against Iran is coming to an end. Share your view of the results of this period of the operation.

— I think that at this point Israel is proving above all that what we are doing was the right thing to do. It seems to me that in the course of this war, two things have been proven beyond any doubt.

Iran has made a final decision to put an end to the State of Israel.

It has been proven that we ensure our own security through our own efforts.

For many years the political and military worldview did not rest on two key paradigms.

Israel must behave as a regional power that can afford a certain measure of uncertainty regarding the outcome of a military confrontation.

The current basic concept of Israel's response ("He who intends to kill you — be first to kill him") rejects the concept of "intermediacy," according to which one must limit oneself to tactical measures, temporary responses, and rounds.

For many years we turned a blind eye to the arming going on in Gaza, the arming going on in Lebanon, the formation of weaponry and extraordinary capabilities in Iran. On October 7th we woke up and realized that tactical means were insufficient. The shock in which we found ourselves under the influence of the rout inflicted on us by Hamas — the weakest army in the Middle East, which killed 1,200 of our country's citizens in a single day — was accompanied by a very heated discussion of whether or not we were capable of dealing with the challenges in Lebanon. That discussion continued until the "pager day." On that day, September 17, 2024, we understood that we could hold our ground, that we had an answer to the threat from Hezbollah and to the capabilities, the potential it had accumulated. And no less important — we were no longer prepared to be in a situation where they accumulate forces, create precision rockets, while we fear confrontation and wait until every five, ten, or twenty years we have an opportunity to strike them.

And the third event, which symbolizes a strategic turn, and above all a turn in thinking — and still more above all, a turn in the thinking of the heads of the political, military, and partly media systems, and most of all a turn in the thinking of the state leader

Benjamin Netanyahu, who has headed the political and state system for the greater part of the last 15 years — is the Iranian story. It shows that a transition has been made from tactical decisions to an active, initiative-based policy with readiness to go into confrontation and pay a price. It also shows the understanding that it is necessary to seek strategic responses commensurate with the challenges that can offer solutions to the strategic problems we face.

And if I try to trace the historical time-line in the Middle East, then starting from the First Lebanon War until October 7, 2023, the Concept held sway. On October 7th it cracked; it became clear that strategic problems cannot be solved that way. In September 2024 the Concept faltered definitively against the backdrop of Israel's active, initiative-based activity in Lebanon, when even the day before the "pager operation" there were those who objected, convinced we were unable to act. And in June 2025 the final understanding crystallized that cosmetic steps were unacceptable for solving strategic problems.

Out of negligence we allowed a gigantic potential to be formed in Gaza, in Lebanon, in Syria, and in Iran. Part of that potential has "leaked" from Iran to the Houthis in Yemen. The end of the war must consist of the liquidation of the potential assembled at those four points and the understanding that one cannot allow those forces to be formed anew. We had grown accustomed to theses built on intelligence data: the deterrence factor has been achieved with Hamas, the deterrence factor has been achieved with Hezbollah, Iran will not intervene, and so on. No — none of that works. One must act against the potential the adversary is building.

The war in Iran has not ended, and I very much hope we did not wait too long before beginning it. In any case, it is too early to celebrate today. Israel's situation is unquestionably better than it was a week ago:

We have destroyed a substantial part of Iran's potential.

We will take care of our own security ourselves, and are prepared to pay a price for that.

Our neighbors fear us again.

— How do you assess Netanyahu and his decision-making process?

— Netanyahu is a leader whose diagnostic abilities are perhaps the strongest in the Israeli public and political arena, and possibly at the international level as well. He possesses a phenomenal capacity for analyzing a situation, separating the essential from the secondary, the genuine from the false. He himself is indeed endowed with a magnificent capacity for correctly assessing a situation, understanding the difference between the desirable and the actual, and with excellent diagnostic gifts.

The other side of the coin is that the practical conclusion Netanyahu always drew was an avoidance of risk — passivity, caution regarding initiative steps, and a striving to limit himself to tactical steps and elevate them to a principle. In his autobiography Netanyahu writes about Operation Protective Edge, about his objection to a ground operation aimed at the demilitarization of Gaza. This took place at the well-known cabinet meeting at which a presentation was given showing that such an operation would cost 500 soldiers' lives. Netanyahu writes in his book that he "made the right decision."

That was how he was before October 7, 2023. That day became shock therapy for the political and military systems, and also for part of the media. They — and first and foremost Netanyahu — came to realize that endless cosmetic solutions were leading them to systemic blindness. To return to Gaza, I can repeat what I said earlier. There was no need to wake anyone at three in the morning, no need for the lookout women's reports. Any sane person understood that one cannot simultaneously watch Hamas creating an army and speak of having achieved a deterrence factor.

Netanyahu understood from the Gaza example that one could not go on that way. The successes in Lebanon revived Netanyahu's faith in the army's capabilities and led to conceptual changes, which contributed to the decision to begin this war against Iran. It is obvious to me that what we are talking about is a historic decision of strategic significance. Before the start of the war with Iran, Netanyahu faced several strategic challenges:

— the rapid development of the Iranian nuclear program;

— the question of Saudi Arabia's nuclear program;

— Turkey taking control of Syria — confrontation with the Turkish-Qatari conglomerate.

— How do you assess the functioning of the defense system?

— The defense system was monolithic; no one challenged its postulates. There was a striking alignment of positions between senior military figures and senior media representatives. All the foundations of the journalist's trade — asking questions, casting doubt — were abandoned. The war correspondents acted as representatives of the IDF press service, only not in military uniform.

After the "Arab Spring" (in 2011 and 2012), millions of Arabs in the Middle East understood that the situation had changed.

The left-wing elite of Israel and its nuclear "only not Bibi" group did not understand this, and did not change their stance on the model for resolving the conflict with the Palestinians. It required dramatic events (October 7, 2023; September 17, 2024; June 13, 2025) that critically affected the political and defense systems, leading to the adoption of strategic decisions, and returning diversity, polyphony, and doubt to public discourse.

"WHISPER IN THE DESERT"

Setting: *A private terminal in Riyadh. Night after the strike on Iran.*

Characters: A high-ranking Saudi prince and his security adviser.

Adviser: *(extending a tablet showing images of burning Natanz) Sir, the Israelis have finished the second wave. Iran's air defense no longer exists. The whole world is now shouting about an "act of aggression."*

Prince: *(studying the screen intently, with a barely perceptible smile) Let them shout. Prepare our official statement. Write about "deep concern," about "the threat to stability" and "the need for restraint." Use the heaviest words from the diplomatic vocabulary.*

Adviser: *Understood. And unofficially? What shall I convey to their liaison at the Mossad?*

Prince: *(rising, gazing out the window at the city at night) Tell them that today they did what we did not have the courage to do for thirty years. They pulled the fangs from the rabid dog. Tell them that our sky remains open for their "stray" aircraft on the return journey. And order the best coffee. Tomorrow there will be a new Middle East, and in it Iran will no longer dictate conditions to us.*

The Arab World in Consternation

Everyone speaks openly or in veiled terms: Israel has stopped restraining itself — it strikes in Iran, in Syria, in Yemen, where it has almost destroyed an entire government — and there is no place protected from Israel's reach, no person in the Arab world who is outside the danger zone. Perhaps it will now eliminate al-Julani, or a high-ranking figure in Lebanon, to force the local government to disarm Hezbollah. Israel is capable of eliminating kings, princes, and grandees. This is being said openly.

"They say Israel has become the 'bully' of the Middle East, and the Arab nation does not understand what is happening," notes Dr. Mordechai Kedar.

The expert underscores that these words sound like "criticism directed at the Arab world," and, to emphasize the scale of what has occurred, explains: "Qatar is a country that drove the Arab world mad from 1996, when Al Jazeera was founded. They triggered the Arab Spring, caused the deaths of millions, and brought down Arab regimes — and nobody dared deal with them directly. For three years attempts were made to impose a boycott on them — it did not work. Qatar survived the sanctions and reigns unchallenged in the Arab world. And then suddenly Israel comes along, strikes at those it particularly loves — Hamas people — right in the Qatari capital, and calmly continues its course. This has thrown the Arab world into complete confusion."

"The whole Arab world is now searching for who is capable of saving it: Egypt? Turkey? Saudi Arabia, suspected of collaborating with Israel and allowing Israeli aircraft to pass through its airspace to reach their target? Saudi Arabia, of course, condemns — but who believes in that condemnation?" he noted. "In

general, mutual distrust and suspicion reign everywhere. They do not trust one another. Formally all have issued condemnations, but none of those who condemned has severed relations with Israel or sent an army against it, with the exception of Egypt, which has slightly strengthened its presence in Sinai, as it had done before. In effect, the Arab nation lies on the ground while Israel treads wherever it wishes and whenever it wishes," added ***Dr. Kedar.***

SYNDROME OF PUBLIC DENIAL

Symptomatology: Arab countries demonstrate classic behavioral splitting. At the level of the "Super-Ego" (official statements) — they are in solidarity with the Islamic world and condemn "Zionist aggression." At the level of the "Id" (survival instinct) — they are celebrating the destruction of Iran as a deliverance from an existential threat.

Mechanics: Israel in this system plays the role of "dirty surgeon." Arab capitals hate the surgeon publicly but pay him with tacit consent for removing the tumor they themselves were afraid to treat.

Verdict: The year 2025 showed: fear of Israel is the foundation of respect in the region. "Peace in exchange for territories" was an illusion. Real peace came as "Peace in exchange for the destruction of a common enemy."

The Role of Bibi in Saving the Country

Benjamin Netanyahu, as Prime Minister of Israel since December 2022, played a central role in the response to the Hamas attack of October 7, 2023 and the subsequent war. Bibi attempted to hold the strategic framework but encountered the sabotage of the "professionals." Generals convinced him (and the nation) that

Hamas was "contained," ignoring his instinct and political will toward harsher actions.

Achievements and Arguments

Decisive leadership of the war. Immediately after October 7th Netanyahu declared a state of war, formed an emergency national unity cabinet, mobilized reserves, and launched Operation Iron Swords. He repeatedly declared the goals: the destruction of Hamas (its military and governmental potential), the return of all hostages, and ensuring that Gaza would no longer threaten Israel.

Military successes under his leadership: By 2025 the IDF under Netanyahu's political direction had eliminated key Hamas leaders (Sinwar, Deif, Haniyeh and others), destroyed 23 of 24 battalions, over 90% of the rocket arsenal, and a significant portion of the tunnels. The war expanded to "seven fronts" (Gaza, Lebanon, Iran, Yemen and others), with the elimination of Nasrallah and strikes on Iranian installations. Netanyahu rejected international pressure for a ceasefire, which allowed the achievement of "sweeping victories that are changing the face of the Middle East."

Return of hostages and deals: By October 2025 approximately 207 hostages had returned (living and bodies of the deceased) thanks to a combination of military pressure and negotiations (including the Trump plan). Netanyahu emphasized: "We withstood colossal pressure and achieved the goals."

Political steadfastness: Despite the failure of October 7th, Netanyahu retained power, strengthened the coalition, and, according to polls in certain periods of 2025, raised his approval rating thanks to successes against Iran and its proxies.

Supporters see in him a leader who prevented a repetition of October 7th, broke the "axis of evil" (Iran–Hamas–Hezbollah), and restored Israel's strategic superiority.

Criticism and Counter-Arguments

Responsibility for the October 7th failure: Many (opposition, hostage families, former generals) accuse Netanyahu of underestimating the Hamas threat (the policy of "containment" via Qatari money, ignoring warnings), which led to the catastrophe.

Humanitarian and diplomatic consequences: The war led to international isolation, protests in Israel, and accusations regarding the absence of a plan for "the day after."

By December 2025 the war had formally concluded with a deal (under the Bibi-Trump plan), with the return of the hostages. Facts from sources across the spectrum confirm both successes and failures.

Changes in the Regional Map

The series of IDF military victories from October 2023 to October 2025 radically restructured the geopolitical map of the Middle East. These victories weakened Iran's "axis of resistance" and strengthened Israel's position as a regional dominant power. By October 2025 the region had transitioned from a balance between Israel and Iran to Israeli dominance, supported by the United States, with the weakening of Shiite influence and the growth of Sunni alliances. The war with Iran in June 2025 became a turning point, destroying the taboo on direct strikes and creating conditions for the restructuring of the region.

The IDF's victories led to territorial, diplomatic, and strategic shifts. The region moved from an "unstable balance" between Israel and Iran to Israeli dominance, with the growth of Sunni forces and the weakening of Shiite ones.

These changes have created a "new map" of the Middle East in which Israel has strengthened its security, but the risk of escalation remains high due to unresolved questions (for example, the status of Jerusalem, the Palestinians). Analysts note that the victories have opened a chance for a real restructuring of the region, but without diplomacy they could lead to new instability.

The Medicine for Social Schizophrenia

The analysis of how the collapse of Assad's regime in Syria (December 2024) and the subsequent dismantling of the Iranian "Axis of Resistance" in 2025 influenced Israel's internal illness is perhaps the most optimistic part of this analysis. This is the moment when the reality of the Middle East brutally broke open the "intellectual bubble" of Israel's elites.

The Collapse of the "Concept of All-Powerful Iran"

For years Israeli media and left-wing intellectuals had convinced society that the "Axis of Evil" was a monolithic, invincible force with which one could only negotiate or "contain."

Shock for the system: The rapid fall of Damascus at the end of 2024 showed that Tehran's enormous investments in Syria evaporated within a matter of weeks.

Medicine for schizophrenia: This forced Israeli society to realize: the enemy is not all-powerful. The fear that for years had paralyzed the will of Israeli leadership (through legal and political restrictions) had in large measure been artificially inflated within the system itself.

The Year of "Surgical Intervention"

Israel's direct war with Iran in 2025 became a moment of truth. When Israel delivered crushing blows to the nuclear facilities and IRGC headquarters, something incredible happened:

All those media experts who for years had frightened Israel with "thousands of rockets on Tel Aviv" and persuaded it not to attack Iran found themselves shamed. Israel held firm, and Iran began to totter.

The army began to recover its hunter's instinct. When the threat of destruction became real, the legal advisers and the "Kaplanists" fell silent for a moment, as the nation united in the face of direct existential threat.

INDUCED HELPLESSNESS

Symptomatology: For decades the Israeli military-political establishment transmitted to society the virus of "impossibility." This is a classic form of social schizophrenia: to acknowledge Iran as a mortal threat ("The Head of the Snake") while forbidding oneself from even thinking about active treatment.

Mechanics of the illness: The elites fell in love with their role as "risk tamers." They began to experience a strange empathy toward the "rationality" of the enemy, unconsciously justifying its aggression.

Therapy: The strikes of June 2025 were a surgical excision of fear. It turned out that "invincible" Iran is a colossus with feet of clay, and "all-powerful" Hezbollah is merely an instrument that can be neutralized by striking the master.

Verdict: Healing will come through the rejection of the "expert opinion" of refuseniks in favor of the hard reality of survival.

The Attempt at Remission: Cleansing the System

The weakening of Iran in 2025 created a unique window of opportunity for treating Israel's internal illnesses:

Discrediting of the "old guard": The heads of intelligence and justice who for years had insisted on "the necessity of containment" lost their moral authority. The victories of 2025 were achieved in large measure against the old doctrines.

Society had matured a demand for leaders who are not bound by the chains of "social schizophrenia." The collapse of Assad proved that decisiveness and military force work better than "legal cleanliness" and endless waiting for deals.

The chance for recovery. The events of 2025 — from the ruins of Damascus to the burning installations in Iran — became shock therapy for Israel. They showed that the main obstacle on the path to Israel's security lay not in the strength of Iran but in the weakness of the Israeli spirit, poisoned by ideological blindness. The collapse of the external threat exposed the internal rot, but simultaneously gave the nation a chance for purification. Israel received the opportunity to rewrite its social contract, discarding from it the clauses about "legal capture" and restoring to it the right to unconditional victory.

Conclusion

Epicrisis. Transition from passive waiting ("the strategy of waiting for collapse") to active surgical intervention.

Clinical effect: The destruction of the Iranian nuclear program and the strike on its infrastructure acted like "electroshock" on the regional psyche. Iran's satellites (Hezbollah, the Houthis), accustomed to the impunity of their sponsor, fell into a state of depressive stupor.

Result: Social schizophrenia within Israel began to recede in the face of an obvious victory. The nation saw that the "impossible" (a direct strike on Iran without a world war) had become a reality thanks to will and technological superiority.

Conclusion: The medicine turned out to be bitter and costly, but it restored the immunity of the state. Israel has once again begun speaking the language of strength — the only sign of mental health in the Middle East.

The conflict of 2023–2025 marked a fundamental shift in the relations between Israel and Iran. If previously their confrontation was conducted mainly through proxy forces, after October 7th it moved into a phase of direct, albeit limited, military conflict.

The 12-day period of confrontation (April 2024, when Iran directly attacked Israel for the first time) became a key moment. It showed that Iran was prepared to violate the "rules of the game" and risk direct escalation. The exchange of strikes confirmed Israel's technological superiority and its status as a regional power. Israel responded with a precision strike on Iranian territory, demonstrating the capacity for strikes while maintaining strategic control over escalation.

Israel strengthened its status as a military power capable of effectively combating the "Axis of Resistance" on five fronts simultaneously (Gaza, Lebanon, Syria/Iraq, Yemen, Iran). However, this victory carries a high price: Despite the success of the air defense, the war revealed the vulnerability of the home front and forced the evacuation of tens of thousands of residents from the north — a strategic failure in deterrence.

Military actions in Gaza and threats of conflict expansion led to diplomatic cooling with key Arab partners (temporarily freezing the normalization process with Saudi Arabia). Israel found itself in a military coalition with the West (in the sky), but in diplomatic isolation (on the ground).

The new map of the Middle East formed as a result of these conflicts is based on the aggressive containment of Iran and its satellites. Israel's doctrine now reduces to the following: Iran must bear direct responsibility for the actions of its proxies. If previously Israel endured the blows of proxies, now any major attack by satellites will be regarded as an act of Iranian aggression. Israel has ceased to be a victim of "a thousand cuts" and has become a force capable of striking at the very heart of the threat. This is the final medicine for schizophrenia: the transition from the illusions of appeasement to the reality of victory.

The Iranian atom was the last lever by which they attempted to hold us in a state of submissiveness. With its neutralization, the era of strategic paralysis has ended, and a return to common sense has begun. We understood that peace in the Middle East is purchased not with concessions but with the ashes on the aggressor's installations. Now, with the existential-level external threat having been neutralized, we can move on to the most difficult task — the analysis of and lessons from the catastrophe, in order to understand how to prevent a new internal explosion. Israel has corrected the map of the Middle East, confirmed its military dominance, and its ability to defend itself against a direct existential threat.

Postscript:

U.S.–Israeli War Against Iran (February–June 2026) — Brief Summary

1. **Timeline**

- **28 February 2026** — launch of the joint operation "Epic Fury" (U.S.) / "Lion's Roar" (Israel). First massive cruise-missile, UAV and air strikes on Iran's nuclear, missile and IRGC infrastructure.
- **1–3 March** — facilities in Natanz, Fordow and Parchin destroyed; IRGC commander-in-chief Hossein Salami reportedly killed.
- **March–April** — daily/wave strikes; Iran responds with ballistic missiles against U.S. bases in Iraq and Syria and against Israeli targets. Hezbollah, Yemen's Houthis and Iraqi Shiite groups become more active.
- **Late April** — Israel strikes Lebanon to suppress Hezbollah rockets; U.S. Navy intercepts Iranian missiles in the Red Sea.
- **May** — campaign shifts to a "suppression mode": fewer but precision strikes; U.S. imposes new sanctions; cyber-attacks knock out power grids in several Iranian provinces.
- **By mid-June** — active phase lasts 100+ days, but strike intensity declines owing to moral-political and economic costs for all sides.

2. **Key U.S./Israeli Objectives**

   1. *Prevent Iran from obtaining nuclear weapons — destroy enrichment centrifuges and stocks of highly enriched uranium.*
   2. *Weaken Iran's missile-and-drone capability — strike factories, silos, SAM sites, UAV depots.*
   3. *Undermine IRGC influence and its regional proxy network — hit infrastructure in Syria, Lebanon, Yemen and Iraq.*

3. **Drivers of Escalation**

   a) *Intelligence that Tehran was ready to cross the "nuclear threshold" (enrichment > 90 %).*

   b) *Surge in attacks by Iranian proxies on Red Sea shipping and on the Ayn al-Asad base in Iraq (Jan–Feb).*

   c) *Collapse of diplomatic efforts to restore the 2015 JCPOA.*

4. **Results by June 2026**

   - *Iran's nuclear program set back at least 2–3 years; key research centers badly damaged.*
   - *Iranian losses: hundreds of missiles/UAVs, dozens of SAM systems, major damage to air and naval forces; ≈ 6–8 k military and 3–5 k civilian deaths (various estimates).*

- *U.S./Israeli losses: several aircraft/UAVs downed; dozens killed at bases in Iraq/Syria; in Israel — hundreds wounded by Hezbollah rockets and Iranian MRBMs.*
- *Iranian economy in recession > 10 %; oil exports halved.*
- *Political outcome unclears: Tehran's regime survives but domestic rifts deepen; Israel meets tactical goals, long-term deterrent effect uncertain.*

5. **Status as of June 2026**

The conflict has shifted to a "limited suppression" phase with low-/medium-intensity reciprocal strike. A Memorandum of Understanding between the U.S. and Iran is described in the media as a framework for ending the war and launching 60-day talks on a final deal.

Main points of the Меморандум

a) *Immediate cease-fire on all fronts, including Lebanon.*
b) *Sixty-day window for negotiations on a definitive agreement.*
c) *Lifting of the naval blockade and restoration of shipping through the Strait of Hormuz.*
d) *Easing or removal of sanctions and unfreezing of part of Iran's assets.*

e) *Iran's commitment not to build nuclear weapons.*

The United States has signed an agreement with a state that openly proclaims its desire to destroy Israel, under which Israel must halt its fight against a terrorist organization seeking its annihilation.

Israel is not a signatory to the memorandum and heavily criticizes it.

There is still no end in sight to the confrontation.

PART VI. ANALYSIS AND LESSONS OF THE CATASTROPHE

CHAPTER 29.
THE CRISIS OF THE PEOPLE'S SELF

The Self of a people denotes the sense of belonging to a particular nation or ethnicity, based on shared language, culture, traditions, and values.

Introduction

Having repulsed the external threats, we move on to therapy of the inner "Self" of the nation — a nation that, having failed to become a "melting pot," has fallen into a state of "social schizophrenia." Israeli (Jewish) identity, forged over centuries of trials in exile, has begun to stratify into warring subcultures that have lost their common language. The problem of Israel in 2023 was not the existence of different sectors (secular, religious, Arab) but that Ben-Gurion's "melting pot" had turned into a "pressure vessel."

The Self (identification) of the people began to dissolve: instead of a common mission of building a refuge for Jews, each group began constructing its own "Israel" that excluded the others. This is the crisis of the Self — when the answer to the question "Who are we?" begins to depend on which rally you attend. We lost the meta-narrative that united the kibbutznik and the inhabitant of Bnei Brak.

Israel is the only Jewish state in the world, combining ancient traditions with modern democracy and innovation ("startup nation"). Its collective self-consciousness was formed from

Zionism, the memory of the Holocaust, immigration, and the "besieged fortress mentality." Over the past two years Israel has experienced not merely a war — it has passed through an internal fracture.

October 7, 2023 divided the country into "before" and "after." Before — confidence that everything was under control; faith in technology, in the army, in barriers. After — a feeling of being exposed, of lost trust and paralyzed power. Israel was not unified. Every group within it — the military, the judicial, the religious, the secular, the media — was building its own small country within the larger one. And when the enemy came, it turned out we no longer had a common wall.

The country, built on the idea of perpetual readiness, turned out to be unprepared for its own illusions. But the tragedy did not arise suddenly. It became the consequence of long years of schizophrenization of consciousness: ideological, institutional, moral.

In the years before the war, society was gradually losing its capacity for agreement. Disputes about judicial reform turned into hatred; protests in the streets became a symbol of pride rather than alarm. The war merely exposed what had long been rotting beneath the surface. Some considered themselves defenders of democracy, others — saviors of the state. Between them "WE" had disappeared. Even in mourning fronts appeared: hostage families whose pain was turned into a political instrument; journalists who had chosen sides; generals whose studio commentaries were louder than the voice of soldiers in the field. The media created a monopoly on tragedy — and, together with that, a monopoly on the interpretation of conscience.

The catastrophe of October 7th also revealed the depth of Israel's strength: soldiers, doctors, volunteers, reservists, and ordinary citizens stood shoulder to shoulder to defend the country on all fronts: confrontation with Iran; war with Hezbollah in Lebanon; elimination of terrorist activity in Syria; fighting Hamas in Gaza; confrontation with the Houthis, the armed group in Yemen; elimination of terrorist activity in Judea and Samaria. These fronts constitute a tectonic challenge. They differ in their nature. Some are visible: borders to the north and south, terrorist enclaves, politically hostile regimes. Others are concealed: world diplomacy, information campaigns, demographic and cultural challenges, internal social division. In each of them Israel confronts not only external adversaries but also itself — confronting the choice of what it wishes to be. The country's security and prosperity depend on how it deals with this trial.

The catastrophe of October 7, 2023 became a watershed, and the monstrous casualties — a warning against further advancement of the delusional ideas of the adherents of left-wing ideology. On October 7th Hamas fighters did not ask who was right-wing and who was left-wing — they killed and tormented all without distinction. Today, twenty years after the expulsion from Gush Katif, Israelis who were children then speak of return. *"This is the heritage of the tribe of Judah, and the Land of Israel will not reject us. We will return, even if it takes time."* Their words are not merely youthful maximalism — they are testimony that memory is stronger than ideology. They are a reminder that, despite all attempts at division, the spirit of the people is alive.

Social schizophrenia in Israel is more dangerous than bullets, and the divide in society is deadlier than rockets. The schizophrenization of consciousness and society demands deep reflection, not superficial solutions.

The book is approaching its end, and the author cannot avoid the main questions he posed to himself before writing it.

Question 1: What is the uniqueness, originality, and resilience of Israel?

Question 2: What happened to Israeli society over the past 35 years?

Question 3: What are the main factors in the schizophrenization of society?

Question 4: How can the division and the crisis of "the people's identity" be overcome?

Question 5: And who is to blame for all this?

The answers to these and other questions are "scattered" across the various chapters of the book. The goal of this chapter is to gather those answers and to summarize the analysis of how the internal division made our society vulnerable, how it turned fellow citizens into enemies, and finally, how the crisis that began with the Oslo Accords brought the nation to a state of "social schizophrenia" and to the catastrophe of October 7th.

"CASE NO. 7-10-2024"

Setting: *A conference room where the failure of the Concept (the "Oslo" Concept or the "Protecting Gaza" Concept) is being analyzed.*

Characters: The Prosecutor of Reality and the Hallucinating Official.

Prosecutor: *You had satellite photographs, intelligence data, observers' warnings. Why did you not scramble the air force?*

Official: *We... we believed Hamas was rational. We created a model in which they wanted economic prosperity. Our analysts said that war was not in their interest.*

Prosecutor: *(hurling a folder onto the table) You created a model, while they created an army. You were treating your own hallucination while they were sharpening their knives. This is not an intelligence error. This is a clinical loss of connection with reality. You are socially schizophrenic.*

Voice off-screen: *"October 7, 2023 is the moment when the 'white noise' fell silent and reality struck a blow to the face. But the problem is that the schizophrenia-producers have gone nowhere. They are already preparing the next portion of hallucinations."*

Question 1: What is the uniqueness, originality, and resilience of Israel?

Many illnesses of society, like those of a person, do not arise suddenly and from nowhere. They are preceded by mutations in the DNA, problems of birth and early development, the accumulation of various experiences over the course of adult life, traumas, errors, and illnesses, and so on. All of this is relevant with respect to society, a people, and a nation as well. The social structure of Israel is determined by a number of features.

The Uniqueness of Israel

"Israel is the only country in which, if you hate the politicians, hate the officials, hate the existing state of affairs, hate the taxes, hate

the quality of service, and hate the weather — this means that you love it." Ephraim Kishon

The Self of the people (collective identity) is in crisis due to accumulated traumas (Oslo, the Gaza disengagement, the judicial reform). This has led to an "autoimmune" condition in which the internal struggle has become more important than the external threat. Israel is unique as the only Jewish state in the world, combining ancient traditions with modern democracy in a region where such values are rare. Here are the key aspects:

Israel is the only country where Jews form a majority, with the Law of Return. This is combined with democracy: free elections, independent courts, a free press. However, the uniqueness lies in the balance: the state is Jewish (the Sabbath is a day of rest; the national anthem "Ha-Tikvah" speaks of the Jewish soul) but democratic for all citizens, including 2 million Arabs.

Hebrew — a revived ancient language used in high-tech; cuisine — from falafel (Arab) to gefilte fish (Ashkenazi); holidays — from Yom Kippur to festivals like Burning Man in the Negev. This creates boldness and directness in communication.

Israel is unique as the "Silicon Valley of the Middle East," with a GDP per capita of approximately $60,000 (higher than Germany). Leadership in cybersecurity and medicine.

As an "island of democracy" in an authoritarian Middle East, Israel is unique in its alliances: from the Abraham Accords with Arab countries to the partnership with the United States.

After the wars of 2023–2025, Israel has become a regional hegemon, having weakened the "axis of resistance."

In general, the uniqueness lies in the capacity to be a bridge between East and West, between the ancient and the new. This makes Israel a "laboratory of humanity," but also a source of global debates. Having a unique history of formation, a constant struggle for its existence, and world recognition, Israel experiences profound social disruptions and deviations from the normal course of events (perturbations), which are explained by the following features.

Israeli society is motley and multi-faceted — owing to immigration from countries of origin with various mentalities, traditions, cultures, and political outlooks among members of society.

A distinguishing feature of Israel is the religious-confessional composition of the population.

Combining within itself the Western and Eastern paths of development, Israel has not followed the customary path of industrial states with clearly expressed class interests and the "circulation of elites."

The existence of clearly expressed partisanship and parties with differing ideologies, which has entailed deep social polarization in the country.

Despite this, the country has learned to survive under the most varied conditions of its contradictory society, maximally satisfying the interests of all categories of citizens, attempting to reconcile the most diametrically opposed and polarized circles.

The collective self-consciousness of Israel is a complex mixture of historical experience, cultural values, and national identity, formed under the influence of thousands of years of Jewish history, the Holocaust, Zionism, and contemporary challenges. Israelis often see themselves as "a people that has returned home" after the dispersion (diaspora), but at the same time as a modern, innovative nation fighting for survival in a hostile environment. This self-consciousness emphasizes resilience, unity in crises, and a balance between tradition and progress. Key elements:

The State of Israel is perceived as the embodiment of Zionism — the movement for Jewish self-determination founded by Theodor Herzl. This creates a collective sense of mission: to be "a light unto the nations," as it is written in the Bible, but in the contemporary context — through technology and democracy.

Many Israelis see themselves as survivors of the Holocaust and persecutions, which reinforces the "never again" narrative.

Israeli society is a mosaic: Ashkenazi (European Jews), Sephardi and Mizrahi (Eastern), Russian-speaking immigrants, Arabs (21% of the population), Ethiopian Jews, and others. However, this is also a source of tension: polls show that 70–80% of Israelis are proud of their country, but internal disagreements (religious vs. secular) cause an identity crisis.

Constant threats (from neighbors, terrorism, Iran) form the "besieged fortress mentality." The IDF is not merely a military force but a "people's army" where service unites society. This reinforces the sense of solidarity but also leads to the militarization of culture.

Israelis see themselves as a "startup nation," a leader in technology, medicine, and agriculture. This self-consciousness emphasizes creativity and adaptability, born of necessity.

The Uniqueness of the People — Psychological Profile

It is impossible to understand the Israeli crisis without exposing the "psychological profile" of the people. We possess a set of qualities that in peacetime earn us Nobel Prizes, but in a period of disorder — social suicide. Psychologists, ethnographers, and sociologists (from Freud and Adler to contemporary researchers of collective trauma) identify several fundamental traits of Jews that form a unique and often contradictory profile.

Jews are characterized by a combination of extreme individualism ("two Jews — three opinions") with a most powerful collective instinct in a moment of catastrophe. The psychological profile is tuned to "high revs."

When there is no external goal (a war or a great construction project), this energy begins to "grind down" internal bonds. Conflict-proneness is not a malfunction; it is the norm of functioning of such a powerful intellect deprived of a common vector.

The Jewish character is an atomic reactor. Without a reliable "lead sarcophagus" of ethics (the very same "Derech Eretz") it turns into a social Chernobyl. But with it — it gives energy to change the whole of human civilization.

Here are the main "ingredients" of this psychological cocktail:

Cognitive drive: "Sacred audacity." This is not mere impudence — it is intellectual fearlessness. A refusal to accept authority in the name of truth. In the Jewish tradition one can (and must) even argue with God (recall Abraham or Job). In science this produces Nobel Prizes and startups. In society — a total inability to "stand in line." Every private soldier considers himself smarter than the general, and every citizen considers himself a better prime minister.

Frenzied thirst for truth: Jewish "truth" is never moderate. It is the striving to reach the very root, down to the atom. In the Talmud this generates brilliant discussions, but in the politics of 2023 it turned into an inability to compromise. If I know the "truth," then my opponent is not merely mistaken — he is the enemy of truth itself.

Existential anxiety: "The survival syndrome." Centuries of persecution formed a hypertrophied vigilance. Psychologists call this "high threat reactivity." We always await a trick from history. This creates an incredible mobilization in a moment of real disaster, but in peacetime it turns into paranoia. We seek enemies in one another when there are none on the horizon, simply because the anxiety mechanism cannot be switched off.

The messianic complex: "Repairing the world." The striving to be not merely a nation but an "example" or a "light." An intense desire to improve reality, to bring it to the ideal. This makes Jews leaders of revolutions, educators, and reformers. But the reverse side is fanaticism. If I believe that I am saving the country (or humanity), I will not compromise. Hence the bitterness of internal disputes: this is not merely politics — it is a battle for the salvation of the soul of the people.

Verbal dominance: "The world as text." For the Jewish psychotype the word is more important than the material object. High intellect oriented toward analysis, interpretation, and criticism. We are a nation of lawyers, writers, and debaters. We can "talk down" any problem, construct a virtuoso logical structure justifying any position. And this is what leads to "social schizophrenia": we so artfully build our ideological barricades that we ourselves stop seeing reality behind them.

Winner at any price: Jewish conflict-proneness is not merely quarrelsomeness — it is a drive for victory. The problem is that in "social schizophrenia" we began to fight for victory over our neighbor with the same eagerness with which we should be fighting the enemy. We became a nation of "winners within ourselves," losing our common future.

"HEAR, O ISRAEL"

Setting: *An airport waiting room. A five-hour flight delay.*

Scene: *The American waits patiently. The German reads a book. After ten minutes the Israeli has already organized a WhatsApp group, found the airport director, explained to him why he is incompetent, simultaneously sold the neighbor an idea for an app, and started collecting signatures for the resignation of the Minister of Transport.*

Voice off-screen: *"We do not know how to wait. We do not know how to submit. We only know how to conquer circumstances. And sometimes in this battle with circumstances we forget to notice that the only one standing in our way is ourselves."*

"THE LABORATORY OF SELF-DESTRUCTIVE GENIUSES"

Voice off-screen: *"Imagine a laboratory where the finest minds of humanity are gathered. They are creating a cure for cancer, launching ships to Mars, and writing brilliant music. But the moment they begin to talk about how to arrange the furniture in the common lounge — they start smashing test tubes, burning blueprints, and cursing one another. Why? Because each of them is a messiah. Each is a pioneer. And each is certain that only his plan for arranging the chairs will save the world."*

Israel in 2023 was precisely such a laboratory, where the sparks of genius ignited the ammunition depot.

"Through the Psychiatrist's Eyes": Overdose of Vitality

Symptomatology: Excessive conflict-proneness against the backdrop of outstanding achievements.

Mechanics of the pathology: The psychological profile of the "pioneer" demands a constant enemy or obstacle. When the external enemy seems "tamed" (the illusion before October 7th), the brain begins to seek an enemy within. The thirst for knowledge turns into interrogations of fellow citizens as to their loyalty to "one's own" truth.

Verdict: Conflict-proneness is a side effect of "Jewish greatness." It brings medals in science, but scorches the social environment. The medicine lies not in becoming "simpler" (that is impossible) but in accepting "Derech Eretz" as a straitjacket for our genius. We must learn to come second in a dispute in order to remain first in history.

Thus:

A. ***We have linked Nobel Prizes with social problems.***

B. ***We have explained why we are such "difficult" partners even for ourselves.***

C. ***We have drawn the conclusion that our salvation lies not in a change of character (it is immutable) but in strict "safety rules" (Derech Eretz).***

Jewish Selfhood is not only history and tradition — it is a unique psychological code operating at superhigh revolutions. Such qualities as the thirst for knowledge, the striving for truth and novelty, revolution, being a winner, an educator, a pioneer, a role model, and so on — conflict-proneness, finally — all of this brings prizes, medals, and social problems.

This is the very epicenter of the "nuclear reactor" of the Jewish soul. This is precisely the aspect that transforms sociology into deep anthropology. *Without this psychological profile we cannot understand the nature of social schizophrenia and the catastrophe of October 7th.* This "cocktail" of the thirst for truth and innate conflict-proneness is an ideal soil for the development of the very social schizophrenia this book is about. In online resources and in scholarly literature this profile is often described as "intellectual hyperthyroidism." We are a nation with an elevated metabolism of the soul.

"THE LABORATORY OF CONTRADICTIONS"

Setting: *A café in Haifa. At the table — two professors and one young startup founder.*

Scene: *They argue so intensely that the crockery shakes.*

Professor A: *"Your approach is intellectual suicide! You are destroying the foundations on which science stands!"*

Startup founder: *"Your foundations are museum exhibits! If we do not make this revolution now, we will lose the future!"*

Professor B: *(interrupting both) "You are both right and both wrong! But look — we have created a solution that will save thousands of lives while we were here tearing each other's throats out."*

Voice off-screen: *"This is the Israeli paradox. We build the greatest things on the energy of pure negation. Our problem is that in 2023 we forgot how to direct this anger toward creation and began using it as acid, corroding the foundation of the house."*

"Through the Psychiatrist's Eyes": Intellectual Hyperthyroidism

Symptomatology: Excess of psychic energy; need for constant novelty and leadership.

Mechanics of the pathology: The qualities that make us "pioneers" and "educators," in the absence of a common vector, turn into social destruction. The striving to "be an example" causes every group within Israel to consider only its own way of life as the only correct one, and everyone else as "the lost."

Social consequences: Medals and prizes are the "by-product" of our restlessness. Conflicts are its "exhaust fumes."

Verdict: The cure for social schizophrenia requires not the suppression of this energy (that is impossible) but its channeling. "Derech Eretz" is a limiter for our hyperactive intellect, enabling us to argue without destroying the laboratory.

"Melting Pot" or "Salad Bowl"?

Debates about the character of the Israeli state — what precisely it should eventually become, given the history, the current real events, the highly complex character of the political arena and society — continue: "melting pot" or "salad bowl"? This is a highly apt question, reflecting the main dilemma of Israeli national construction and its future. The dispute between the "melting pot" and "salad bowl" models is a dispute about what the unity of the nation should look like: through assimilation or through the recognition of diversity.

The "Melting Pot" model was the dominant ideology in the first decades of Israel's existence (1950s–1970s). The essence of the model:

- Creating a unified, new "Israeli" person (Sabra), who would abandon the Diaspora (galut) character traits and distinctions.
- State institutions (the army, schools, kibbutzim) actively sought to erase the cultural differences between Jews who had arrived from Eastern Europe (Ashkenazi) and Jews from the countries of the Middle East and North Africa (Mizrahi).
- A unified, secular, socialist, Zionist culture was to emerge, with a single language and common values.
- In practice this process failed and led to social and cultural trauma, especially among Mizrahi communities, whose culture was often discriminated against and considered "backward" in comparison with the dominant Ashkenazi culture.
- Today this model has been almost completely rejected, as it does not account for the growth of the ultra-Orthodox (Haredim) and religious-Zionist sectors, who have no desire to assimilate into the secular mainstream.

The "Salad Bowl" model is a contemporary, multicultural concept that is gaining strength as the rifts in society deepen. The essence of the model:

1) Recognition of the plurality of sectors as having equal status: Secular Israel, Religious Zionism, the Ultra-Orthodox (Haredim), Mizrahi, Ashkenazi, Russian-speaking, Ethiopian Jews, Arab citizens Unity through diversity.
2) The nation recognizes and respects the coexistence of many different groups who maintain their unique culture, language, traditions, and identity (like ingredients in a salad, which retain their flavor but together constitute a single dish).

The main drawback of this model is that it does not answer the question: what unites these sectors, besides a common border? The sectors, especially the secular and the Haredim, serve together, study together, and work together less and less, which undermines national resilience.

Diversity ("salad bowl") can easily turn into "social schizophrenia" — a state in which different groups live in different informational, moral, and political realities (for example, on questions of security or the rule of law).

Debates about what the Israeli state should eventually become continue. Professor Khanin proposes moving toward planning a society composed of four main "tribes," roughly equal in size: secular, religious-Zionist, ultra-Orthodox, and Arab. This multi-tribal society must nonetheless be united by a common state idea.

Israel 2025: Between Ideals

As of today, Israel functions as a discordant "salad bowl." The future of Israel depends on finding a compromise model. Israel needs to preserve the diversity of the "salad bowl" (respect for cultures) while at the same time creating a minimal "melting pot" of common obligations (service, work, respect for democratic institutions) in order to ensure the functionality of the state and prevent its self-destruction.

The Self

> *"This is the only country in which the majority of its inhabitants cannot explain why they live here specifically, but have a*

thousand explanations for why it is impossible to live anywhere else."

Ephraim Kishon

The term "Self," proposed by the psychologist Carl G. Jung, in the context of a people points to the deep striving toward wholeness and harmony of the individual person as well as of the entire ethnos.

The Self is that which we perceive as ourselves. It includes that part of our personality that we know about ourselves. The ego, meanwhile, is that part of the Self that we show to those around us and give them the opportunity to evaluate. Human consciousness strives to eliminate cognitive dissonance, reconciling beliefs and behavior.

The crisis of the Self is a period in a person's life characterized by a feeling of having lost oneself, of doubts about one's values, goals, and place in the world. This state may be accompanied by emotional instability, loss of interest in life, apathy, and even physical symptoms.

"The Self of the People" (or "the identity of the people") is a metaphorical expression denoting the collective identity, values, and unique essence of a people that unites its members and distinguishes it from other peoples. Although the concept of the Self more often refers to the inner, psychological integrity of the individual, in the context of a people it denotes its collective self-consciousness and uniqueness.

Question 2: What happened to Israeli society over the past 35 years?

Over the past 35 years Israel has experienced three mega-traumas, which are examined in detail in the book:

1) **The Oslo Accords (1992–1993) and the assassination of Rabin in 1995.**

2) **The expulsion of Jews from Gaza (2005).**

3) **The Hamas attack of October 7, 2023.**

These events led to a tectonic fracture in society and to a crisis of the people's Self.

The crisis of the people's Self is a state in which a nation loses its common values and direction of development, which leads to internal uncertainty, doubts about fundamental beliefs, the loss of cultural points of reference, and the absence of common goals — making the people vulnerable to external influences and internal conflicts, up to and including schizophrenization.

The essence of the crisis of collective identity (distinctiveness) is the diminution of individuals' identification with the collective reality they previously supported.

The crisis of the Self in Israeli society is a many-faceted problem, the roots of which lie in the history of the founding of the State of Israel as a Jewish national home, but which has sharpened in recent years under the influence of political, social, and military events. This is not only an internal conflict between different groups of the population, but also a deeper question of what it means to be an "Israeli" in the modern world: is this a Jewish identity, a secular one, a national one, or a combination of all of these?

The crisis of the Self is caused by fundamental contradictions embedded in the Zionist project itself, and was sharply exacerbated by internal political divisions and the unceasing external conflicts of recent years. It is the accumulated effect of unresolved ideological disputes, deep political fragmentation, and the shock of recent military events, which called into question the basic principles of its existence as a secure, Jewish, and democratic state.

The Social Schizophrenia of Society

Such an anamnesis and such mega-traumas launched, in my view, the process of schizophrenization of consciousness and society in Israel, which reached its peak in the split of 2023.

The main pathological factor is the "peace process"; the trigger is the identification crisis, when "I am an opponent of Bibi" or "I am a defender of the reform" became more important than "I am an Israeli." The nation entered a state of autoimmune illness. The organism began to attack its own vital organs (the army, the economy, unity), regarding them as "foreign."

Until the fateful morning of October 7, 2023, Israel was at war with itself. The state was paralyzed by the deepest crisis in its history: hundreds of thousands of citizens came out into the streets every Saturday, torn by disputes about judicial reform. The army — the backbone of the nation — found itself split by threats of service refusal. Society was in a delirious state that many called a "civil war" — blind and deaf to external threats. The catastrophe of October 7th became a brutal, bloody interruption of that internal battle. By October 7, 2023, Israeli society was in a state of the deepest and most unprecedented internal crisis.

The Main Problems Tormenting Society

The "Oslo Peace Process" split the people, and Rabin's readiness for territorial compromises provoked acute polarization, dividing Israelis into supporters of peace and defenders of Israel. His policies and actions intensified the conflict.

The split between left and right in Israel is a fundamental ideological conflict that has sharpened sharply in recent years. Left-wing forces support three principles: a Jewish state, democracy, and peace with the Palestinians. Palestinian terror undermined the platform of the liberal parties. The center-left can no longer offer a peaceful solution.

Israel was proclaimed as both a Jewish and democratic state, but the tension between the secular majority and the religious Orthodox (Haredim) grew incessantly. The increased influence of ultra-Orthodox (Haredim) and religious-Zionist parties in the coalition provoked the indignation of the secular part of society. Disputes about the financing of ultra-Orthodox educational institutions, exemption from army service for the Haredim, as well as attempts to change the status quo regarding the Sabbath and religious laws — all of this deepened mutual distrust and hostility between sectors.

The majority of Israelis (about 55%) identify themselves as "traditionalists" — not strictly religious, but observing some customs — which creates a "gray zone" between Orthodoxy and secularism.

From January 2023 until the very attack, Israel was experiencing the most serious political crisis in its history, connected with the plans of the left-wing "peace camp" to overthrow the newly elected right-wing government that had planned to carry out judicial reform — of mass protests against the newly elected right-wing government that had planned to carry out judicial reform in order to restore the balance between the Knesset, the government, and the Supreme Court.

The events of 2023–2025 (October 7th, the war in Gaza, the war with Iran) sharply shifted the public focus to the right — toward security, deterrence, and retribution. This led to an unprecedented split between the two largest camps.

The protest camp (secular, center/left) saw in the reform a threat to democracy, the independence of the judicial system, and the transformation of the country into a theocracy. Every Saturday hundreds of thousands of people took to the streets, blocking main arterial roads.

The coalition camp (right-wing, religious) considered the reform necessary for restoring the power of the elected majority and limiting the activism of the Supreme Court — with the aim of putting an end to the overreach of an elite (unelected) group of progressive judges.

The crisis penetrated the army. Thousands of reserve officers and air force pilots threatened to cease service (the so-called "refusal of voluntary service") as a protest against the reform, which created tension and, in the view of many, weakened the IDF's combat readiness.

Before October 7th there existed a deep crisis of trust in the political leadership. Five elections in four years (from 2019 to 2022) led to social fatigue and cynicism. Netanyahu, whose tenure as prime minister was overshadowed by court proceedings, became a polarizing figure. For some he was the only leader capable of governing; for others — the source of the entire political crisis.

Thus, by October 6, 2023, Israeli society was deeply divided on questions of religion, democracy, and the role of the Supreme

Court. This split became a factor creating the impression that Israel was focused on internal struggle rather than external threats. In this way a tectonic social crisis of society occurred, which led the country to social schizophrenia.

Experts call for a healthy discourse in order to overcome a polarization that has become personal and toxic. The crisis led to social collapse: protests against the judicial reform, a rise in emigration, and loss of faith in the state. However, some see hope in new forms of Jewish identity, where people are united by religion, culture, and politics without dogma.

How Was the Country Sinking into Social Schizophrenia?

Internal division was plunging the nation into a state similar to "social schizophrenia" through several interrelated psychological and social processes. This process undermines social cohesion and destroys the basic trust necessary for the functioning of a democratic society.

"A VOICE FROM 2023"

(The point of "social schizophrenia" from which we began the journey.)

Setting: *A news studio, September 2023. On air — a furious dispute.*

Characters: A popular TV presenter and a political activist.

Presenter: *(almost shouting) Do you understand that your reform is the end of Israel? You are destroying democracy, you are turning us into Iran!*

Activist: *It is you who are destroying the country with your calls not to go on duty! You have taken the army hostage!*

Presenter: *If it is going to be "your" army, we don't need it!*

(At this moment, on the monitor behind them there flashes a brief intelligence message about "strange movements in Gaza." The director into the presenter's earpiece: "Skip that, it's a minor piece of news. Let's continue about the Supreme Court — the ratings are through the roof!")

The Destruction of the Common Narrative

A nation sinks into "social schizophrenia" when:

Citizens begin to live in two different informational realities. Each group consumes only those media outlets, social networks, and opinions that confirm its picture of the world (**echo chambers and filter bubbles**). As a result, facts, history, and even moral imperatives become mutually exclusive.

Members of the opposing side cease to be perceived as misguided fellow citizens and ***become enemies of the nation.*** Their motives are interpreted not as political disagreement but as ***malicious intent or betrayal.*** This removes the moral constraints on aggressive behavior and rhetoric toward them.

Identity ceases to be defined by common national characteristics (citizenship, culture) and begins to be defined by camp affiliation (for example, "***I am not merely a citizen, I am an opponent of the reform" or "I am not merely a citizen, I am a fighter for traditional values***").

The Transition from Politics to Existential Threat

The key moment when fellow citizens become enemies arrives when political disagreements transform from a dispute about methods into a battle for survival.

Each side convinces itself that the victory of ***the opponent will lead to the death of the nation, democracy, or the traditional way of life.*** This justifies the use of any means, since the stakes are "all or nothing."

Opponents are declared agents of external or internal forces working to undermine the state. In Israel's case this manifested in accusations that protesters were "working for Iran" or "undermining the army," while the coalition was "destroying democracy."

Basic social trust is undermined (for example, trust in the Supreme Court, the police, the army). Citizens begin to believe that state institutions have been captured by the hostile camp, and refuse to recognize their authority.

The Destruction of Society's Functionality

Social schizophrenia manifests in the nation becoming incapable of making unified decisions on questions requiring national consensus, even in the face of external threat.

The government spends time and resources fighting the internal opposition rather than addressing real problems or countering external threats. This creates a power vacuum and strategic weakness (as occurred before October 7, 2023).

In the Israeli context this manifested in the dichotomy of "The Religion of Hostages" vs. "Victory over Hamas." Society cannot arrive at a unified moral decision: saving lives at any price (universal moral duty) or refusing to be blackmailed (national security ethos). These two moralities coexist simultaneously, tearing the nation apart.

Thus, the internal division does not merely divide — it redefines the adversary from a political opponent to an existential enemy, making the joint governance of the country practically impossible.

"DINNER IN AN INTERRUPTED FORTRESS"

("How a nation sinks into social schizophrenia" or the moment of "dissolution of the Self" through an ordinary family scene)

Setting: *An apartment in Tel Aviv. Friday dinner. September 2023 (a month before the catastrophe).*

Characters: Father (an old Zionist, a veteran), Son (a Kaplan protest activist), Daughter (returned from a settlement for the weekend).

Son: *(throwing down his fork) I am not going to report for reserve duty! I am not going to serve a dictatorship. If they push through the reform, this country will cease to be mine. I would sooner go to Berlin than defend "messianic madness."*

Daughter: *(calmly, adjusting her headscarf) And did you ask us? Those of us living on the front line while you drink lattes on Rothschild Boulevard? For you "democracy" is only your right to decide the fate of the country. You are prepared to burn our house down just so as not to lose in court.*

Father: *(slapping his hand on the table) Both of you be quiet! Do you hear yourselves? You speak to each other like enemies. In '73 we did not ask in the tank who voted for whom.*

Son: *That time has passed, Dad. Your Israel is dead. Now it's either "The State of Tel Aviv" or "The Kingdom of Judah." Together we no longer exist.*

(The camera pulls back. Through the window the lights of the city are visible, and on the television in the background there flash footage of Hamas drills by the fence. But at the table no one is looking out the window. They are too busy destroying each other.)

"Through the Psychiatrist's Eyes": State Autoimmunity

Symptomatology: The organism (the nation) ceased to recognize its own cells (fellow citizens) as "its own." The immune system (the army, the police, the courts) began to attack itself.

Mechanics of the illness: Self-identification ("Selfhood") narrowed to the size of a sector. "I am an Israeli" was replaced by "I am secular," "I am a settler," "I am an opponent of Bibi." At this stage of schizophrenia, the common good is perceived as a threat to personal comfort.

Result: Hamas on October 7th did not create the divide — it merely walked through an open door. It attacked a body that was already paralyzed by internal conflict.

Verdict: The only salvation is a return to **"Derech Eretz"** (the Way of the Land). But for this the patient must recognize that his reflection in the mirror is precisely the one he hates.

Question 3: What are the main factors in the schizophrenization of society?

My answer: the schizophrenization of society before 07.10.2023.

1) **The illusion of the "peace process"** that began with the Oslo Accords (1993–1994), followed by the expulsion of thousands of Israelis from Gaza (2005).

2) **The political blindness of the left-wing "peace camp,"** which promoted these processes while ignoring our enemies' plans to destroy Israel.

3) **The decline of public trust in the power structures of the state** (the Knesset, the Government, and the Supreme Court) and their leaders.

4) **Weekly riots — the protests** ("Nukhba of the Kaplanists") throughout 2023–2025, which deeply split society.

5) **The left-wing doctrine, which led to the loss of offensive fighting spirit among the IDF's generals.**

6) **The systemic failure** of the IDF, AMAN, SHABAK and government leaders before and after 7/10/23.

7) **The erroneous strategic "Concept" of the Government and the heads of the security agencies over many years.**

"THE MIRROR IN AN EMPTY ROOM"

(Showing the moment of awareness of the collapse of the Self through an official or officer who realizes he has become too caught up in politics.)

Setting: *An office in the General Staff. Night of October 7th. Telephones are ringing off the hook with reports of the border breach.*

Characters: A senior officer who only yesterday had supported "refusenik" protest.

Officer: *(looking at the screen showing footage from the kibbutzim, his hand trembling) We just wanted to put pressure on the government... We thought it was a game. That we were the "elite," without whom the country would not survive.*

Adjutant: *(entering) Sir, the reservists from the refuseniks are calling. They're asking what they should do.*

Officer: *(bitterly) Tell them the enemy doesn't care about our petitions. While we were looking for a "dictatorship" in Jerusalem, the real dictatorship of death walked into our homes.* ***We cured our schizophrenia in the most terrible way — through the amputation of illusions. Go, issue weapons to everyone. Without exception.***

Why Are Ideals Being Displaced by Progressivism and Anti-Zionism?

Because progressivism offers a comfortable illusion: it is easier to be a "citizen of the world" than a Jew in a besieged fortress. This is intellectual corrosion. Zionism was declared "old" and "aggressive" and replaced by a post-Zionist desire to become a "normal country" (like Sweden or Belgium). But in our region "normalcy" is the shortest path to liquidation.

The crisis of the Self came when a significant part of the elite began to be ashamed of its own exceptionalism and its right to this land. This question touches on deep sociocultural and political shifts occurring in the Western world and affecting Israel and the Jewish diaspora. The displacement of religious and Zionist ideals by progressivism and anti-Zionism can be explained by a combination of demographic, academic, and media factors.

At the root of the process lies a change in the dominant cultural and ethical paradigms in Western societies and Israel.

Contemporary progressivism places universal human rights, individualism, and multiculturalism at the top of its hierarchy. Zionism and religion are often perceived as particularist (based on the unique identity of one group), which conflicts with universalist demands.

The level of secularism is rising, and younger generations tend to be critical of any traditional structures of power — whether religious institutions or nation-states.

The progressive movement focuses on the categories of "oppressor" vs. "oppressed." In the eyes of many Western intellectuals and activists, Israel, as a strong state, is perceived as the "oppressor" (a colonial project), while Palestinians are the "oppressed" party — regardless of the specific circumstances.

However, Israel's actions are based on the legitimate historical right of the Jewish people to the Land of Israel and on international legal foundations. The majority of Israel's actions with respect to Palestinians that the West calls "oppression" are defined by Israel as necessary security and self-defense measures. The construction of the separation barrier (wall) was a direct response to the wave of suicide bombers during the Second Intifada. The barrier sharply reduced the number of terrorist attacks and saved thousands of lives, justifying its necessity from a national security standpoint.

Freedom from occupation (Gaza): in 2005 Israel unilaterally withdrew all its troops and settlements from the Gaza Strip. If Israel were striving for oppression or control, it would not have done so. The subsequent rule of Hamas and the rocket fire, however, forced Israel to maintain partial control over the airspace and borders.

A unique situation: no other state faces the situation where entire territories under or near its control are used as a launching pad for rocket and terrorist attacks with the declared aim of its destruction. Thus, Israel's actions represent the protection of legitimate sovereignty and its citizens from terrorist threats — not the oppression of the Palestinian population.

Global media and social networks tend to simplify complex conflicts into binary oppositions. The visual component of the conflict (Palestinian suffering) fits easily into the narrative of the oppressed, which emotionally attracts a progressive audience.

Zionism is regarded as part of a global system of oppression (white, Western colonialism), which makes it the enemy for the entire progressive alliance.

These processes represent a collision between national and religious self-determination (Zionism) and the universal humanitarian ideal (progressivism), with the latter currently dominating the formation of political culture in the West.

Question 4: How can the division and the crisis of "the people's identity" be overcome?

Israeli society is experiencing a prolonged period of social schizophrenia and a deep internal division. This affects the religious, ethnic, ideological, economic, and political dimensions. What are the possible paths to the restoration of public trust?

"BROTHERS IN THE TRENCH"

Setting: *A reservists' assembly point. October 8, 2023.*

Characters: Itay (a yoga instructor from Tel Aviv, participant in the protests) and Yoni (a resident of a settlement, father of five children, supporter of the reform).

Itay: *(tightening his bulletproof vest, not looking at his neighbor) A month ago I was shouting on Kaplan that I would not serve in "your" army.*

Yoni: *(loading magazines) And I was writing on Facebook that people like you are "overfed traitors."*

Itay: *(raising his eyes) At Kibbutz Be'eri this morning I saw something that erased all those slogans. They didn't care whether we were for the reform or against. They slaughtered us simply for being what we are.*

Yoni: *(extending his hand) It seems we have a common Self again, Itay. Only the price for this reminder has turned out to be immeasurable. Let's go. We'll sort out in the APC who's more right-wing.*

Steps Toward Rapprochement

- National dialogue: structured discussions between representatives of different strata and sectors.
- Education for coexistence: reform of school curricula — adding courses on Judaism, democracy, law, and pluralism.
- Service for all: military, social, medical, and educational.
- A new political culture. Limiting demagoguery and incitement in the speech of leaders and media.

- Economic equalization. Support for peripheral regions and sectors (Arab towns, the Haredim, young people). Integration into the labor market: training, employment of women and young people from all sectors.
- Justice and equality before the law. Independence of the courts and anti-corruption bodies. Ensuring equality of rights and responsibilities for all citizens.
- Israel is capable of overcoming internal conflicts. The divide can not only be mitigated but transformed into a source of strength — given the will, dialogue, and real steps.

How to Overcome the Crisis?

Rethinking of values: it is necessary to return to the roots while also rethinking one's values in the context of the modern world.

Formation of a new national narrative: creating a shared image of the future that would unite and inspire citizens.

Support for national culture: active preservation and development of national art, language, and traditions.

Civic activity: participation in public life and dialogue helps to form collective identity and find common goals.

Education: transmitting knowledge about one's history and culture to a new generation, as well as developing critical thinking.

The Imam's Recognition

I, a son of Ishmael, an imam, a Muslim, a man of peace, give here my sincere testimony about this remarkable people:

I must confess: I believe in religions and in miracles. But there is in this people — the people of Israel — something that feels like a genuine living miracle. A people that the pharaohs tried to erase from the face of the earth 3,000 years ago... and failed.

A people that the Babylonians tried to destroy 2,500 years ago... and could not.

A people that the Romans wanted to erase 2,000 years ago... and did not succeed.

A people that the Nazis tried to exterminate 80 years ago... but could not destroy.

A people against whom the Arabs waged five wars, striving to wipe it from the world map... and were defeated.

This is a small people in number, but with a special strength, with a divine blessing. Whatever direction it turns its efforts toward — it achieves success. In finance, trade, science, philosophy, literature...

In a desert land it created a paradise, without oil or gas, but with will, democracy, intellect, and a striving for freedom.

This is a people that gave the world Einstein, Newton, Kafka, Karl Marx, Nietzsche, Spinoza, Freud... and many others who have left their mark on the history of humanity.

There are realities that neither reason nor logic has the power to explain. There is only one word for this: miracle.

For a year and a half now, this people has been waging war on five fronts. People said it was tired, that it was about to collapse... and yet it continues to astonish the world, opening a new front against the Iranian enemy that even some Arab regimes fear.

This people, despite its small numbers, possesses the courage of aristocrats, the wisdom of prophets, the patience of the righteous, and the determination of survivors. How could it be otherwise, if these are the descendants of Abraham, Solomon, David, Moses, Jacob, Joseph... and 1,523 prophets and messengers from their lineage?

This is a people that brought monotheism and faith in the One God to the world. A people driven by a thirst for life, labor, innovation, and continuity that has already lasted more than 4,000 years. Truly, I cannot find another word to describe it, except: a people-miracle.

If the Arabs had clear vision, they would choose to unite with this people, to learn from it, to cooperate with it... perhaps they would be infected by its knowledge, wisdom, and dignity.

Hassan Chalghoumi — an imam from Tunisia, serving at the municipal mosque of Drancy in Seine-Saint-Denis, near Paris.

Israel in 2050

Israel in 2050 is a society of healthy pragmatism. This is by no means a utopia in which everyone loves one another. It is a society in which people from different sectors live and serve the country together — not out of affection, but out of the understanding that the alternative is a common grave.

Forecasting Israel's future through 2050 involves the analysis of durable demographic, economic, technological, and geopolitical trends, many of which are already radically transforming the face of the country.

The reinvention of Israel is impossible without recognition of every other citizen's right to be different. We must transition from "surviving in spite of one another" to "building together." The idea of universal national service is not only about the army — it is about creating shared memories. By 2050, being Israeli must be not a party affiliation but a civic religion founded on mutual respect (Derech Eretz). Either we will learn to argue without dehumanizing one another, or the crisis of the Self will become chronic and lead to a lethal outcome. Here are the principal forecasts for key areas:

The Demographic Explosion and Shift in Identity

Demography is the most predictable factor in Israel's future and will serve as the primary engine of internal change:

Israel's population is expected to surpass fifteen million people (compared with approximately ten million in 2025).

The fastest growth is occurring in the ultra-Orthodox (Haredim) sector. By 2050, the Haredim may constitute 20–25% of the population, and the Arab population approximately 21–25%.

The secular, high-technology middle class — the backbone of the tax base and military service — will become a minority. This poses an existential economic challenge for the country, associated with the low productivity and educational attainment of the ultra-Orthodox sector.

A strengthening of the religious-nationalist character of the state is anticipated, deepening the divide with the liberal-secular population.

The Technological Core and Social Inequality

Israel will retain its status as a global technology leader but will confront the challenge of distributing its benefits equitably.

The high-tech sector will remain the primary driver of the economy, concentrated around artificial intelligence, cybersecurity, and biotechnology. Israel will be one of the world's leading powers in the field of AI.

Social inequality will intensify. The economy will be divided between a prosperous, globalized high-tech sector (predominantly secular) and a dependent, low-productivity sector (predominantly ultra-Orthodox) that requires ever-growing state subsidies.

Israel will likely achieve complete energy independence through natural gas, and retain world leadership in desalination technology and water-resource management — critically important assets in an era of climate change.

"LUNCH IN 2050"

Setting: *A café in a "mixed" neighborhood of Jerusalem. The year 2050.*

Characters: Amir (grandson of a secular Tel Avivian) and Levi (a young ultra-Orthodox man in rescue-service uniform).

Amir *(sliding the menu across): Did you hear there was trouble on the border again yesterday?*

Levi *(calmly): Yes — my reserve battalion "Judea" was on full alert. The systems handled it routinely. You know, my grandfather used to say that back in 2023 people were genuinely arguing about whether I should wear a uniform at all.*

Amir *(smiling): And my grandfather was convinced yours wanted to turn the country into a theocracy. What a mad time that was. How did they survive with such a mess in their heads?*

Levi *(adjusting his kippah): I suppose they had to lose everything to grasp one simple truth: "Derech Eretz" is not about how we pray — it is about how we cover each other's backs. Anyway, I have to get to my hospital shift. See you at the muster next month?*

Amir: ***Without fail. Take care of yourself, brother.***

Geopolitics and Security

The Iranian threat — the nuclear programme and the "Axis of Resistance" — will persist. Israel will be compelled to maintain a state of constant high-technology warfare against proxy forces and, quite possibly, a limited direct military conflict with Tehran (as occurred in 2024 and 2025).

The Palestinian Conflict. By 2050 the situation will most likely remain unresolved. The "Two States" scenario will have become extremely unlikely owing to settlement expansion and demographic realities. Instead, some form of limited Palestinian self-governance will probably emerge, with periodic outbreaks of violence.

The Abraham Accords — the normalisation of relations with Arab states — will consolidate, and the Israel–Sunni-states axis will become a key defensive bloc against Iran.

Thus, Israel in 2050 will be a powerful, technologically advanced country, but its internal life will be defined by an acute conflict of identities and a competition for the distribution of resources.

The Antidote to Division and Extremism: Derech Eretz

The concept of Derech Eretz — literally "The Way of the Land" or "The Way of Peace and Society" — is one of the foundational Jewish concepts that extends far beyond strictly religious prescription. It can be understood as a set of redemptive values and ethical norms that ensure social cohesion, respect, and humanity in society, making the very existence of the state and the nation possible. In the context of a contemporary Israel torn by internal conflict, Derech Eretz acquires special urgency as an antidote to division and extremism. ***It is not merely good manners; it is a code of ethical conduct and respect for others that precedes even the fulfilment of religious commandments:***

1) *Recognising in every human being the image of God, regardless of religious or political affiliation.*

2) *Rejecting arrogance, boastfulness, and the public humiliation of others — including the ability to speak gently and to listen.*

3) *Prizing personal responsibility and self-reliance.*

4) *Practising mutual aid, honesty in commerce, and the honouring of agreements.*

The contemporary divide in Israel is in large measure caused by the absence of Derech Eretz in public discourse. Were it to prevail, the adversaries in the judicial-reform debate would cease to regard each other as enemies and traitors, allowing critique of ideas rather than persons.

It would eliminate the public dehumanisation and aggressive rhetoric that fans hatred and undermines the legitimacy of political opponents.

Talmudic wisdom teaches that Derech Eretz precedes the Torah — meaning that even the highest spiritual or legal principles are futile if they are not preceded by basic human respect and ethics.

When ideological differences reach the breaking point, Derech Eretz remains the minimal common ground that enables people to live and work together, preserving the state as a functional unit.

It is the capacity to set aside political grievances in order to focus on mutual aid and respect for another person's pain, regardless of that person's political camp.

Only through Derech Eretz is it possible to restore the trust in institutions — the army, the courts, the government — that was eroded by the internal struggle, because it demands restraint and honesty from all participants.

Derech Eretz is thus a redemptive value: it offers an ethical and behavioural framework capable of stitching together a society torn apart by ideological and political conflict.

As Alexander Hayat — rabbi and chairman of the "Turei Zahav" Association — has observed, preserving Israel as a state requires opposing the ontological bubbles with values and principles that unite secular and religious Israelis alike. **He has identified Derech Eretz as precisely such an approach: a bridge between religious and secular Israelis.**

In Judaism, Derech Eretz implies:

- *Respect for the dignity and rights of every person as a creation of God;*
- *A harmonious union of Torah (spirituality) with "earthly" concerns and obligations;*

- *The primacy of the common good over selfish interests.*
- *As a universal ethic, Derech Eretz provides:*
- *Basic principles of humanity relevant to people of all persuasions;*
- *A standard for moral conduct in society;*
- *An antidote to fanaticism, intolerance, and moral absolutism;*
- *A foundation for dialogue and cooperation across all dividing lines;*
- A path toward harmonising Israeli society in all its diversity.

The "Dor Moriah" Association, the "Samuel Schwarzbard" Foundation, and the "Turei Zahav" Association have resolved to join forces within the framework of an all-Israeli "Derech Eretz" movement. Its goal is to preserve and strengthen the state, to resist the formation of ontological bubbles, and to unite the healthy forces of Israeli society. The movement believes this path is possible, and invites all people of goodwill to walk it together — for the sake of Israel's future and our children.

"Derech Eretz is not merely politeness. In Israel's conditions, it is a safety protocol — like oxygen masks on an aircraft: put yours on first, then help your neighbour. Respect for one's opponent is precisely the oxygen mask the state requires."

Question 5: And who is to blame for all this?

This is a complex — and, in part, rhetorical — question.

In the catastrophe of October 7th, blame does not rest with any single individual. It is a tragedy that became the sum of many years of a "peace process" (without a partner), a confluence of circumstances, and the errors and delusions of many people, compounded by the systemic failures of an incompletely constructed state.

I am prepared to answer without political censorship. The cause of the tragedy is the disruption of the normal functioning of our society.

My metaphoric diagnosis is social schizophrenia. *This "disorder" is multifactorial in nature, and the responsibility lies not with some abstract "they" but with "us" — a country shaped by its own history, its people, and their collective psychology. For decades we lived under the illusion that internal conflicts could be left unresolved, that time could be played for indefinitely.*

Social schizophrenia contributed to political opponents becoming existential enemies. Each side convinced itself that the opponent's victory would mean the nation's death. *We all became complicit in this social schizophrenia the moment we allowed political fanaticism to displace common sense.* The result was a paralysis of will and the society's inability to unite before an obvious external threat. The unprecedented split — caused by the sabotage of the judicial reform and the attempt to overthrow the legitimate government — undermined trust in the institutions and the rule of law, and created in our enemies' eyes the illusion of strategic vulnerability.

The following parties bear responsibility:

The crisis of Self (identity) in Israeli society — tied to the very concept of the State of Israel as the Jewish national home and to the sharpening of its political and social tensions.

1. The architects of the Oslo deal and of the expulsion of Jews from Gaza.
2. Those who demonized entire sectors of society — religious or secular.
3. The protest forces — the Kaplanists' intifada.
4. The judicial overreach, the media, and the deep state.
5. Political leaders who placed partisan survival above national security.
6. The blind faith in "the wall" — both concrete and digital.
7. Those who turned the army into an instrument of political blackmail.
8. The very "method" of living in a state of permanent division.

The catastrophe of October 7th is the bankruptcy of the entire system of relations we built over the thirty-five years following Oslo.

The tragedy returned us to reality. October 7th became the moment when the energy squandered on internal battles over "truth" was forcibly returned to the real world. It was a brutal reminder that our Self is not a choice but a destiny. On that Saturday, the enemy did not ask who was for the reform and who was against it.

Blood on the doorsteps of homes restored the nation to a state of primordial unity. The shock became a moment of truth: beneath the thin layer of social schizophrenia and hatred, a single people's heart was still beating. But the tragedy lies in the fact that this revelation required a catastrophe.

The lesson is this: if we cannot find internal cohesion — the Self — in peacetime, the enemy will forge it for us through our blood.

"THE QUEUE FOR THE MIRROR"

Setting: *An empty room. On the wall hangs a single large mirror.*

Characters: Opinion leaders, politicians, generals, and ordinary citizens enter one by one.

Politician: *"It's the fault of the left — or the right! They split the people with their slogans; they incited hatred for the sake of ratings!" (The mirror is silent. In the reflection, the politician sees himself signing the budget for yet another project that divides the sectors.)*

General: *"It's the fault of the intelligence! We slept through the threat because politicians dragged us into their games. We trusted in technology instead of people!" (The mirror shows the general who yesterday supported the refusenik protest, or who ignored the lookout-women's border reports.)*

Citizen: *"It's Bibi's fault! The demonstrators' fault! The fault of those who don't serve!" (The mirror shows the citizen who yesterday posted on social media: "Let them burn in hell — they are no longer my brothers.")*

Voice off-screen (the Doctor's): *"Everyone who believed that his own piece of truth constitutes the whole truth is to blame. The system* *that for decades fed us the illusion that one can live in a single state while hating half of it is to blame."*

Through the Psychiatrist's Eyes

Symptomatology: Displacement of blame — mechanism for avoiding acknowledgment of one's own contribution to the catastrophe.

Mechanics of the pathology:

The media is guilty of having turned political dialogue into gladiatorial combat for the sake of audience reach.

The elites — military and judicial — are guilty of having begun to regard themselves as "power above power," forgetting what it means to serve the people.

Politicians are guilty of making "divide and rule" their sole survival strategy.

Verdict: *October 7th is the outcome of all layers of society simultaneously deciding that their private interests outweighed national security. Schizophrenia is when the left hand does not know what the right hand is doing. The Israeli "left hand" (the protest forces) and "right hand" (the government) were, in 2023, attempting to strangle each other while the enemy tightened the noose around both their necks.*

Conclusion

The crisis of the people's Self is a growth disease, complicated by external interference and internal pride. We approached the edge of the abyss, looked into it on October 7th, and recoiled. The task now is not merely to "forget and move on" but to undertake a profound reconstruction of the national consciousness. The Israel of the future is a union of those who have understood: we are one boat on an ocean of fire. I call for a ceasefire within the nation — for the sake of victory over death.

The world looked at us in 2023 as though we were finished. We were written off, called a "collapsing project." But we did what no one expected: we used our catastrophe as fuel for rebirth. We cured our schizophrenia not with pills but with deeds. This book began with the acknowledgment of the profound trauma inflicted upon Israel on October 7, 2023, and with a search for the causes that made the catastrophe possible. Before that day, Israeli society existed in a state of social schizophrenia, division, and internal weakness.

Justice is not when everyone is the same — it is when everyone pays the same price for the same mistake. On October 7th, a terrorist's bullet did not choose between a liberal from Tel Aviv and a Hasid from Bnei Brak. It saw only a Jew. October 7th was an existential warning. Israel is a fortress that its external enemies could not destroy, but one that was nearly brought down by internal self-destruction. Salvation lies in learning anew to respect one another, to serve together, and to speak with one another.

We are a nation that does not know how to "just live." We need either to save the world or to rebuild it. This "high fever" of the spirit makes us invincible in innovation and insufferable in close quarters.

The restoration of the nation requires not merely a ceasefire but a return to common, non-politicised values that held Israeli society together before its disintegration. The key to reducing the divide is the revival of **Derech Eretz — the Way of the Land:** a return to basic human ethics and respect that must precede any religious or political disagreement; the recognition that one's opponent, even when he thinks differently, remains a patriot and a fellow citizen.

The unequal distribution of burdens among the sectors is the primary source of internal anger and division.

The introduction of universal national service — military or civil — for all citizens, including the ultra-Orthodox and Arab sectors, would not only advance social equity but compel representatives of different sectors to interact and serve side by side, overcoming segregation.

Israel in 2050 is not paradise. It is a place where people argue until they are hoarse — but where they know: if darkness descends tomorrow, we will meet it shoulder to shoulder.

Because our "Self" is now not only a shared history but a shared determination never again to bring ourselves to the edge of the abyss.

In 2050, historians will write that Israel of the early twenty-first century stood on the brink of extinction — not because of Iranian rockets, but because of the loss of its Self.

Yet we proved that a start-up nation is capable of the most ambitious "upgrade" in history.

We integrated our contradictions.

We created a society in which religion and progress, tradition and freedom, do not wage war on each other but complement each other.

We passed through darkness in order to learn to value the light of our common home. We are Israel — and we are finally home, not merely in geography but in spirit.

CHAPTER 30.
PALESTINOMANIA

Introduction

Social schizophrenia does not stop at Israel's borders. It is a pandemic: the West, blinded by left-wing progressivism, voluntarily inoculates itself with the "virus" of self-destruction by lending support to those who dream of its destruction.

This essay was not part of the book's original plan. Yet once all the intended chapters had been written, it became clear that I could not pass over in silence the social schizophrenia that has engulfed the countries of the Western world — countries whose masses have been seized by "Palestinomania" and whose streets have been filled with brainwashed pro-Palestinian demonstrators.

Two global themes — Palestinomania and antisemitism — have been deeply implanted in the minds of the obsessed citizens of these countries through the mechanism of Islamization and the process of schizophrenization. Three interrelated but distinct ideological and social processes are fuelling the growth of social schizophrenia across the globe, and all three reinforce one another.

Islamization provides ideological and military support to the Palestinian narrative — and not only to it. The terrorism emanating from the Muslim world did not arise from nowhere; it is the direct consequence of a culture that has preached hatred, jihad, and antisemitism for generations.

Antisemitism is a toxic process that targets not only the State of Israel but Jews throughout the world.

Palestinomania mobilises global masses and furnishes external legitimacy to anti-Israeli actions.

What follows is a concise, reasoned account of each of these processes in the context of the contemporary world.

Islamization

This process describes the growing influence of Islamic norms, identities, and political ideologies in public life — not simply an increase in the number of practising Muslims.

Islamist movements such as the Muslim Brotherhood, Hamas, and the IRGC, which seek to use Islam as the basis of governance, have gained significant political influence.

The conflicts of recent years have become powerful mobilisation tools for Islamist movements against Western and Israeli influence, strengthening Iran's "Axis of Resistance" and its proxies.

Antisemitism

Contemporary antisemitism frequently takes the form of anti-Zionism or criticism of Israel that goes beyond legitimate political debate and escalates into demonisation, double standards, and denial of Israel's right to exist.

The war in Gaza (2023) and Israel's war with Iran (2025) provoked an unprecedented surge in antisemitic incidents worldwide, particularly in the West — in universities and on social media — where criticism of Israeli policy rapidly transformed into direct threats against Jewish communities.

Antisemitism is a foundational element of the ideologies of both Hamas and Iran, making it a direct weapon in the current conflict.

Moscow: The Headquarters of Terror

Moscow's role in this spectacle is that of a cynical puppeteer. The Kremlin, which itself flattens cities with rockets, has suddenly expressed "concern" for the inhabitants of Gaza. This is not mere double standards — it is the complete absence of any standards whatsoever. By receiving Hamas leaders as honoured guests, Russia has definitively chosen its side in the global confrontation: it has placed itself at the head of an internationale of death. Moscow trades on Western fear, using the Palestinian question as a smokescreen for its own crimes. **This is geopolitical schizophrenia: claiming the mantle of "guardian of tradition" while sponsoring those who hold those traditions in contempt.**

The following account draws on the article by Lieutenant General Ion Mihai Pacepa— the highest-ranking intelligence officer of the Warsaw Pact countries ever to defect from the Soviet Bloc to the West — author of "Red Horizons," published in twenty-seven countries. The article was published on 24 August 2006 in National Review Online.

Today's international terrorism was conceived in the KGB offices on the Lubyanka immediately after the Six-Day War of 1967. In 1972, the Kremlin resolved to turn the entire Muslim world against Israel and the United States. We were directed to plant in the Muslim world a hatred of Jews comparable to that which the Nazis had cultivated, and to use that hatred as a weapon of mass bloodshed against Israel and its principal partner, the United States. The plan stipulated that no one "in the American-Zionist sphere of influence" should ever feel safe again.

According to Andropov, the Muslim world was the nutrient solution into which the bacillus of deadly anti-American hatred — grown on the yeast of Marxism-Leninism — was to be introduced and cultivated. And indeed, antisemitism took deep root in the natural medium of Islam. Muslims are accustomed to the tastes of nationalism, jingoism, and sacrifice. Suppressed and depersonalised masses can easily be whipped into hysteria.

Terrorism and acts of violence against Israel and the United States would, according to Andropov, be the "natural" consequence of religious zeal. We had only to repeat familiar slogans — that the USA and Israel were "fascist, imperialist, Zionist countries" in thrall to "Jewish capital." Islamic rhetoric centres on preventing the seizure of Middle Eastern lands by "the godless"; these slogans would easily be absorbed — and the US Congress portrayed as a malevolent instrument of Zionists bent on turning the entire world into their dominion.

In the mid-1970s we began flooding the Muslim world with copies of an Arabic translation of the Protocols of the Elders of Zion — a Tsarist-era Russian forgery that Hitler had used with great effect in constructing his antisemitic philosophy. We also distributed a KGB-fabricated article in Arabic claiming that Israel and its principal patron, the USA, were Zionist countries intent on reducing the entire Islamic world to a Jewish colony.

The role of Moscow in feeding "Palestinomania" is not diplomacy but geopolitical trolling. By receiving Hamas leaders in the Kremlin within days of the October 7th massacre, Russia signalled to the entire "Global South": terror against the West and its allies is legitimate. Moscow uses the Palestinian question as a battering ram against American hegemony, converting human suffering into a bargaining chip in its war against Ukraine and NATO. This is a cynical alliance of two "schizophrenias": imperial nostalgia and radical Islamism.

Palestinomania — Part One

Palestinomania is the terminal point of the cognitive disintegration of Western liberalism. When LGBT activists and feminists march with placards in support of Hamas, we are witnessing clinical Stockholm syndrome on a civilisational scale. These are people marching under the banners of those who would throw them off a rooftop first. This is not solidarity — it is civilisational schizophrenia: the desire to destroy one's own foundations (Israel as the West's forward operating base) in order to earn the approval of the barbarism that styles itself "the oppressed."

The term Palestinomania does not belong to mainstream contemporary political discourse, though it does appear in literature of the 1970s, where it is used critically or ironically. Israeli and Jewish publications of that era — such as the journal Zion (1974) — describe it as "a new, strange illness": an obsession with the idea of Palestine closely associated with anti-Israeli sentiment. The book The Third Temple (1975) refers to it as a "probable illness" born of political illusions surrounding Palestine. In contemporary usage the term surfaces as a metaphor for the "irrational" or "disproportionate" global support for Palestine — particularly in social media, where critics see in it a systematic disregard for Hamas's terrorist character. According to The Economist (2023), social-media support for Palestine is four times greater than support for Israel.

Palestinomania describes the process by which the Palestinian narrative becomes the central, unifying theme for disparate global movements and political forces — a universal lens for criticising colonialism, global inequality, and Western dominance, in which Palestinian identity and suffering become the symbol of the "Global South's" struggle against the "Global North."

It unites Islamist movements, left-wing activist groups, and human rights organisations. As a result, any conflict involving Israel automatically acquires a global, moral-political dimension that transcends regional boundaries.

It is not, however, justified by facts, nor grounded in genuine humanitarian principles.

Solidarity with Murderers

Solidarity with the Palestinian people is routinely conflated with support for Hamas or Hezbollah. Such conflation provides indirect justification for terrorism. Critics argue that support for Palestine constitutes a form of Stockholm syndrome for those who fear comparable outcomes in their own societies. Accusations of "supporting murderers" are frequently deployed to discredit the movement as a whole.

Ultimately, legitimacy depends on context: supporting the civil rights of Palestinians is lawful under international law; solidarity with terrorist acts is not.

Double Standards

Global attention to the Israeli-Palestinian conflict is disproportionate relative to other armed conflicts — in Nigeria, Sudan, or Ukraine. This disproportion is explained by an unprecedented convergence of factors.

For the first time, a major armed conflict is being transmitted in near real time through social media. Video footage of civilian casualties and destruction circulates immediately, bypassing the traditional editorial filters of mainstream media and creating a previously impossible sense of emotional immediacy.

Many countries in Asia, Africa, and Latin America perceive the conflict through the prism of their own colonial histories. For the Arab and Muslim world, events in Gaza carry the weight of a profound personal tragedy and national humiliation, evoking powerful emotional responses and mass mobilisation.

A Resonant Speech at the United Nations

Rawan Osman — a civic activist of Lebanese-Syrian background — has earned international recognition for her uncompromising stance on the Middle East. Having grown up in an environment saturated with anti-Israeli propaganda, she absorbed hostile views toward Jews from childhood. After relocating to Europe, however, her worldview changed: direct encounter with Israeli society and study of Jewish history led her to the realisation that her peoples' true adversary was not Israel. She appeared before the UN Human Rights Council and directly declared the hypocrisy of the states of the region:

"If you are outraged by the war in Gaza — so am I. My name is Rawan Osman; I am half Lebanese, half Syrian. Since October 7th I have visited Israel nine times and can state with complete certainty: Israel is not the problem. But those who accuse Israel would do well to look in the mirror."

She then addressed the governments of several Arab states with pointed questions:

To Qatar: "Why, instead of arresting Hamas's leaders in Doha, do you continue to finance them?"

To Iran: "Why do you send billions of dollars to Hamas and Hezbollah rather than liberating your own people from oppression and poverty?"

To Egypt: "You charged Gaza residents thousands of dollars for the opportunity to flee the war. How do you speak of morality while condemning the displacement of Palestinian Arabs?"

To Jordan: "Why did you refuse to receive Gaza residents? Are they not your people?"

To Lebanon: "Instead of debating Hezbollah's political role — ban it!"

To Syria: "If your new president is sincere in his desire for change, I ask him to return the body of Eli Cohen. Six decades have passed. Allow his wife to bury him while she is still alive."

Her unsparing remarks caused visible shock among the Arab delegations; the video spread rapidly across the internet. (Source: Rami Madrich.)

"A ONE-WAY TICKET"

Setting: *A tent encampment on the Columbia University campus. Placards: "Queers for Palestine."*

Characters: Chloe (an activist in pink-rimmed glasses) and Ahmed (a radical protest coordinator).

Chloe *(enthusiastically): Ahmed, we're winning! The university will soon agree to our divestment demands. Together we will build a free Palestine — a place for everyone: gay people, feminists, all of us!*

Ahmed *(with a barely perceptible smirk): Of course, Chloe. Your energy is very... useful. Right now.*

Chloe: *I dream of going to Gaza and organising a Pride festival there — to show them our solidarity!*

Ahmed *(turning his back, whispering in Arabic): If you come to Gaza, you foolish girl, the only thing you will see is the bottom of a pit before they stone you. But for now — shout louder. We need your voice on CNN.*

Voice off-screen: "Schizophrenia at its terminal stage: defending a regime that will destroy you first, simply to feel like a 'good person' on TikTok."

Who Organises the Protests?

Western universities have ceased to be temples of knowledge and have become incubators of social schizophrenia. The mechanics are straightforward: over the past two decades, Arab states have invested billions of dollars in American universities. This is not philanthropy — it is the purchase of intellectual space. The funds have created academic departments where Marxist professors teach students the "correct" history — one in which Israel is "white colonial evil." The result is a generation of intellectual zombies. When a Harvard student shouts "Globalize Intifada!" he does not understand that he is calling for massacre. He is merely executing a Qatari grant that has been embedded in his brain under the guise of "fighting for justice." It is intellectual prostitution disguised as academic freedom.

Why do eighteen-year-old Harvard students parrot jihadi slogans? Because the Palestinian narrative has been perfectly packaged for social-media algorithms. Complex historical facts have been replaced by fifteen-second clips with emotionally charged montages, in which the aggressor is invariably a victim and democracy invariably an oppressor. This is induced psychosis delivered through a smartphone screen.

Palestinomania has become the new religion for those who have lost their faith — offering them a simple and poisonous binary picture of the world: black and white, oppressor and oppressed. The mass pro-Palestinian demonstrations that began after the Hamas massacre of October 7, 2023, are organised in character, coordinated through networks of activists, NGOs, and social movements.

Key players, based on available data: in the United States, the principal organisers include the U.S. Campaign for Palestinian Rights (USCPR), Jewish Voice for Peace (JVP), Within Our Lifetime, and student groups such as Students for Justice in Palestine (SJP). In Europe and the United Kingdom, the Palestine Solidarity Campaign (PSC) is a leading force; in the UK, Palestine Action — supported by private donors — coordinates many actions. In India, the Communist Party has led demonstrations. The Palestine Action Group organises events in Australia, and the Global March to Gaza coordinates activity internationally.

"DINNER AT HARVARD"

Setting: *A prestigious American university campus; a tent city in the student quarter.*

Characters: Sara (a sociology student, keffiyeh draped over a branded hoodie) and her Professor.

Sara *(enthusiastically): Professor, did you see yesterday's march? We are finally on the right side of history! Death to colonialism! From the river to the sea!*

Professor *(nodding): Brilliant, Sara. You are the voice of conscience. You do understand that Israel is an anachronism?*

Sara: *Yes! It is so inspiring! By the way, I plan to volunteer in Gaza after the semester — I want to help women in their struggle for rights...*

(The Professor pauses for a second, knowing that in Gaza Sara would at best find herself in a basement, and at worst face the fate of the hostages taken on October 7th. He merely adjusts his glasses and smiles.)

Professor: *A courageous decision, Sara. Just don't forget to post stories — that is very important for our "struggle."*

Voice off-screen: *"Schizophrenia in its purest form: travelling to those who despise your way of life in order to defend their 'right' to destroy you. A generation raised on TikTok has lost the instinct of self-preservation along with its history textbooks."*

Umbrella Coalitions and Financing

The pro-Palestinian movement is sustained by a broad coalition: left-wing and anti-globalist organisations traditionally opposed to US and Israeli foreign policy; the BDS (Boycott, Divestment, Sanctions) movement and allied groups; and organisations of Muslim and Arab diaspora communities, who play a central role in mobilising participants. In a number of countries, protests are directly organised or patronised by political leaders —

in Turkey, for instance, large Istanbul rallies have been held under the patronage of President Erdoğan's administration.

Qatar occupies a particularly significant position: a Trojan horse embedded within the Ivy League. Over the past twenty years, Doha has channelled more than thirteen billion dollars into American universities — a long-term investment not in philanthropy but in the systematic erosion of critical thinking. With this money, academic chairs were purchased, curricula financed, and "institutes of justice research" established that have spent years instilling in students the idea that Israel is the root of all global evil. In 2024, Qatar received its dividends: thousands of Harvard and Columbia students took to the streets chanting "Allahu Akbar," unaware that they were serving as infantry in someone else's religious war.

Additional financing flows from private donors and foundations — among them major liberal sponsors such as George Soros, the Rockefeller Brothers Fund, the Pritzker family, and the Bill and Melinda Gates Foundation, whose grants often reach pro-Palestinian organisations by indirect routes. Iran encourages and funds some protests through proxies such as Hezbollah. Reports also document Chinese Communist Party influence on pro-Palestinian activism in the United States, with links to Singham-associated networks. Crowdfunding platforms and organisations such as the Tides Network — which, according to Congressional investigations, channelled support to groups connected with Palestinian activism — complete the picture.

Schizophrenization

"Schizophrenization through Palestinomania" describes a state of deep cognitive and social rupture on a global scale. The same events are perceived in radically opposite ways by opposing sides, generating parallel realities and an inability to dialogue — a condition exacerbated by social-media echo chambers and media polarisation.

The loss of a unified, widely accepted understanding of truth, morality, and the legitimacy of actions leads to a crisis of international law and institutions. In Europe, signs of schizophrenization are intensifying, driven by migration crises, digital deviance, and political polarisation.

Metaphorically, schizophrenization manifests in the dominance of simulacra — signs without a real referent — and a regression to primitive thinking. EU societies exhibit a growth in "negative symptoms": social withdrawal, loss of motivation, and cognitive deficits.

Psychological, Social, and Cultural Signs

Psychological signs: a split in consciousness — events perceived as "real" on the basis of media imagery rather than verified facts; permanent frustration, manifesting as anxiety, irritability, and despair; and negative symptoms including social withdrawal, loss of motivation, and emotional flatness.

Social signs: a degradation-and-crisis pattern marked by rising unemployment, declining living standards, and the collapse of governmental legitimacy; deviant behaviour adopted as political protest; and stigma-driven isolation, particularly among migrants, who experience systemic barriers to integration.

Cultural and ideological signs: the dominance of simulacra in culture and politics; gender and identity distortions normalised through activist propaganda; and a regression to primitive thinking, enabled by postmodernism as the ideology of schizophrenization.

Through the Psychiatrist's Eyes

Symptomatology: selective blindness. The patient sees "genocide" where a defensive operation is under way and "freedom" where terror reigns.

Mechanics of invasion:

The Qatari financial syringe — billions of dollars poured into American universities over decades have produced an army of compliant "zombies."

The Russian-Iranian alliance — Moscow supplies the ideological framing ("anti-colonialism"); Tehran supplies the "cannon fodder."

Media narcosis — the BBC, CNN, and Al Jazeera function as a single intravenous drip, administering poison around the clock.

Verdict: "Palestinomania" is a form of collective insanity in which the survival instinct of a civilisation has been completely paralysed. The West has become the "useful idiot" in the hands of those who are already sharpening a knife for its throat.

Palestinomania has become, for the Western man in the street, a new form of civic religion. In a world that has lost its meanings, the "struggle for Palestine" provides the illusion of moral superiority at zero personal cost.

This is schizophrenia by calculation:

For Ivy League students — it is a way to feel like "revolutionaries" without leaving the comfort zone.

For the European left — it is an attempt to atone for colonial guilt by designating Israel as "the last coloniser."

For Islamist structures — it is an instrument of soft expansion, with Western liberals willingly serving as "useful idiots" in the service of the caliphate.

The Islamization of Europe, 1990–2025

The term "Islamization" denotes not only the growth of the Muslim population in Europe but also the cultural, social, and political changes associated with its integration — or, increasingly, its deliberate non-integration. Over the past thirty-five years, Europe has faced a succession of crises and protests that illustrate the complexity of this process.

The demographic transformation is stark: France has between six and eight million Muslims (approximately 10% of the population); Germany, approximately 5.5 million (6.5%); the United Kingdom, 4.4 million (6.5%); Sweden, approximately 800,000 (8%).

Millions of Muslims have no intention of integrating, and are actively imposing their way of life on the host societies. What is under way is a strategic expansion of radical elements without an adequate defensive response from populations, legislators, or governments. European countries that today are not stinting in their condemnation of Israel will soon be compelled to study our bitter experience of "peaceful coexistence" with populations that feel not like guests in the house but like its owners.

The culture war has not been slow to arrive. Key episodes:

Denmark, 2005–2006: The "Cartoon Crisis." Mass protests by Muslims across Europe following the publication of caricatures of the Prophet Muhammad. Danish Islamists called for jihad and the introduction of sharia law, waving flags bearing the shahada and Al-Qaeda insignia: "One umma — one victory."

Germany, 2014–2016: The PEGIDA movement (Patriotic Europeans Against the Islamization of the West) began street demonstrations in Dresden, expressing a significant section of the population's anxiety about Islamization and mass migration.

United Kingdom, 2017: Protests following the terrorist attacks in Manchester and London — mixed demonstrations, for and against Islamism.

France, 2023: Mass riots following the death of Naël M., a seventeen-year-old of Algerian descent. Disorder spread to dozens of cities; special police units were deployed. Underlying causes: social isolation and deep-seated grievances over perceived injustice.

BLM Europe, 2020: The wave following the murder of George Floyd — marches, toppling of monuments, sit-down protests, decolonisation debates, and street renamings.

France — "Block Everything", spring–autumn 2025: Major actions involving road blockades, sabotage, and barricades, resulting in hundreds of arrests, the deployment of water cannons and tear gas, and serious political destabilisation.

The Islamization of Europe is not a single process, but a complex interplay of demographics, politics, and cultural conflicts. It manifests itself most clearly in protests, laws, and social transformations.

Britain for the British

On 13 September 2025, London hosted the largest anti-illegal-migration rally in decades. More than one hundred thousand people, rallying under the leadership of far-right activist Tommy Robinson, demonstrated against migrants and called for the resignation of the government. A peaceful action ultimately gave way to clashes with police and dozens of arrests. Anti-immigration sentiment in Britain had been building gradually, reaching a peak in August after an Ethiopian immigrant was charged with raping a schoolgirl.

Far-right outbursts and demands to deport migrants and asylum seekers are not new to the United Kingdom: they flare up reliably whenever the press reports crimes committed by migrants or those of migrant background. In summer 2024 the right-wing wave was inflamed by the Southport massacre, in which an assailant whose parents had emigrated from Rwanda burst into a children's dance studio with a knife and stabbed three young girls to death.

Simultaneously, a counter-demonstration of approximately five thousand left-wing activists marched in favour of open borders. Experts note that the migration question has become the central driver of Britain's social divide and ultimately of Brexit.

This year, the Emmy Awards ceremony was also transformed into an anti-Israeli performance by hypocritical figures who have no understanding of the realities of the Middle East but who understand perfectly that identifying with Palestinians will earn them support within their own industry. Once again they wore red "bloody-hand" badges — devised as a counter to the yellow hostage badges. Javier Bardem appeared in a keffiyeh; Jewish actress Hannah Einbinder, accepting an Emmy for best supporting performance in a comedy, concluded her speech on stage with the cry "Free Palestine!" When one sees a Jewish woman trying to win their approval and instead becoming a useful idiot, she too deserves an award — for best actress in a tragicomedy.

Antisemitism in Europe

The period from 2020 to 2025 was marked by a substantial rise in antisemitism across Europe, confirmed by data from the Anti-Defamation League (ADL), the European Union Agency for Fundamental Rights (FRA), and national monitoring bodies. Antisemitism took the forms of physical violence, vandalism, online harassment, and discrimination.

Key triggers included the COVID-19 pandemic, the Russia-Ukraine conflict, and, most powerfully, the events of October 7, 2023, after which the number of incidents rose sharply and, in some countries, severalfold. According to ADL data, the sharpest rises — particularly in violent incidents — were recorded in countries with the largest Jewish communities.

2020–2022: Rising against the pandemic backdrop. Pew Research recorded anti-Jewish incidents in ninety-four countries; approximately 371 violent incidents were registered globally, a significant proportion within the EU.

2023–2025: Explosive growth after October 7, 2023. The FRA reported increases of up to 400% in some countries. In the UK alone, more than 1,500 incidents were recorded in the first half of 2025. Online antisemitism accounted for 35–62% of all cases in 2024–2025.

Causes of the surge: the Middle East conflict (30–62% of incidents referenced Israel/Palestine); pandemic-era conspiracy theories blaming Jews for a "world plot"; political extremism of both left and right, including Islamist groups; social-media algorithms amplifying hate content; and, in some analyses, the social tensions generated by immigration from the Middle East.

Antisemitism in Europe reached a historic peak in the period 2020–2025, threatening both democratic values and the security of Jewish communities.

Why Did the World "Normalise" the October 7th Massacre?

The world has not merely "normalised" the October 7th massacre — it has institutionalised it. Western universities, the press, and international organisations have converted rape and the murder of children into a "contextually justified act of resistance." This is the highest point of moral disintegration: the moment when a civilisation that built itself on humanism begins to kiss the boot of the one who has come to slaughter it.

"A LECTURE ON SELF-LIQUIDATION"

Setting: *An auditorium at Yale University.*

Characters: A professor of political science and a student from Israel.

Professor *(dictating to the hall): "Thus, decolonisation is not a metaphor. It is a violent process, and on October 7th we saw it in action. We must evaluate this through the prism of the struggle of the oppressed..."*

Student *(rising, voice trembling): Professor — my friend was shot dead there. My sister was kidnapped. What "prism" justifies rape?*

Professor *(coldly)*: *You are too emotional, young man. You cannot see the "structural oppression." Your personal tragedy is merely a* *statistical rounding error in the process of liberating the Global South. Sit down.*

Voice off-screen: *"When elite education becomes a factory for the rationalization of barbarism, civilisation forfeits its claim to a future. This is intellectual suicide, paid for out of someone else's pocket."*

***

"Palestinomania" is not a struggle for human rights. It is a virus of self-hatred, in which the white European or American attempts to expiate imaginary past sins by sacrificing the only democracy in the Middle East. They do not love the Palestinians — they simply hate themselves and fear those who are prepared to kill.

In the global discourse following October 7th, a paradox is evident: despite the condemnation of the attack by many world leaders, solidarity with Palestine rapidly became a viral trend in social media, protests, and mainstream press, often eclipsing the horror of the attack itself.

I interpret this as the "normalisation" of the massacre. It comprises: the denial of facts (videos of the rapes dismissed as "fakes"); relativisation ("the context of occupation justifies it"); a focus on disproportionality (1,200 victims of October 7th versus 40,000-plus in Gaza, framed so as to marginalise the original crime); and conspiracy theories, with 20–30% of respondents in Europe and the United States, according to polls, believing in "exaggerations" about October 7th.

In Africa and Latin America, the attack has been framed as an "anti-imperialist act" against a "US ally." The BBC and CNN were accused of bias — devoting more coverage to Gaza and less to October 7th. For pro-Israeli analysts, the trend represents support for terror; for neutral observers, it reflects a polarisation in which the events of October 7th dissolve into the broader narrative of occupation.

Solidarity with Palestine

After October 7th, the "Free Palestine" hashtag exploded across TikTok, Instagram, and X, amassing billions of views, and global protests multiplied. The key drivers were:

The humanitarian crisis in Gaza as the dominant narrative. Israel's military response (Operation Iron Swords) caused extensive destruction of Gaza's infrastructure, a blockade, and many thousands of casualties including children. Images of ruins and Palestinian suffering — particularly among young people — generated strong empathy. According to Pew Research (2024), 60% of millennials and Generation Z in the United States approach the conflict by focusing on casualties in Gaza rather than on October 7th.

Anticolonial and anti-imperialist framing. The attack was incorporated into the narrative of "resistance to occupation": Palestinians and their Western supporters describe it as a "response to seventy-six years of apartheid" (Amnesty International's term). This resonates with the Black Lives Matter movement and climate activism, in which Israel is positioned as "the coloniser." Reuters (2023) noted that support for Hamas among Palestinians rose from 12% to 42% after October 7th, reinforcing the "liberation struggle" narrative.

The role of social-media algorithms. Platforms amplified pro-Palestinian content: TikTok was accused of systematic bias.

Posts on X range from Palestinian condemnations of October 7th to celebrations in Gaza, demonstrating the full depth of the polarisation.

In Europe and the United States, left-liberal circles — universities, celebrities, cultural institutions — saw in October 7th a revival of the Palestinian cause that had been forgotten since Oslo.

The UN and UNRWA — The Black Hole of World Conscience

The UN and UNRWA are not merely international structures — they are the black hole of world conscience, where humanism has definitively been inverted into its opposite. Here, social schizophrenia has been given the force of law and a budget of billions of dollars.

"The Virus of Self-Liquidation"

(A Psychiatric Diagnosis for Groups Such as JVP — Jewish Voice for Peace)

The most grotesque manifestation of 'Palestinomania' is the participation of Jews themselves in it. In psychiatry this resembles 'auto-aggression.' This is a pathological turning of destructive impulses against oneself.

Syndrome of Acquired Deficiency of Meaning

Symptomatology: complete loss of the instinct of self-preservation in the elite of Western society and part of the Jewish diaspora. Mechanism of invasion: Qatari financial virus — the replacement of education with propaganda. Social mimicry: the need to 'be like everyone else' in the liberal milieu forces one to switch off logic. Traumatic alienation: anti-Zionist Jews attempt to cure their 'inferiority' through betrayal. Verdict: this is not politics — it is pathology.

The Qatari financial virus: the replacement of education with propaganda.

Social mimicry: the need to 'be like everyone else' in the liberal milieu forces logic to shut down.

Traumatic alienation: anti-Zionist Jews attempt to cure their 'inferiority' through betrayal. Verdict: this is not politics — this is pathology.

"SALARY FOR DEATH"

Setting: *UN Headquarters, Geneva or New York. A lavishly appointed office.*

Characters: A UN official (in an expensive suit) and a field coordinator from Gaza.

Official (reviewing a report): *We have a complaint here from Israel. They claim that a Hamas command centre and a data facility were discovered under your school in Gaza. What am I to tell them?*

Coordinator *(impassively): Tell them we are "deeply concerned." And remind them that we have run out of fuel. If they don't provide more, we will declare a humanitarian catastrophe live on CNN.*

Official *(stamps it "APPROVED"): Reasonable. By the way, please tell the staff: when they are filming videos for TikTok against the* *backdrop of rubble, they should remove the UN-logo vests. It looks... inelegant in reports for EU donors.*

Voice off-screen: *"When evil dons a blue helmet, it becomes untouchable. This is the moral paralysis of the world community — too afraid to acknowledge that it is financing its own destruction."*

***

The contemporary UN is a collective psychotherapist for dictatorships. Countries in which human rights are entirely absent sit on human rights commissions and stamp out resolutions against Israel. The number of UN condemnations directed at Israel exceeds the total number of resolutions against all other countries in the world combined. This is not politics — it is manic obsession. The UN has become the headquarters of social schizophrenia, a place where the words "peace" and "justice" are deployed to legitimise medieval barbarism. The Secretary-General's statement that the massacre "did not occur in a vacuum" amounted to issuing a global licence for terror.

Double Standards

The accusations against the ICC of bias and double standards are well documented.

Critics point out that the ICC devotes a disproportionate amount of attention to Israel, while governments and military commanders of other states — responsible for far greater losses among civilians — escape prosecution.

Israel and its allies argue that antisemitic and anti-Israel movements are using international legal instruments to delegitimize the Jewish state.

Israel faces an unprecedented legal challenge: it is waging war against a group that deliberately uses civilian infrastructure — hospitals, schools, mosques — as military bases, forcing Israel into an impossible choice: defend itself or be accused of attacking civilians.

The Hamas Massacre of 7 October

The key argument against unconditional support for the Palestinians is the terrorist character of Hamas and the crimes committed on 7 October 2023.

The cause of the war: Israel's military operation in Gaza, which triggered a global wave of protests, was the direct response to the Hamas invasion of southern Israel on 7 October 2023 — the largest massacre of Jews since the Holocaust.

The use of civilians as a 'human shield': Israel and its supporters argue that Hamas deliberately uses civilian infrastructure as military bases, making any military response to Hamas fire appear to be an attack on civilians.

The refusal to recognize Israel: the ideology of Hamas and Iran (the foundation of the 'Axis of Resistance') denies Israel's right to exist and openly calls for the destruction of the Jewish state and the killing of Jews — everywhere in the world.

The Right to Self-Defense

International law and the basic principles of security permit a state's retaliatory actions following an attack.

Compliance with international law: Israel argues that, although its actions do result in tragic losses among civilians, it complies with international humanitarian law, providing warnings before strikes and coordinating humanitarian corridors.

A unique threat: no other country in the world faces a constant threat from forces positioned so close to its population centers, so deeply embedded in the civilian infrastructure of a neighboring territory.

Criticism of Double Standards

This argument concerns the global 'schizophrenic' focus on Israel, which ignores other, far larger humanitarian crises.

Ignoring other conflicts: supporters of Israel point to the double standards of the world community. Against the backdrop of millions of victims in the wars in Syria, Yemen, Libya, and Myanmar, the world is focused precisely on Israel — a country that is defending itself after the bloodiest terrorist attack in the history of the state.

Morality in geopolitics: many moderate Arab states (such as Saudi Arabia and the UAE), while criticizing Israel, are nevertheless establishing ties with it, recognizing that stability in the region requires the inclusion of Israel rather than its destruction.

Moral Agnosia of the United Nations

Symptomatology: Complete inability to recognise and condemn evil — specifically, terror — when it is directed against Israel.

Mechanics of the pathology: Bureaucratic parasitism — thousands of UNRWA employees depend on the continuation of the conflict; peace is their principal enemy, for it would eliminate their positions. ***Diplomatic schizophrenia — decisions made on the basis of a "majority" composed of tyrannies and autocracies.*** Corruption of meaning — the conversion of humanitarian aid into resources for terrorist infrastructure.

Verdict: The organisation created to prevent catastrophes has become their primary catalyst. The UN today is an institution afflicted with gangrene that, rather than healing, transmits the infection of madness to the entire planet.

The Destructive Role of Iran

Support for Israel is frequently motivated by the need to confront the wider, destabilising force in the region — Iran and its ideology.

Iran as the root of the problem: Iran is alleged to be the principal sponsor and coordinator of all forces hostile to Israel, constituting the "Axis of Resistance." The direct war of 2025 made Iran's intentions unmistakable. For many countries, supporting Israel is the means of containing Iranian regional hegemony and its nuclear ambitions.

The antisemitism dimension: the global surge in antisemitism documented above demonstrates that many protests that began as solidarity with Palestine rapidly degenerate into direct antisemitism and threats against Jewish communities. For Western governments, supporting Israel is both a moral obligation in light of the Holocaust and a practical necessity in the face of contemporary antisemitic hatred.

Palestinomania — Part Two

This phenomenon is not merely a "mania" but a compound of antisemitism, historical grievance, media dynamics, geopolitics, and social factors. It is a complex global phenomenon — the disproportionate worldwide attention devoted to the Palestinian conflict, which genuinely stands apart from other tragedies (the wars in Sudan, Ukraine, and the humanitarian crisis in Yemen). Let us examine it methodically, drawing on data available as of September 2025.

Jews Were Palestinians

Before the establishment of the State of Israel, the term "Palestinians" was applied to the Jews living in the region of Mandatory Palestine under the British Mandate (1920–1948). The Jewish newspaper The Palestine Post (founded in 1932) later became The Jerusalem Post. Arabs in the region predominantly identified themselves as "Arabs" or "Southern Syrians" rather than as a distinct "Palestinian people" — a concept that crystallised only in the 1960s, with the founding of the PLO.

Why "Palestinomania"?

Global attention to Palestinians is indeed disproportionate relative to other conflicts — hundreds of thousands have died in Sudan, yet far fewer protests have been held. The key drivers as of 2025:

Media and social networks: the conflict is highly visual — video of destruction in Gaza and protest footage spread virally. TikTok, Instagram, and X algorithms amplify content and create echo chambers. Demonstrations often have a "festive" quality — music, flags, performance — drawn from the activist playbook of movements like BLM, making the topic "fashionable" among young people and left-wing circles.

Geopolitics and symbolism: Palestine symbolises struggle against colonialism, imperialism, and "Western hegemonism." UN resolutions on "occupation" give the topic global institutional standing.

The BDS movement (Boycott, Divestment, Sanctions) and campus pro-Palestinian groups keep the issue permanently visible. The Palestinian conflict has lasted decades, commands a substantial diaspora, and enjoys the financial and political backing of Iran and Turkey — advantages that conflicts in Sudan or the Congo lack.

Recognition of Palestine as "Schizophrenism"

Recognition of Palestine as a state is a diplomatic instrument; it is not the literal creation of a viable, functioning state. ***The recognition of Palestine by European countries in the wake of October 7th is the highest expression of political schizophrenism.*** In psychiatry, a split personality is characterised by the suppression of reality in favour of hallucination. Europe's "hallucination" consists in recognising a "state" that:

1) **Has no unified authority — Fatah is in open conflict with Hamas;**
2) **Has no recognised borders;**

3) **Has a significant portion of its political spectrum openly committed to the destruction of a neighbouring state.**
4) **To recognise a "state" in response to massacre, rape, and mass kidnapping is to reward terror.**
5) **This is social schizophrenia: Europe believes it is treating the conflict; in reality it is feeding the virus that will tomorrow arrive in its own cities under the same flags.**

By September 2025, more than 140 countries have recognised Palestine, including recent additions: the UK, Canada, Australia, France, Belgium, and Portugal. The decision is deeply contradictory — simultaneously an expression of diplomatic "schizophrenism" (internal incoherence) and a calculated political instrument.

Critics' central argument: recognition of Palestine in the aftermath of October 7th is perceived as a reward for terrorism, undermining the principle of negotiated peace in preference to violent pressure. What is being recognised is a state that controls neither of its principal territories — Gaza being governed by Hamas (a designated terrorist organisation) and the West Bank by a weakened PA — and that is economically non-self-sufficient, with a GDP per capita of approximately $3,000 and unemployment in Gaza running at 25–50%.

Supporters counter that with the peace process dead and settlement expansion on the West Bank continuing to undermine the two-state solution, recognition is an attempt to keep the option alive, to exercise non-violent diplomatic pressure, and to strengthen the moderate PA against the radicals. In the end, recognition of Palestine is an act of diplomacy aimed at preserving a political solution — but its timing (in the midst of active warfare) leads critics to regard it as precisely the kind of schizophrenism described here.

Palestine as a Symbol for the Masses

Palestinomania is not a political position — it is a surrogate religion. In the postmodern era, when the old gods have died and the great ideologies have been discredited, the Western subject needed a new object of devotion and hatred. Palestine was the perfect candidate for the role of "eternal victim" and Israel for the role of "absolute evil" — because it allows adherents to:

- Experience moral ecstasy without rising from the sofa.
- Find a simple explanation for the world's complex problems.
- Legalise covert antisemitism by repackaging it as "anti-Zionism."

The world chose Palestine as its fetish because it enables Western liberals to feel like heroes fighting "colonialism" while actually sustaining the most obscurantist forms of fundamentalism. For left-wing and anti-colonial activists, Palestine is the arena in which the West is put to the test of its own proclaimed values. The protests of 2024–2025 amplified this dynamic: the Palestinian flag became an icon of resistance, and Palestinian identity a screen onto which anti-American and antisemitic ideas are projected.

What truly drives the "fuss" over Palestinians, beneath the surface humanitarian concern, is a set of ideological and psychological needs: the pursuit of moral capital and social belonging (the keffiyeh as virtue-signalling, protest as a substitute for genuine engagement); antisemitism and a displaced hostility toward "the West" routed through the proxy of Palestinians-as-victims and Israel-as-evil; and an anti-colonial identity politics that offers the "Global South" and the Western left a readymade narrative of "the oppressed against the oppressor."

"THE MIRROR OF PALESTINOMANIA"

Setting: *A coffee shop in Oslo or Dublin.*

Characters: Thomas (a humanist intellectual) and Mark (a journalist recently returned from the Middle East).

Thomas *(signing a petition): We are obliged to recognise Palestine now. It is the only path to peace — an act of the highest justice.*

Mark: *Thomas, I was there. Hamas turned schools into rocket depots, and their leaders openly say October 7th will happen again and again. Who, exactly, are you recognising? Those who hold children as hostages?*

Thomas *(irritably): You are too fixated on details, Mark. That is mere "context." The point is the idea. Palestine is a symbol of oppression. We are recognising the dream of freedom!*

Mark: *But this "dream" intends to kill your reality. If they come here with sharia, you will be the first one they arrest.*

Thomas *(smiling): You are simply an Islamophobe. Justice is above fear.*

Voice off-screen: *"This is Palestinomania — the willingness to sacrifice real people and one's own safety for the sake of a beautiful but poisonous symbol."*

Through the Psychiatrist's Eyes: Inversion of Meaning

Symptomatology: the aggressor is perceived as victim. Documented facts (Hamas's own footage) are ignored; disinformation is accepted as truth.

Mechanics: the world gazes at "Palestine" as into a distorting mirror. Western leftists see the "struggle against oppression"; Islamists see a "holy war"; Russia sees the "collapse of the West." No one sees the actual Palestinians, or the actual Israelis.

Verdict: "Palestinomania" is the world's mechanism for avoiding the resolution of its own problems, by projecting all its accumulated hatred and failure onto a tiny patch of land. It is a collective psychosis — curable only by collision with hard, irrefutable reality.

The Pro-Palestinian "Bacchanalia"

At the Glastonbury music festival in the United Kingdom — broadcast live by the BBC — the crowds chanted, among other things, "Death to the IDF." The rapper Bob Vylan was "warming up" the audience before the headline performance of the Northern Irish band Kneecap, widely regarded as purveyors of rock antisemitism. The crowd, waving Palestinian flags, took up the chant. Organisers and police pretended not to notice. When Bob Vylan proceeded to sing about "Jewish bastards," "fucking Zionists," and "sages weaving conspiracies," the BBC broadcast continued uninterrupted. The British government expressed "shock" and "deep concern" and issued a formal rebuke to the BBC — and that was the end of the matter.

"THE CARNIVAL IN LONDON"

(The surrealism of what is taking place)

Setting: *Trafalgar Square. An enormous crowd.*

Characters: Claire (an LGBTQ+ activist) and Mohammed (a radical street preacher).

Claire *(holding a placard: "Queers for Palestine"): We are here to stop genocide! Freedom for Gaza! We stand for inclusivity and human rights!*

Mohammed *(through a megaphone, in Arabic): Allahu Akbar! We will cleanse this land of the infidels! Sharia is the only solution!*

Claire *(smiling at Mohammed): We are with you! We stand for justice!*

Voice off-screen*: "She does not understand that in the Gaza she is 'liberating,' she would be thrown from a rooftop within five minutes. This is the highest point of social schizophrenia: supporting those who dream of your destruction in exchange for a false sense of solidarity."*

What was all this? In the assessment of Jake Wallis Simons in The Telegraph — a demonstration of how gravely ill Britain and the entire Western world has become. Several arguments from his article, "Middle-class youngsters chanting for death shows how sick Britain now is":

The spectacle of crowds calling for Jewish blood is more closely associated with Islamist dictatorships than with Western democracies. Yet after October 7th, something rotten stirred in the West.

Less than two years on, we are witnessing thousands of young British people chanting "death, death to the IDF" at a music festival — the very IDF that, according to the head of MI5, helped restrain Iran at minimal civilian cost.

What the Jewish attendees of that festival must have felt amid this sabbat of hatred should make every decent person ashamed of their country. In any sane world, an Israeli flag would have been raised over Glastonbury and chants demanding Hamas's destruction would have rung out — in solidarity with the victims of the Nova music festival.

The twelve-day war against Iran demonstrated what the IDF can accomplish when the enemy is not using civilians as human shields to generate media outrage. It is entirely evident that Israel is not trying to kill innocents.

However, crude the propaganda, sheer volume eventually prevails: Hamas transforms from murderer into "hero." There is no form of evil that will not find enthusiastic support among Western leftists — provided that Jews suffer first.

Antisemitism is a disease, and at its root there frequently lies self-hatred. Glastonbury's founder, Sir Michael Eavis, brushed aside all criticism. The festival's character is now established: a carnival of radicalism and antisemitism impossible in the Britain of previous generations.

Through the Psychiatrist's Eyes: "Palestinomania"

Symptomatology: inversion of reality. Killers are perceived as freedom fighters; a democratic state is perceived as an aggressor. Complete loss of empathy for the victims of October 7th.

Mechanics of the illness: Islamization of meaning — the embedding of the terms "apartheid" and "genocide" in contexts where they have no legal application. Media virus — social-media algorithms, fuelled by external financing, generate bubbles of hatred. Moral relativism — the rejection of objective truth as a concept.

Verdict: the Western world is afflicted with an autoimmune disease: it attacks Israel — its own forward line of defence. In destroying Israel in its imagination, the West signs the death sentence of its civilization.

The "Bacchanalia" Through the Psychiatrist's Eyes

As a psychiatrist, I seek a balanced analysis — one that integrates "combustible material" into an understanding of the collective psyche without sensationalism, while focusing on mechanisms. The phenomenon of pro-Palestinian demonstrations cannot be reduced to Gaza alone. It is deeply intertwined with archaic antisemitism — a prejudice activated in crisis situations and masquerading as political protest.

The Hamas attack of October 7, 2023, is not merely a set of statistics (approximately 1,200 killed, the majority civilians; 253 taken hostage, held in tunnels). It constitutes a mass trauma that failed to produce a global "shudder" in any way comparable to September 11, 2001. This demands an explanation in terms of selective empathy, selective indignation, and the psychological mechanisms that enable the suffering of one group to be systematically disregarded.

Antisemitism in pro-Palestinian demonstrations is not a peripheral feature but a frequent hidden "driver," rooted in stereotypes — "Jews are elites," "aggressors," "outsiders." Psychologically, this is a combination of prejudice, dehumanisation, and conformism. In crisis conditions, empathy for Palestinians displaces compassion for Israelis, and protests slide toward antisemitic slogans ("From the river to the sea") and attacks on Jewish institutions. In the United States in 2024–2025, systematic harassment of Jewish students on campuses was documented.

Why the World Did Not Shudder on October 7th

Emotional numbness and desensitisation: an oversaturation of violence in the news cycle has blunted response.

Cognitive dissonance: the framing of October 7th as "resistance" allows bystanders to avoid confronting their own indifference to the victims' pain.

Social-media echo chambers: in young people's media environments, pro-Palestinian content dominates; October 7th is "dissolved" into the broader "context of occupation."

The results: a surge in hate crimes; growing emigration sentiment among European Jews; a pervasive sense of insecurity within Jewish communities.

Consequences for the Psyche

For Jewish communities: secondary traumatisation, anxiety, intrusive thoughts, and a profound sense of isolation. For Palestinians: the trauma of war, bereavement, and deprivation. Antisemitism pours fuel on the fire, closing the cycle of violence and reciprocal radicalisation.

Dan Ariely, the Israeli-American economist and professor of behavioural economics, explains what he terms the "visibility effect": like weather, sport, and celebrity, Israel has become an "international celebrity" — a small country with permanent news traction, easy to talk about. Negative news delivers emotional charge and "stickiness" — hence the impression of relentless hyperfocus on Israel, and its escalation, at times, into antisemitic discourse.

Through the Psychiatrist's Eyes: Jewish Pro-Palestinians — Betrayal of the Self

A particular form of pathology within this global madness is represented by "Jewish Voices for Palestine." In psychiatry, this resembles the Stockholm syndrome elevated to the absolute. These individuals are the product of extreme estrangement from their own identity. In seeking to become "good Jews" for the Western left establishment, they renounce their own people at the moment of its deepest pain. They stand with placards reading "Not in My Name" while their brothers are being tortured in the tunnels of Gaza. This is not humanism — it is fear of ostracism. It is easier for them to stand in the ranks of the executioners than to bear the burden of victimhood alongside their people. ***This is the final stage of the dissolution of the Self: the "I" so terrified of the crowd's censure that it is prepared to help that crowd tighten the noose around the neck of its own father.***

Symptomatology: support for the enemy by members of the targeted group.

Mechanics: the desire to belong — fear of exclusion from the progressive camp — overrides the survival instinct. Cognitive dissonance — the mind suppresses the facts of October 7th in order to preserve a comfortable picture of "peace and goodness."

Verdict: Jewish pro-Palestinians are social "mutant lymphocytes." They attack their own body (Israel), believing they are purging it of "toxins." In reality, they are the primary instrument of Israel's delegitimisation, since the world says: "Look — even Jews themselves are against it."

Conclusion

It is impossible to ignore the global echo of the Israeli conflict — manifesting as deep social and ideological instability far beyond the borders of the Middle East. This essay has focused on how three processes — **Islamization, antisemitism, and Palestinomania** — act in concert to create a state of "social schizophrenia" in Western countries, where rational thinking yields to emotional-ideological obsession.

Islamization in this context means not merely demographic growth but the consolidation of the radical Islamist narrative as a political force, especially in relation to Israel. It provides the theological and ideological foundation for the Palestinian narrative, transforming a territorial conflict into a holy war — a Jihad — thereby giving it an absolute moral weight that cannot be contested by secular argument or empirical fact. Islamization creates an ideological bridge between radical elements within Muslim diasporas and left-wing movements in the West, providing both motivation and a mobilisation base for mass protests.

Antisemitism is the fuel that powers the entire mechanism. Pro-Palestinian activists routinely erase the distinction between Israeli policy and Jews worldwide. The attack on Israel — on Zionism — rapidly and easily transforms into an attack on Jewish identity, on synagogues, on businesses, and on university campuses. Antisemitism in its progressive guise makes it possible to ignore the historical status of Jews as a minority, recasting them as "oppressors" — a classic example of the social displacement of reality.

Palestinomania — mass obsession with the Palestinian narrative — is the social catalyst that translates ideology and hatred into mass action. It emotionally engages progressive Western audiences who, following the doctrine of intersectionality, cast Palestinians as the victims of global white colonialism and racism. The Palestinian banner becomes a universal symbol of resistance against all forms of oppression: capitalism, racism, the climate crisis. It furnishes external legitimacy for anti-Israeli actions, enabling them to attract broad constituencies entirely remote from the Middle East. It is here that the West's schizophrenia is most nakedly visible: people who advocate for LGBTQ+ rights and women's rights massively support organisations that deny those very rights — Hamas — simply because those organisations are embedded in the narrative of the "oppressed struggling against oppressors."

The three forces — Islamization, Antisemitism, and Palestinomania — have generated a perfect storm of irrationality that is destroying Western public discourse. On the streets of European and American cities, we are witnessing not merely political protest but mass social disorder rooted in a rupture with reality. Just as individual schizophrenia is defined by an inability to distinguish reality from fantasy, global social schizophrenia manifests as the inability to distinguish aggressor from victim, terrorist from freedom fighter, and self-defence from genocide. When people march under the banner of "liberation" while demanding the destruction of an entire nation, and when their rhetoric is fed by ancient hatreds, this is no longer politics.

The West has ceased to distinguish defence from genocide, and truth from manipulation. When university campuses become incubators of hatred, the immune system of Western civilisation is dead. Palestinomania is not about Arabs and not about borders — it is about the capitulation of reason before ideological fanaticism. Israel in this situation is merely the canary in the mine: if we permit this "mania" to devour the truth about October 7th, the next victims will be Paris, London, and Washington themselves.

It is a matter of deep regret that Western societies, succumbing to this invasion, have voluntarily abandoned their foundational values: rational dialogue, consistent morality, and historical memory. In doing so, they have condemned themselves to fruitless internal wars in which fellow citizens become enemies, and truth and facts become casualties of emotional and ideological obsession. ***Until these societies find within themselves the strength to reject this toxic symbiosis and return to Derech Eretz — the way of respect and reason — they will remain prisoners of their own global social schizophrenia.***

CHAPTER 31: THE PROTOCOL OF RECOVERY

"The world is divided into two classes — those who believe in the incredible, and those who accomplish the impossible."

Oscar Wilde

From Shock to Reboot

The reboot of Israel is impossible without a rigorous disinfection of the legal and bureaucratic system. *We must return to the model in which the people are the source of power and the official is its executor. The judicial reform must be carried through to its conclusion — not as a political slogan but as a condition of national survival. Judges must judge by law, not by "reasonableness," and legal advisors must advise rather than block. Only in this way shall we cure the institutional splitting of consciousness.*

The Concept of a Societal Rehabilitation Plan

The concept of a plan for the rehabilitation of society after conflict, trauma, or social schizophrenia — a deep internal schism — has a long but not always systematized history. Over the centuries it has developed from purely medical assistance to the wounded toward complex programs encompassing psychological, social, and political reintegration. Three key stages in the development of this idea may be identified.

1. At the initial stage the concept of rehabilitation was applied very narrowly. The focus was principally on servicemen and the disabled. The concept of rehabilitation in the legal sense — the restoration of rights — has been known since ancient times (for example, the rehabilitation of Joan of Arc in the fifteenth century). In the twentieth century it became a key instrument in countries with a totalitarian past, where millions of citizens were restored to their rights after political repressions (for example, in the USSR from the 1950s onward).

2. The establishment of comprehensive rehabilitation (1940s–1970s). The Second World War was a turning point when the scale of traumas demanded a systemic approach. It was in this period that the concept of "rehabilitation" was officially enshrined in medicine and gained wide currency. An enormous number of people — physically, mentally, and spiritually maimed — were in need of comprehensive support. The Marshall Plan (1947) was the largest plan in history for the economic and social rehabilitation of an entire continent, Western Europe. Its fundamental goal was not only economic but political: to prevent social destabilization and the growth of radical moods in postwar societies. Military and clinical psychology directed toward the restoration of speech, thought, and the mental health of soldiers was actively developed for the first time, alongside assistance to the civilian population in the rear.

3. Post-conflict reconstruction and social integration (from the 1980s to the present). The modern concept of societal rehabilitation is focused on overcoming the psychological and social consequences of internal and interstate conflicts. Rehabilitation has gone beyond assistance to individuals and concentrated on social reconstruction and reconciliation. Key concepts include: post-conflict reconstruction (with a division into stages — crisis, post-crisis, settlement, and long-term recovery); programs directed toward increasing social trust, supporting dialogue and civic participation; de-radicalization programs for former combatants and populations caught up in conflict; and the creation of truth and reconciliation commissions (as in South Africa), which serve as a key mechanism for collective healing from national trauma and the restoration of a shared moral narrative.

At present a plan for the rehabilitation of society after deep schism encompasses work not only with traumatized individuals but also with narratives, institutions, and the overall level of social trust.

Reconciliation and the restoration of society require both institutional and cultural steps simultaneously. This plan sets out concrete benchmarks for each source of schism, ensuring measurability, accountability, and political neutrality.

A Sample Rehabilitation Plan

Despite the trauma, Israel remains a phenomenally vital organism. The average income, the high life expectancy, and above all the willingness of 62 percent of citizens to invest in their own housing — these are indicators of faith in the future. Our task in the rehabilitation process is to transform this economic potential into social unity. The Israeli paying off a mortgage and serving in the reserves is the Atlas upon whom the Self of the nation rests.

The rehabilitation of Israel will require overcoming a deep crisis of internal Self and external legitimacy.

Loss of Trust in Government and Institutions

A portion of the population experiences distrust of the authorities — security decisions, management of the war, transparency. This is a key factor of political schism. It is necessary to restore transparency of decisions and a sense of accountability, and to demonstrate that the state is capable of listening and correcting its errors.

How? An independent commission on the facts; public reports; a law on accountability; training of crisis managers.

KPI: the index of trust in government; the speed of publication of reports.

"The Code of the New Elite: Five Principles of Regeneration"

I. Priority of Self over approval. The leader of the new formation does not seek praise in the pages of The New York Times or at Davos buffet tables. His sole criterion of success is the security and agency of the Jewish state. We are no longer an "object" of international pity; we are the "subject" of our own history.

II. Intellectual honesty. A prohibition on euphemisms that distort reality. The enemy is called the enemy; victory, victory; and terror, terror. The new elite is obliged to call things by their names, even if it sounds "politically incorrect" to Western sponsors.

III. The coefficient of solidarity. Only one who shares the fate of the nation in deed and not in word alone can be a leader. The entry requirement for the elite is personal service — military or civilian — and life within the reality of Israel, not in the "bubble" of gated communities.

IV. Unity through diversity ("Salad Bowl," not "Melting Pot"). The new elite does not try to "re-educate" the Haredi into secular citizens or vice versa. It builds a system in which each sector contributes its share to the common security. Respect for tradition is not a concession — it is the foundation of resilience.

V. The responsibility of "Derech Eretz." Argument is a tool for the search for truth, not a means of destroying the opponent. The new elite introduces strict internal etiquette: criticism of the government or the army must not become delegitimization of the state.

"The New Examination"

Setting: A senior state appointments commission.

Characters: Candidate (a graduate of a prestigious university with an impeccable résumé) and Commission Member (a weathered reserve veteran).

Candidate: *I have three degrees; I consulted European foundations on questions of "regional stability." My strategy is deep retreat in exchange for long-term recognition.*

Commission Member: *(interrupting) Tell me — where were you on 8 October?*

Candidate: *(stumbling) I... I was coordinating a Zoom conference on human rights in London. It was important to convey our position to the world.*

Commission Member: *I see. Whereas that man over there — (points to another candidate sitting in the corridor in uniform) — on 8 October was pulling the wounded out under Sderot and then commanded a company for three months in Khan Yunis. He has no London diploma, but he has a "diploma of reality." Your "stability" is a hallucination. His experience is our life. You are dismissed.*

Voice-over: *"This is how the changing of elites occurs. Not through decrees, but through a change of values.* ***When "the ability to reach agreement with outsiders" ceases to be valued above "the ability to defend one's own.""***

"Through a Psychiatrist's Eyes": Formation of the Immune Layer

Symptomatology: *The old elite is afflicted by "agnosia" — the inability to recognize a threat.*

Mechanics: *The introduction of the "Code" makes it possible to filter out social parasites and ideological schizophrenics at the approaches to power.*

Verdict: *The new elite is not "right-wing" against "left-wing." It is the sane against the hallucinating. The rehabilitation of society will be complete when the key posts are occupied by people for whom Israel is not a project but a destiny.*

Social Problems

- Exemption from army service for the Haredi.
- Imposition of kashrut norms, Sabbath rules, and gender separation.
- Inequality in funding, infrastructure, and security.
- Suspicions of disloyalty in the Arab sector.
- The dominance of Ashkenazim in politics and economics.
- Left versus Right — different approaches to the Palestinian question.

- A predominance of investment in the center of the country.
- Gaps in education, medicine, and wages.

Paths to Resolution

- Creation of platforms for national dialogue.
- Joint initiatives in civil society.
- Equal civil rights with respect for faith.
- Universal mandatory civil or military service, with the possibility of an alternative.
- Equality in funding, infrastructure, and the labor market.
- Counteracting the demonization of opponents.
- Investment in transport, medicine, and education in the periphery.
- Incentivizing business outside the center.
- Integration programs for youth from disadvantaged areas.
- **Recognition of the error of the left-wing approach to security and peace.**

Media Fields and the Narrative Monopoly

- Reduce the "narrative monopoly" effect and expand media pluralism.
- How? A media ethics code; funding for independent investigations; joint journalism projects; social-media partnerships with Israeli media.
- KPI: the media pluralism index; the number of items that have undergone independent fact-checking.

The Ideological Rift

(Judicial Reform, Right vs. Centre/Left)

The conflict over the reforms has intensified distrust among social strata.

- Relieve the tension through institutional guarantees and civic dialogue.
- How? A national consensus forum; constitutional consultations with a referendum.
- KPI: the number of agreed points; a reduction in protest activity.

"A Conversation in a Queue"

Setting: The corridor of a state clinic — a queue for the doctor.
Characters: Rakhel (a settler from Judea) and Darya (an activist from Tel Aviv).

Darya: *(looking at her phone, sighing) These news stories again... When will this ever end? Because of your fanatics we are trapped in this.*

Rakhel: *(calmly) My son is in Gaza right now, Darya. And he is covering the back of a guy from Tel Aviv who probably also thinks I am a fanatic.*

Darya: *(raising her eyes, a pause) My brother is there too... in the same brigade.*

Rakhel: *You see. Over there they have already recovered from this schizophrenia. They know that if one of them falls, both fall. Perhaps it is time for us here to stop waiting for politicians to cure us?*

Voice-over: *"Rehabilitation does not begin in the Knesset. It begins in a queue for bread or at the doctor's, when we realize that shared pain is the most durable glue."*

Centre and Periphery

- The feeling of inequality and marginalization.
- Reduce the sense of alienation and give the periphery genuine participation.
- How? A reconstruction fund; mobile assistance services; co-management of budgets; cultural exchanges.
- KPI: reconstruction of infrastructure; satisfaction of residents.

The Religious-Secular and Ethnic Schism

- Intensification of friction between groups.
- Preserve civic coexistence.
- How? Interfaith initiatives; youth projects; integration of education; exchanges.
- KPI: the number of joint projects; the level of trust between communities.

Youth and Online Polarization

- Viral radicalism on social networks.
- Refocus attention on critical thinking.
- How? Media literacy in schools; youth media; partnerships with platforms.
- KPI: engagement; a reduction in disinformation.

Cross-Sector Measures

- A National Centre for Recovery and Dialogue.
- A platform for truth and documentation.
- Large-scale psychological support (MHPSS).
- Youth participation programs.
- Monitoring and public evaluation.

Key Performance Indicators (KPIs)

Index of trust in institutions; media pluralism; number of inter-community cooperation projects; coverage of psychological support programs (MHPSS).

"Through a Psychiatrist's Eyes": The Technology of Unity

Symptomatology: *Residual fear and suspicion.*

Mechanics:

(1) Education: replacing textbooks of "peace at any price" with textbooks of "respect for the Self."

(2) Economics: investment in the periphery not as alms but as the creation of new centres of strength.

(3) National service: transforming service into a "university of solidarity." If 7 October was a shared grief, then service must become a shared duty. Universal national service — for the ultra-Orthodox, for Arabs, for the secular — is not only about security; it is about the creation of a unified cultural code. ***When people from different sectors together build, rescue, or defend, social schizophrenia retreats.***

Verdict: *Rehabilitation is not a return to the condition of "before 7 October." It is the creation of Israel 2.0, whose immunity to internal strife is greater than the politicians' thirst for power.*

The Thirty-Day Roadmap

- Creation of the National Recovery Centre.
- Launch of MHPSS (Large-Scale Psychological Support).
- Commission on the facts (mandate: six months).
- Media ethics code.
- A media literacy pilot for schools.

Three Key Directions

Internal rehabilitation (restoration of the Self).

The most critical and complex stage — restoration of unity and trust within Israeli society after the deep political schisms and the shock of the security failure of 7 October 2023.

- *New political leadership is needed, not tied to the errors that led to the crisis of 2023. This presupposes elections, the formation of a broad, stable coalition, and the adoption of unpopular but necessary decisions.*
- *It is necessary to restore the basic social contract. The state must once again become the absolute guarantor of security for its citizens — something that was gravely undermined on 7 October. This includes reform and strengthening of the security and intelligence services.*

- *A search for compromise on the character of the state ("Jewish and democratic") and the achievement of national consensus.*

Regional rehabilitation

Rehabilitation requires the reformatting of relations with the Middle East.

- *The successful outcome of the war with Iran (June 2025), including the destruction of part of Iran's nuclear and missile infrastructure and the dismantling of the main Hamas structures, has restored military deterrence. Israel must maintain this status without allowing the complete destruction of stability in neighboring countries.*
- *For rehabilitation it is necessary to find a path for the renewal and expansion of the Abraham Accords.*
- *Israel will be required to present a realistic, long-term strategy that can be accepted by key Arab partners.*

International rehabilitation

The tendency toward the isolation of Israel in the international arena is one of the most acute challenges.

- *It is necessary to change the global narrative and effectively counter disinformation.*
- *This requires greater transparency in military operations and more effective public diplomacy.*
- *Rehabilitation depends directly on Israel's observance of the norms of international law and the provision of humanitarian assistance in conflict zones.*

The rehabilitation of Israel is possible, but it cannot be purely military. The success in the conflicts of 2023–2026 created a window of opportunity for the restoration of security and deterrence, but now the focus must shift toward internal unity and regional diplomacy. If the internal schisms remain unresolved, military victories will have only a short-term effect.

The Right–Left Vector of Schizophrenization

When consulting Benjamin Netanyahu, the American political strategist Arthur Finkelstein expressed this in the form of a purely political equation: "Ask someone who he is more — a Jew or an Israeli." If the answer is "an Israeli," those are the left, and "we are the Jews."

According to this division, Jews love Israel; will always believe that Israel is right; possess a communal sense of unity and shared destiny; respect Jewish traditions; are close to "the religious light"; and will always look upon Arabs with suspicion.

An "Israeli" is typically an "awakened," secular, cosmopolitan Ashkenazi — of European origin — who feels equally at home in Tel Aviv, Berlin, or New York; cares about the LGBTQ community and the Palestinians; is prepared to criticize his own country at any moment; and is, from a cultural standpoint, a patronizing snob.

It is well known that the left and the right do not understand one another. Some people in both groups live in echo chambers in which all the media they consume and all the opinions they encounter in everyday life coincide with their own. To understand other positions one must step outside one's comfort zone: read articles with which one disagrees, listen to speeches by politicians one dislikes, and speak with people from the opposite side of the political spectrum.

The catastrophe of 7 October 2023 not only exposed failures in the security system but radically changed the political landscape.

Left-wing ideology, traditionally associated with peace through negotiation, concessions to the Palestinians, and support for a two-state solution, was subjected to sharp criticism and lost significant support. Many Israelis who had previously sympathized with left-wing views turned away from them, accusing them of naivety and an inability to ensure security.

Having good intentions, but ignoring the hostile intentions of the terrorists, the left-wing political forces brought the country to the crisis of 7 October 2023, splitting and befogging the minds of a considerable part of society. Thus, a picture formed of a society suffering from social schizophrenia and dangerous to itself.

Many residents of the southern kibbutzim, traditionally left-wing and supportive of "peace with the neighbors," were the first to suffer. In Kibbutz Be'eri, where many residents held left-wing views, dozens of people were killed. This led even survivors and relatives of victims to reject their former views, seeing in them the cause of vulnerability. Left-wing parties such as Meretz and Avoda, which had traditionally championed the two-state solution and negotiations with the Palestinian Authority, are losing influence. Polls show that support for the idea of a Palestinian state has fallen to almost zero.

"Almost no one supports the old idea of a Palestinian state," *sociologist Manny Nir has noted. Left-wing activists who previously went out to protest against the government now face accusations of betrayal, and the term "leftist" has become a term of abuse. Critics of left-wing ideology link the failure of 7 October to its key principles. The unilateral disengagement of 2005 — when Israel withdrew its forces and settlements from Gaza — is now seen as a mistake. Instead of peace, Gaza became a Hamas base, leading to the catastrophe of 2023. Many Israelis consider that concessions only strengthened the enemy.*

The Four Conceptual Errors Behind 7 October

1. **Faith in technological superiority:** ignoring signals about Hamas's preparations due to overestimation of the "smart fences."
2. **Ignoring the enemy's ideology:** Hamas and its sponsors (Iran, Hezbollah) saw concessions as weakness, not as a step toward peace.
3. **Focus on internal reforms:** the protests against the judicial reform distracted attention from external threats.
4. **The idea of "land in exchange for peace"** (Oslo, Camp David) collapsed, confirming the right-wing thesis about the necessity of strength.

IDF investigations confirmed the largest intelligence failure, emphasizing that Hamas had been planning the attack for years, coordinating with Iran, while Israel ignored the warnings.

The failure of the left strengthened the right-wing bloc. By 2025, Israel had become more conservative: the expansion of settlements reached a record level (13,000 units in 2023), and the ideas of "Greater Israel" entered the mainstream. The left is trying to revive itself through social reforms and anti-war protests, but is encountering nationalism.

In the final analysis, 7 October became the "death" of left-wing ideology in its classical form: from naive pacifism to realism through strength. Although some elements of the left are evolving, the societal shift to the right seems irreversible in the coming years.

Personal Stories of Disillusionment

"The Moment of Truth"

Setting: *A kibbutz on the border with Gaza. The morning of 7 October.*

Character: Michal, an activist of the "Peace Now" movement who for years transported Palestinian children to Israeli hospitals.

Michal: *(hiding in the safe room, hearing shouts in Arabic outside the door) I knew their names... I believed that if we were kind, they would see us as human beings. I believed in two states.*

(The door begins to be broken down. Through the window Michal sees a Palestinian who worked in their garden yesterday, and today is pointing out to the fighters where the wealthiest families live.)

Voice-over: *"At that moment, the "apple" did not merely fall — it shattered.* ***The schizophrenic illusion of peace with those who want to erase you evaporated together with the smoke of the fires.*** *Michal did not simply "leave the left" — she returned to* *her Self. She remembered that she is a Jew, and her life is not small change for other people's utopias."*

The Israeli left is in disarray after 7 October; they are not so much "changing camp" as undergoing changes within their own political camp, as their former positions yield to new challenges and internal schisms against the backdrop of the war in Gaza. Many mainstream Israelis who always voted for left-wing parties have found refuge in the vast, comfortable space called the "centre," where they believe a synthesis of left and right ideas will prove politically attractive.

Personal Testimonies

Almog Holat, Kibbutz Nirim: Previously held left-wing views and believed in peace with the Palestinians, teaching her children that "most people in Gaza are good, just like us." After the attack, when Hamas fighters threw grenades into her home, she called her former convictions "naive." She now says: "I no longer know what to believe, but certainly not in peace. I can no longer say that 95 percent of them want to live in peace."

Avida Bahar, Kibbutz Be'eri: Before 7 October believed in coexistence and the two-state solution. Having lost his wife, his teenage son, and a leg in the attack — in which 100 of the kibbutz's 1,100 residents were killed — he radically changed his views. He now believes Israel must "raze Gaza to the ground and take full control." He acknowledges that such a position would earlier have surprised even himself.

Daniela (22, Ashkelon): Called herself a "leftist" and believed that Palestinians acted out of poverty. After the attack, she stated: "After that Saturday, people who believed in peace no longer believe. It became personal. They broke into the kibbutz and just killed people."

Aldema, photographer, 30, from a kibbutz: Emphasizes that Hamas attacked not settlers but "primarily pro-Palestinian communities." Although he still wants peace, he believes the left needs to be more realistic about the necessity of a military response.

Nira Herman Sharabi, Kibbutz Be'eri: Initially supported the war in Gaza, but later changed her view, demanding that the hostages be returned first: "If you do not return them, it will tear us apart from within."

Dafna from Kibbutz Re'im: Cultural director of the kibbutz and one of the organizers of the Nova Festival. She was the sole survivor of her family — her mother and children, Shira and Meir, were killed; her home was burned; she herself was taken captive. A militant atheist before 7 October, she cried out in the tunnel: "I am a Jewess, I am a Jewess!" — and for the first time experienced a crisis of Self. "For the first time in my life I saw my soul; I saw that I am a Jewess," she says. Now she wants to build a synagogue in her kibbutz.

These stories illustrate how the personal experience of trauma led to a rejection of left-wing ideas in favor of pragmatism and firmness, intensifying the general rightward shift in Israel.

The table contains the stories of other real people who represent what remains of the left-wing or peace forces in Israel. These are not abstract slogans but personal fates and words. These stories show: the "left-wing forces" in Israel today carry almost no political weight, but there are individual people who, despite personal losses and pressure, continue to believe in the possibility of dialogue and peace.

Name	Story	Position
Maoz Inon	Entrepreneur. Lost both parents on 7 October.	Even after personal tragedy, advocates for peace and dialogue.
Rami Elhanan	His daughter was killed in a terrorist attack.	"My loss must not become fuel for hatred." Works for dialogue with Palestinians.
Hagit Ofran	Activist of "Peace Now," monitors settlements, receives threats.	Advocates for Israel as a Jewish state with equal rights for Palestinians.
Robi Damelin	Her son was killed by a Palestinian sniper.	"I turned the pain of loss into motivation for reconciliation." Works with Palestinian families.
Rela Mazali	Feminist and pacifist writer, opposes militarism.	Believes the culture of the army destroys civil society; writes and lectures.
Vivian Silver	Peace activist, killed on 7 October.	Worked in "Women Wage Peace," building bridges between Jews and Arabs.

Testimonies

Maoz Inon: "My parents were killed on 7 October. I lost what was most precious to me. And yet I say: I do not want revenge.

If we respond only with war, we will lose again and again. The only path is peace."

Rami Elhanan: "I am an Israeli who has lost a daughter in a terrorist attack. I met a Palestinian who had lost his brother. We both sat and wept. I understood: our pain is the same. From that moment I decided that my life would be devoted not to revenge but to bringing people together."

Robi Damelin: "My son was killed by a Palestinian sniper. When the military informed me, I said: You will not have my child in the name of hatred. I do not want my son's death to be used to continue the war. I want it to be the beginning of dialogue."

Disillusionment

Political science research is well acquainted with the phenomenon of disillusionment. It refers to the cognitive and moral rupture that occurs when a normative ideology — based on good intentions, universalism, and abstract morality — again and again collides with stubborn facts. In such situations a person can choose between denial, rationalization, and emotional radicalization — or a painful but honest revision of their world-view. The disillusioned are those who chose the second path.

The peculiarity of Israeli disillusionment lies in the rupture between what is experienced in the private sphere and what is permitted to be said publicly. In the left-wing camp a broad stratum of "anusim" has formed — rational, educated people closely connected with reality who understand that the formula of unilateral concessions does not lead to peace, but are afraid to say so aloud. In the high-tech sector they are silent so as not to find themselves in isolation. In the academic environment — so as not to suffer professionally. In the judicial system and in the juristocracy—because the price may be personal and immediate.

The deep problem is that the left-wing Kaplanists merged with the radical left and adopted a total moral discourse admitting of no doubt, correction, or revision. Thus the former left-wing Zionists disappeared — those who believed in peace but understood that it is attainable only from a position of strength; those who knew that in the Middle East, peace is not achieved through a bowed head but through the inspiring of respect and fear. Research in the fields of security and international relations shows again and again: stability and political arrangements in our region arise when one side demonstrates clear and unambiguous strength, not moral weakness wrapped in beautiful slogans.

The reconstruction of the country will become a home for the disillusioned. For citizens who love this country, believe in freedom and equality, but also understand that our existence here cannot rest on good wishes. For those who recognize that strength does not contradict liberalism but is the condition of its existence. And for those who understand that our connection to this land is not a colonial project of a century ago but a historical, cultural, and moral bond of thousands of years.

Disillusionment is not a betrayal of values. It is a return to reality.

Thousands Still Want a Palestinian State

The Zazim initiative has already collected 8,866 signatures in favor of the recognition of Palestine — the organizers want to present 10,000 at UN headquarters during the conference on the Palestinian question (22 September, under the auspices of Saudi Arabia and France). Among the signatories are families of victims of 7 October: Yotam Kipnis (Be'eri), Liora Eilon (Kfar Aza), Maoz

Innon (Nativ HaAsara), and Yonatan Zeigen — son of the killed activist Vivian Silver.

Commentary: Is 7 October not enough for them?

On 18 July 2024 the Knesset adopted a declaration categorically rejecting the establishment of a Palestinian state west of the Jordan River. Such a state "would represent an existential threat to the State of Israel and its citizens, would prolong the Israeli-Palestinian conflict, and would destabilize the region." Vote: 68 in favor, 9 against. This was not the first such decision: on 21 February 2024 the Knesset had already adopted a resolution (99 in favor, 9 against) rejecting the unilateral recognition of a Palestinian state without negotiations with Israel.

Is De-Schizophrenization of Consciousness Possible?

Protocol: Rehabilitation of the National Self

Stage 1 — Cleansing: Annulment of the Oslo legacy — not as a political act but as a hygiene of consciousness. Recognition that the model of "territories in exchange for peace" in the conditions of the Middle East is a suicidal hallucination.

Stage 2 — Integration: Transition from segregation to shared responsibility. Universal service — military or alternative — is the "social glue."

Stage 3 — Reform of trust: Elimination of the "Periphery-Centre" gap. Economic rehabilitation must proceed in parallel with psychological rehabilitation.

Verdict: *De-schizophrenization is possible only through radical honesty. We stop treating symptoms and begin to build a state founded on reality, not on the expectations of European sponsors.*

Reducing the Intensity of Conflict Between Left and Right

A reduction in the intensity of conflict between the carriers of left-wing and right-wing ideology could serve the cause of societal rehabilitation. An important role belongs to citizens from the left-wing camp who, after the catastrophe of 7 October, experienced a shock and revised their world-view. Here are several examples.

Oded and Yokheved Lifshitz, kibbutz members.

The Lifshitzes fought for the rights of Gaza's residents, drove them to Israeli hospitals for check-ups and operations, and believed in peaceful coexistence. But Yokheved was mistaken — she had no friends in Gaza. She was released after sixteen days of captivity only because a contagious disease had been discovered in her; Oded, like all the other hostages, received no help from anyone. Even in the most antisemitic countries during the Holocaust there were Righteous Among the Nations. There was not a single righteous person in Gaza.

"Oded, my dear, it is strange and unimaginable to stand before people and deliver a eulogy for you. The stage was always yours, and I was at your side. You wrote with such talent, and I was your personal photographer. I want to thank you for sixty-seven years of happy life together. We created a wonderful family, a posterity to be proud of! All our lives we fought for justice and

peace. Unfortunately, we received a cruel blow from those to whom we strove to extend a hand on the other side. I stand here shaken, seeing the number of graves and the terrible destruction of our community, which was left completely without protection on 7 October. I do not lose hope. I shall continue our path and fight for the liberation of all the hostages, to the last of them." — *Yokheved Lifshitz (https://t.me/besedergamur/6519)*

Vivian Silver — "Women Wage Peace."

Vivian Silver devoted the greater part of her life to building understanding and cooperation between Jews and Arabs in Israel. She was the founder of the "Women Wage Peace" movement and the "Ajeec" organization, and was a member of the board of "B'Tselem." She lived in Kibbutz Be'eri on the outskirts of the Gaza Strip. She had left her home in Winnipeg more than fifty years ago to live in Israel and work on peace initiatives. Her body was identified by forensic experts, who confirmed that the 74-year-old activist was killed during the massacre of 7 October by Hamas-led terrorists.

The Betrayed Leftist — Avida Bahar, Kibbutz Be'eri.

On 7 October Avida Bahar lost his wife and his fifteen-year-old son. He survived, but lost a leg. He had been very much a leftist, like his friends in Be'eri, but radically revised his views. In December he even said he was fortunate the massacre had occurred in Be'eri rather than in Gush Etzion: "I would have said: 'Why do they live there?' I would have said: 'They deserve it.' I would have said all the worst things in the world."

"Take their land. Take their land, don't blink. Push them into Egypt... The volcano will erupt again. When? We don't know. But it will happen. I endured endless torture in the bomb shelter for twelve

hours. Next to me was my wife, who was killed in the afternoon, and my son, who was killed at around 4:30 p.m. I am a leftist who was betrayed. That is what happened to me on 7 October — I became a betrayed leftist, and I have no compassion for anyone." This is called shock therapy. Many recover.

https://dusiznies.blogspot.com/2025/03/betrayed-leftist-warns-of-situation-in.html

"Why I Left the Left"

Leaving left-wing ideology in Israel after 2023 is not a "shift to the right" — it is the recovery of the instinct of self-preservation. When people say "I saw that I am a Jew," they mean that the external threat erased the artificial constructs of the "citizen of the world." The rehabilitation of society begins with the recognition of a simple fact: we are a nation waging a war of survival. Any policy that ignores this fact is toxic.

The departure from the left is not a betrayal of values. It is a return to reality.

"I Saw That I Was a Jew"

Daphna from Kibbutz Re'im

This is a story of spiritual rebirth, one of those that became a mass phenomenon over the past year. By 7 October, Ami Magazine reports, Daphna had spent 20 years making coexistence programs for Arabs and Jews. She never identified as a Zionist and never felt 'particularly Jewish.'

And then Daphna found herself in a tunnel with her captors.

'Why are you tormenting me? For 20 years I have been making programs for Arabs and Jews. Jews are your cousins,' I said to the elderly guard.

'You are not a descendant of Ibrahim! You are not a Jew! — he answered angrily and spat. — 'You are a European colonizer who stole our land!'

'I began to scream: I am a Jew, I am a Jew!' The guards held her, sealing her mouth with duct tape. This shook her. 'In that moment I realized: they do not care that I made peace programs. They hate me only for being a Jew, whatever I do or do not do.'

https://dusiznies.blogspot.com/.../dafnah-leftist-secular...

"Bibi Came Out to Save Israel"

Extraordinary! Former Labor minister Eli Goldschmidt, a long-standing opponent of Netanyahu, is saying remarkable things about him. He quotes Nahum Barnea — one of Netanyahu's most prominent critics.

'We were probably wrong about Netanyahu,' says Barnea. It is hard not to appreciate such an astonishing compliment from an ideological opponent.

The phrase that 'there is no politician in the world today who comes even close to him' is one we fully share. Look at what Goldschmidt says:

Can a Palestinian State Be Created?

The creation of a fully functional Palestinian state today remains extremely unlikely, believes orientalist Mikhail Yakubovich, a research fellow at the Oriental Studies Department of the University of Freiburg. He declared that neither Israel nor its key ally — the United States — would permit the emergence of a new independent Palestinian statehood. Concessions on Israel's part, especially in territorial matters, are practically impossible: "I cannot imagine how it would be possible for Israel to cede territory in any way." Even in the future, one can speak at most of a partial expansion of the Palestinian Authority's powers, not full sovereignty. He also noted that the creation of a Palestinian state is complicated not only by political circumstances but also by the geographic fragmentation of the territories.

The Abolition of Oslo

The following is an approximate plan for the annulment of the Oslo Accords and the transition to a cantonal system in Israel, while ensuring the central government's control over security, foreign policy, and economics.

Legal-Political Basis

- Adoption in the Knesset of a declaration recognizing the agreements as having lost force, on the basis of systematic violations by the other party and national security threats.
- Introduction of amendments to the Basic Laws to enshrine the new administrative structure.
- Confidential consultations with key international partners to minimize diplomatic damage.

The Canton Model

Each territory receives canton status with limited self-governance in the social-cultural sphere. Security, foreign policy, and economics remain under the central government. Types of cantons:

- Jewish cantons: integrated into the national system.
- Arab cantons: internal self-governance while subject to the general laws of Israel.
- Mixed cantons: a special regime in areas of mixed population.

Phased Transition

Stage 1 — Preparation (0–12 months):

Map of future cantons; a cantonal organization bill; reinforcement of security during the transition period.

Stage 2 — Transitional period (1–3 years):

Replacement of PA institutions with a transitional administration; creation of cantonal councils; integration of services.

Stage 3 — Full integration (3–5 years):

Transfer of powers under the new arrangement; achievement of international recognition of the new status.

Advantages: Removes the ambiguity of the two-state idea; grants local communities self-governance; centralizes security.

Risks: International pressure and sanctions; internal escalation during the transition period; high demands on the security system and economic support.

Should Religion Be Separated from the State?

In my view: No. In a state such as Israel — the Holy Land in the understanding of Judaism, Christianity, and Islam — where, in addition to Jews, there live Muslims, Christians, Druze, and representatives of other faiths, religion must not be separated from the state, because this would hollow out the Jewish character of the state and might be negatively perceived by the religious minorities, whose relations with the state are built on religious self-identification. Modern society must be free from religious coercion, since religious beliefs and way of life come from the heart and must not be imposed. Moreover, religious coercion leads to the moral defeat of religion.

From what has been said, it follows that the Jewish character of our state can be expressed through:

1) Symbolism.
2) Holidays and days off according to the Jewish calendar.
3) Kosher food in the army and in state institutions.
4) Matrimonial services (marriages, divorces) must be provided by the state; religious services available only by the desire of citizens.
5) The state administration must recognize marriages, divorces, and conversions performed by rabbis of all streams of Judaism.
6) A unified kashrut certificate must be agreed upon.
7) Shops must remain closed on Saturdays and holidays.
8) The question of freedom of transport on Saturdays and holidays must be resolved at the municipal level.
9) In the name of national unity it is necessary to elect a single Chief Rabbi for both Ashkenazim and Sephardim (as is customary in the IDF).
10) All citizens of the country, regardless of religious affiliation, are equal before the law, including in military or alternative service.

For Arabs, service in the army must be voluntary, but alternative service obligatory.

11) Financial privileges based on religious affiliation must not exist and must be commensurate with the general financial policy of social solidarity.

Are these goals attainable? Today no, but this is what we must strive for. The experience of recent years — when we have changed five governing coalitions in three years — clearly demonstrates this. Any prime minister becomes a hostage and an object of blackmail by the parties making up his coalition. The split in our society, combined with economic, diplomatic, and military dependence on the USA, makes our situation as an exclusively Jewish state more than problematic.

The Abolition of the Monopoly on Meaning

The old "apple" is not merely people; it is a network of influence that for decades has controlled the media, the judicial system, and the senior military command. This network lived in the paradigm of "peace in exchange for territory" and "a state of all its citizens" without regard for the national Self.

Intellectual deprivation: We need a new intellectual elite that has emerged not from the hothouses of the Ivy League or Qatari grants, but from the trenches of 7 October and the volunteer centres of the periphery. These are people whose social contract is signed in blood, not at Oslo buffet tables.

A change of "firmware" in the IDF: The army must cease to be a place where senior officers dream of political careers in left-wing parties. The "new growth" consists of combat commanders of the middle echelon who see the army as an instrument of victory, not a platform for social experiments.

The IDF must undergo a process of de-Harvardization. We need to return the spirit of the "Iron Wall" to the General Staff. The fundamental lesson of rehabilitation: security is provided not by fences but by the enemy's fear of retribution. Military Doctrine 2.0 must officially enshrine the priority of destroying a threat over "monitoring" it. The judicial castration of the army must be halted by legislation: on the battlefield the commander answers before God and his orders, not before a lawyer.

"The Handover of the Keys"

Setting: *The General Staff or the office of a major media outlet.* **Characters: Alon (an old functionary, certain that "one simply needs to negotiate") and Eitan (a reserve officer returned from Gaza).**

Alon: *Eitan, you don't understand the big picture. The world demands restraint of us. We must preserve the status quo, otherwise we will lose the support of the USA and Europe.*

Eitan: *(placing his dusty helmet on the table) Your "big picture" burned on 7 October in Kibbutz Be'eri. For thirty years you fed us the illusion that the enemy could be bought. You built a system in which the survival of the nation is secondary to your image in the New York Times.*

Alon: *You are too radical...*

Eitan: *No, I am simply real. Your time is up. From now on, decisions will be made by those who know the price of every metre of this land. Keys on the table, Alon.*

Voice-over: *"This is not a rebellion. This is the natural process of cleansing, when reality displaces hallucination. The old apple has shrivelled because it no longer contains the juice of life. The new generation is not an ideology — it is a biological fact of survival."*

"Through a Psychiatrist's Eyes":

The Phase of Active Regeneration

Symptomatology: Resistance from old structures: judicial activism, media pressure.

Mechanics:

Direct democracy — expansion of the periphery's influence on decision-making.

Meritocracy — appointment to posts on the principle of performance on 7 October, not belonging to the "right families."

Educational detox — a complete revision of textbooks restoring the concepts of "enemy," "victory," and "national pride."

Verdict: The old tree cannot be healed if its roots have rotted in the swamp of Oslo. "New growth" consists of those 300,000 reservists who returned home as different people. They are the new backbone of Israel.

A Model of Political Reform

In my view, yes. But for this it is first necessary to determine what we want. The state needs stable governance resting on the will of the people. Therefore it is necessary to abandon the parliamentary republic system, which has become outdated for our country. The following is one realistic and widely discussed reform in Israel that could substantially change the political system for the better, without revolutions and without the destruction of the Zionist character of the state. It is being actively promoted by both the right and the centrists.

Reform: "Regional Districts + 4% Threshold + Direct Election of Prime Minister"

The essence — a package of four interrelated changes.

Transition to 15–20 regional electoral districts instead of one nationwide "basket."

At present all 120 seats are distributed proportionally throughout the country, allowing small parties and political extortionists to thrive. In the new system approximately 80–90 mandates would be elected by a majoritarian-proportional system in districts (for example, Haifa, Be'er Sheva, Galilee, Judea and Samaria). The remaining 30–40 mandates remain national party-list seats. Result: parties with 3–5 mandates that currently decide the fate of coalitions will disappear. Larger parties will be compelled to field genuine local leaders.

Raising the electoral threshold to 4 percent (from the current 3.25 percent).

This would immediately remove from the Knesset micro-factions that currently hold the whole country to ransom.

Return to the direct election of the prime minister (with amendments to avoid repeating the failure of 1996–2001). The prime minister would be elected directly in two rounds, like the President of France. To prevent him from ignoring the Knesset — a vote of no-confidence is retained, but constructive and with a high threshold (at least 65–70 votes, not 61). This gives the prime minister a personal mandate from the people and makes him far stronger than the small coalition partners.

Limitation of the "Norwegian Law" and the number of ministers: a maximum of 18–20 ministers (at present there can be 35+). A Knesset member who becomes a minister vacates his seat for the next person on the list.

What this will yield in practice within 5–10 years:

- ♦ Instead of 10–12 parties in the Knesset there will be 4–6 large ones.
- ♦ Coalitions will command 70–90 mandates instead of the current 64–65 "on the edge."
- ♦ The prime minister will receive real power and accountability to voters, not to Shas or Mansour Abbas.
- ♦ Settlements and Arab towns will receive direct representatives, not "appointees" from Tel Aviv headquarters.

This reform was already on Netanyahu's desk in 2021–2022. Most importantly — it does not require amendment of the Basic Laws on the Jewish character of the state and passes by an ordinary majority in the Knesset.

On the eve of the Jewish New Year 5786 (Rosh Hashanah), the population of Israel exceeded 10 million people, the Central Bureau of Statistics reported.

Over the past year, the country's population grew by 1.2%, compared with 1.6% the year before.

- Arabs: 2.104 million (21.4% of the population)
- Jews and others: 7.7 million (78.6%)
- Foreign nationals: approximately 260,000

Immigration and emigration

In 2024, more people left the country than arrived:

- New immigrants: 31,000
- Emigrants (permanent): 82,000

For comparison, in 2023: 46,000 arrived, 55,000 departed. Also in 2024, 24,000 people returned to Israel (in 2023 — 21,000).

Population Growth

Indicator	Figure
Total population	Over 10 million
Jews and others	7.7 million (78.6%)
Arabs	2.104 million (21.4%)
Average monthly gross income	22,013 shekels
Average monthly net income	18,237 shekels
Average monthly expenditure	14,526 shekels
Life expectancy — men	81.4 years
Life expectancy — women	85.5 years
Birth rate	2.87 children per woman
Births in 2024	181,614
Homeownership	62.7% in owner-occupied homes

Secular / non-religious (aged 20+)	42.7%
Ultra-Orthodox (Haredi)	11.4%

Religious self-identification (among those aged 20+)

- Secular and non-religious — 42.7%
- Traditional, not very religious — 21.5%
- Religious — 12%
- Haredim (ultra-Orthodox) — 11.4%

Family and birthrate

- In 2023: 48,025 marriages and 15,283 divorces
- In 2024: 181,614 births
- Average fertility rate: 2.87 children per woman

Households

- In 2024: 2,979,400 private households
- Average household size: 3.18 persons
- Families (parents + children): 2,330,800

Standard of living

- 62.7% live in owner-occupied apartments
- 34% of these are paying a mortgage

Finances:

- Average gross family income per month: 22,013 shekels
- Average net income: 18,237 shekels
- Average monthly expenditure: 14,526 shekels

Average life expectancy:

- Men — 81.4 years
- Women — 85.5 years

In 2024, 51,881 people died; almost a quarter of deaths were caused by cancer.

The figures do not lie: Israelis are voting for the future with their families. A high birth rate and standard of living are our principal strategic reserve. The task of the state is to direct this energy not toward internal strife but toward expansion and innovation. We must become not merely a start-up nation but a "fortress-nation with a human face," where high technologies serve the protection of traditional values. This is the final "upgrade": the integration of our ancient identity with the power of the modern state.

Conclusion

The shock of 7 October was a defibrillator that restored the stopped heart of the nation to life. The reboot is painful, lengthy, and requires the courage to acknowledge mistakes. But the data of 2024–2025 shows: Israel has not merely survived — it is being reborn. We are emerging from this catastrophe as different people — tougher, hopefully more consolidated, and finally rid of illusions. This is not a full stop; it is the beginning of a new chapter in our history, in which the word "Victory" once again acquires its true, definitive meaning.

The concept of the rehabilitation of society has traveled from the provision of physical and medical assistance to individuals to the creation of a comprehensive program for the restoration of social trust and political stability. At present this is a holistic approach directed not only toward the healing of individuals from trauma but toward the reintegration of fractured social, psychological, and political spheres. Modern societal rehabilitation is a strategic imperative for the restoration of national unity and the functionality of the state after a deep internal crisis or conflict.

We say: NO to schism. NO to hatred. NO to schizophrenism. NO to the dictatorship of the Supreme Court and the bureaucrats. YES to democracy and tolerance. YES to a renewed Israel.

Afterword

"One must write either about what one knows very well, or about what no one else knows."

The Strugatsky Brothers

I thank all those who have read this book. I hope your time was not spent in vain. A psychiatrist, thanks to close contact with patients and their families, has a unique opportunity to observe, study, and understand human dramas. The clinical method of the psychiatrist resembles in many respects the creative method of the writer: both are interested in the psyche, the behavior, and the destinies of people. The principal distinction between them is that the psychiatrist deals with real people, while the writer creates images and plots by the force of imagination, taking care of plausibility. It is no wonder that every doctor is a little bit of a writer, and every writer a little bit of a doctor.

I wrote this book wishing to understand how and why it proved possible to implant the illusions of the "peace process" into public consciousness, leading Israel to the catastrophe of 2023. It is based on real events and decisions by well-known leaders who, despite their sincere desire for the prosperity of the country, committed a series of fatal strategic errors. The so-called "peace process" with the Arabs of former Palestine, begun by the Oslo Accords and continued by the "disengagement," encountered the fierce hatred and brutal terror of the "partners for peace."

How, and by whom, was it possible to befuddle a pragmatic people and carry out in practice deals that today look criminal? *The architects and contractors of the "peace process" initiated destructive processes that split Israeli society and plunged it into a state of "social schizophrenia." Examining the manipulations of public consciousness over the last thirty-five years, I never ceased to marvel at the persistence of political leaders in carrying through their corrupt deals despite the existence of criticism that PREDICTED ALL THE TRAGIC CONSEQUENCES.* I can understand their thinking and behavior only as that of people with a splitting of political consciousness — an ignoring of facts in the service of ideology, a loss of contact with reality, and an absence of critical insight into their own decisions. ***Rabin, Peres, and company knew about the criticism and the real threats, but preferred ideology and their own morally elevated narrative about peace. This cognitive dissociation led to decisions that, from a historical distance, seem reckless and self-destructive.***

One can only regret that the left-wing "peace camp" succeeded in creating a parallel reality in which Arafat was a "partner for peace" and not a terrorist who used the peace process to strengthen his military potential. Criticism warning of the growth of terror was demonized as "incitement" and "hostility to peace."

The creation of the Palestinian Authority headed by the terrorist Arafat, and the expulsion of Jews from the Gaza Strip, constitute a sacrifice on the altar of a mad left-wing ideology and its obsessive idea of creating a Palestinian state on the Land of Israel. Gush Katif, like the Second Temple, was destroyed because of the paranoid hatred of the left for the carriers of right-wing ideology. Their blindness reminded me of delusional patients; their faith in an imminent peace with the Palestinians was insane, and the consequences were tragic for both sides. The assumption that, if Israel ceded land, the Palestinians would renounce violence ignored the ideological and religious character of the Palestinian movement, which rejects Israel's right to exist within any borders. The cession of territory did not lead to a change in the ideology of Hamas or the PLO but only strengthened their military potential and provided springboards for attack.

For our enemies, we are all settlers for whom there is no place in the Middle East — and that includes the left! This is one of the most bitter but fundamental insights for Israeli society, dramatically confirmed by the events of 7 October 2023. For our enemies there are no distinctions between left and right, religious and secular, settler from Gush Katif and liberal resident of Tel Aviv. This fact — that the enemy sees us as a single bloc — is the most powerful argument in favor of the immediate cessation of internal "social schizophrenia." If the external threat makes no distinctions, the nation cannot afford to be divided on questions of security and national survival.

7 October 2023 was the moment when social schizophrenia in Israeli society received confirmation in the most brutal manner — through the electroshock of reality. For too long we tried to combine incompatible things: the striving for European liberalism with the necessity of Middle Eastern survival. On that tragic day these two worlds collided head-on. There are no longer "two Israels" disputing legal subtleties; there is one Israel standing before an existential choice: to be or not to be.

As a doctor I can say: the shock has passed, and now the most difficult stage begins — recovery through truth and compromise. October 7, 2023, became not just a tragedy — it was an earthquake that shattered the illusions of 'normality' in Israel. As a psychiatrist, I know: such a shock can either destroy a personality entirely, or become a starting point for healing. We witnessed the collapse of the previous system, but at the same time saw the birth of a new solidarity.

The social schizophrenia of which I wrote on these pages arose from the attempt to live simultaneously in a world of illusions — the "New Middle East" — and in the reality in which we are wanted destroyed. There is no longer any room for hallucinations. The reboot is not merely a change of government or a judicial reform. It is a return to a healthy national identity. We have finally understood who we are, who our enemy is, and in what our strength lies.

Political debates have not yet lost their meaning, and the nation, finding itself face to face with absolute evil, encountered an unresolvable moral dilemma that merely exposed the full depth of the schism in society. Two years on, the war on several fronts — with Iran, Hamas, Hezbollah, and the Houthis — has abated but not concluded. The moral dilemma remains everywhere: how to avenge the massacre without becoming a monster in the eyes of the world? How to preserve the Jewish character of the state? How to choose between "an eye for an eye" and the search for peace?

Around 1,200 killed, 253 hostages, breaches of the border, the tragedy at the 'Nova' festival... This was a blow not only to borders but to the national identity. On the ruins of kibbutzim and amid the ashes of the tragedy there arose a genuine, popular solidarity — precisely what the structures of the 'deep state' had for years been trying to dissolve. We saw: social disintegration stops before the face of absolute evil. This is our main resource. If we preserve this capacity to see in one another brothers, rather than political opponents, no rockets and no 'conceptions' will ever again be able to break us.

The disputes over the High Court of Justice (HCJ; BAGATS), the criminal proceedings against Netanyahu, the confrontation between the Haredim and the secularists — in my view, these are insignificant in the face of absolute evil: Hamas, Iranian proxies, and the surge of global antisemitism that poured into the streets of New York, London, and other cities. The shock did not erase the internal split — it merely exposed it, like an X-ray. The moral dilemma 'how do we live on with this?' is tearing society apart. On one side stands the thirst for justice and security; on the other, a humanitarian crisis and accusations of genocide from a part of the Western public that has forgotten about 7 October. This is a tectonic fault, forcing Israel to redefine itself.

Two years on, the war on multiple fronts — against Iran, Hamas, Hezbollah, and the Houthis — has quieted but has not ended: ceasefires remain fragile. And the moral dilemma? It is everywhere: how does one avenge a massacre (reports of systematic rape and torture by Hamas are not 'fake' — they are fact) without becoming a monster in the eyes of the world? The West accuses Israel of 'famine' and 'genocide' in Gaza, echoing Hamas propaganda. How does one preserve the Jewish character of the state? Israel has held firm, Hamas has been beaten but not broken. Continuing 'an eye for an eye' risks the soul; seeking peace risks security. The creation of a commission of truth and unity could be a step toward healing. To escape this impasse, what is needed is not merely reform — the entire nation requires therapy.

"THE FINAL APPOINTMENT"

Scene: a doctor's office. On the desk, a manuscript. The window is open — voices and the noise of an Israeli street drift in.

My voice off-screen: 'The Great Patient,' or 'Israeli society,' has endured the most severe episode. There were moments when collapse seemed irreversible. But today, looking out the window at these young people in uniform, at volunteers, at those who debate the future without forgetting the past, I see: consciousness is clearing. We are emerging from the state of social schizophrenia. Yes, the scars will remain forever. Yes, rehabilitation will be long. But the hallucinations have disappeared. We see reality as it is again. And in this reality, we are the masters of our own destiny.

***

This book is only one of the possible perspectives on the problem. Its purpose is to prompt the reader to reflect: what happened to our society, where did we go wrong, and — most importantly — what can each of us do to restore inner peace and harmony. No country can exist if its people does not trust those who protect and judge it. Israel has faced a crisis of both kinds of trust. The BAGATZ has come to be perceived not as a judicial arbiter but as a political actor. The army's leadership — as part of an ideological camp. The President, who was supposed to be a symbol of unity — as a participant on one of the sides.

This book is not about finding the guilty parties, but about how to restore society's trust — in the law, in the army, in the truth. How to build a commission of inquiry free from the dictate of elites, how to reform institutions without destroying the country, and how to restore to the army the spirit of victors that cannot be measured by approval ratings.

The reader who holds left-wing views will find in these pages considerable criticism of them, particularly of the flawed decisions taken. This criticism applies only to ideas and decisions, not to people. A healthy society cannot consist solely of representatives of the right or the left — it needs all its citizens and all their ideas!

Israel knows how to defeat enemies. But now it faces an enemy of a different kind — an internal one. It is not outside, it is not armed. It lives in apathy, in fatigue, in cynicism. Israel's rehabilitation after the war is not about restoring buildings — it is about restoring faith. Faith in the meaning of service, in justice, in the possibility that society can be united without coercion. For this a new understanding of 'Israeli solidarity' is needed: not a slogan, but a system of mutual responsibility. Not a ritual of remembrance, but action.

This book is not an indictment and not a rehabilitation program. It contains a preliminary 'diagnosis' and its justification. We cannot allow social schizophrenia to continue celebrating its 'victory' over the memory of those killed and humiliated, over the collective intelligence of the most ancient of peoples, and over its Holy Books.

I had no intention of writing a historical work or providing a particular political analysis — that is not my field of expertise. I saw my task as applying the expertise of a psychiatrist and scholar to understanding the mental split in society, in its collective psyche. What was happening resembled the degenerative disintegration of a personality, but on the scale of an entire nation. Common sense was yielding to dogma, and hope to mutual hatred. I know that behind the external manifestations of aggression and protests there typically lie anxieties, fear, pain, and psychological trauma. In this book I tried to record the symptoms of this 'disease' and to show how we all found ourselves its unwitting participants — how ideals, not supported by a real understanding of human nature, can lead to an even greater split.

This book was written for those who strive to understand what is happening; who believe that from 7 October one can emerge not weaker but stronger and wiser; who know that the future of Israel depends not on its enemies, but on the extent to which we can overcome our disagreements and complete the building of the state. The book was also composed so that we do not forget: the path to peace cannot be paved through hatred and mutual alienation. And although it deals with a dramatic period in the life of the country, I hoped that, by looking truth in the eye, we would find the strength to overcome the split and restore a unity based not on ideology and illusions but on mutual respect and acceptance of one another.

Israel as it ought to be is not a state without mistakes. It is a country that knows how to acknowledge mistakes and correct them. A country where the lesson of tragedy does not become a new ideology, but is transformed into responsibility. Israel can once again become whole, if it stops fearing itself — its faith, its strength, its right to be. Peace begins with the healing of the soul and mind, with the return to dialogue and humanity. This is where I see the hope for the future. For only through acknowledging our shared trauma can we find the path to its healing.

Our future depends on whether we can overcome the internal split, stop the schizophrenization of society, and complete the building of the state. I want to believe that YES, we can!

Israel must remain a strong warrior and at the same time a wise psychologist. Perhaps it is precisely in this that the main lesson of its modern history lies.

In this book I tried to record the symptoms of this "disease" and to show how we all found ourselves its unwitting participants; how ideals, not backed by a real understanding of human nature, can lead to an even greater schism.

Israel must remain a strong warrior and at the same time a wise psychologist. Perhaps it is precisely in this that the main lesson of its contemporary history lies.

This book is my analysis, my diagnosis, and my protocol of therapy. "Derech Eretz" is not merely politeness; it is our national immunity. It is the ability to hear another without losing oneself. It is the recognition that our diversity is not a disease but a resource, if we have a common backbone of responsibility.

This book is my contribution to our shared rehabilitation. I wrote it not to reopen wounds but so that we might learn to heal them correctly. Concluding this work with a prayer for our soldiers, I believe: the Israel of 2026 is a country that has finally opened its eyes. We have completed the examination. The patient is alive; his pulse is stable; and he is ready for a great future.

Take care of one another. And remember: truth is the only medicine that works.

Epicrisis: Israel After the Shock

Condition: *stable; consciousness clear.*
Recommendations: *constant hygiene of meanings;*
rejection of political hallucinations;
daily strengthening of "Derech Eretz."
Prognosis: favorable.
"The Great Patient" possesses a unique will
to live that surpasses any medical prognosis.

Why Are They Uncomfortable with Israel?

Response by Allister Heath (Editor of The Sunday Telegraph):

There is something about Israel that makes people uncomfortable, and it is not what they say. They will point to the politics, the settlements, the borders, and the wars. But dig beneath the outrage, and you will find something deeper. The discomfort is not about what Israel does, but about what it represents. Such a small country should not be this powerful. Full stop. Israel has no oil. No particular natural resources. A population barely the size of an average-sized American city. They are surrounded by enemies. They are hated at the United Nations. They are subjected to terrorism. They are condemned by celebrities. They are boycotted, defamed, and attacked.

And yet they thrive, as if tomorrow will never come.

In the military. In medicine. In security. In technology. In agriculture.

In intelligence. In morality. In pure, unbreakable will.

They turn desert into farmland.

They make water from the air. They intercept rockets in the air.

They rescue hostages from under the noses of the worst regimes in the world.

They survive wars that were supposed to destroy them.

And they win! The world watches this and cannot understand.

So they do what people do when they see a power they cannot understand. They assume it must be a trick.

It must be American aid. It must be foreign lobbying. It must be oppression. It must be theft.

It must be some dark trick that gave the Jews such power. It must be blackmail. Because God forbid it is something else. God forbid it is real. God forbid it is deserved.

Or, worse still, foretold by destiny.

The Jewish people should have disappeared long ago. That is how the story of the exiled, enslaved, despised minorities is supposed to end. But the Jews did not disappear. They genuinely returned home, rebuilt their land, revived their language, and brought their dead back to life — in memory, in identity, and in strength. This is not normal. This is not political. This is biblical.

There is no cheat code that explains how a group of people returns to its homeland after 2,000 years. There is no rational path from the gas chambers to global influence. And there is no historical precedent for surviving the Babylonians, the Romans, the

Crusaders, the Inquisition, the pogroms, and the Holocaust, and still showing up to work on a Sunday in Tel Aviv. Israel makes no sense.

Unless you believe in something beyond mathematics. That is what drives the world mad. Because if Israel is real, if this extraordinary, ancient, despised nation somehow continues to be chosen, protected, and prospering, then perhaps God is not, after all, a myth.

Perhaps He is still in history. Perhaps history is not random.

Perhaps evil does not get the last word.

Perhaps the Jews are not merely a people... but a testimony.

This is what they cannot endure. Because the moment you acknowledge that Israel's survival is not merely impressive but divine, everything changes.

Your moral compass must reset.

Your assumptions about history, power, and justice collapse.

You realize you are not watching the end of an empire.

You are witnessing the beginning of something eternal.

So they deny it. They defame it. And they rage against it.

Because it is easier to call a miracle a 'trick' than to admit the possibility that God will keep His promises. And He is still keeping them.

***

This book is my analysis, diagnosis, and treatment protocol. 'Derech Eretz' is not merely politeness — it is our national immunity. It is the ability to hear another without losing oneself. It is the recognition that our diversity is not a disease but a resource, if we share a common backbone of responsibility.

This book is my contribution to our shared rehabilitation. I wrote it not to reopen wounds, but so that we might learn to heal them properly. Concluding this work with a prayer for our soldiers, I believe: Israel in 2026 is a country that has finally opened its eyes. We have completed the autopsy. The patient is alive, his pulse is stable, and he is ready for a great future.

There is something about Israel that makes people feel uncomfortable, and it is not what they say. They will point to policy, settlements, borders, and wars. But dig beneath the indignation and you will find something deeper. What makes people uncomfortable is not what Israel does but what it represents.

Such a small country should not be this strong. Full stop. Israel has no oil. No special natural resources. A population barely the size of an average American city. They are surrounded by enemies. They are hated in the UN. They face terror. They are condemned by celebrities. They are boycotted, slandered, and attacked.

And yet they flourish as if there were no tomorrow.

In the army. In medicine. In security. In technology. In agriculture. In intelligence. In morality. In sheer, unbreakable will.

They transform desert into farmland. They make water from air. They intercept rockets in flight. They rescue hostages from the very dens of the world's worst regimes. They survive wars that should have destroyed them. And they win.

The world watches and cannot understand. So they do what people do when they see a strength they cannot comprehend — they assume it is a deception. It must be American aid. It must be foreign lobbying. It must be oppression. Because God forbid it is something else. God forbid it is real. God forbid it is deserved.

The Jewish people should have disappeared long ago. That is how the story of exiled, enslaved, despised minorities is supposed to end. But the Jews did not disappear. They truly returned home, rebuilt their land, revived their language, and brought their dead back to life — in memory, in identity, and in strength. This is not normal. This is not political. This is biblical.

There is no cheat code that explains how a group of people returns to their homeland after 2,000 years. There is no rational path from the gas chambers to world influence. And there is no historical precedent for surviving the Babylonians, the Romans, the Crusaders, the Inquisition, the pogroms, and the Holocaust, and still turning up for work on Sunday morning in Tel Aviv. Israel does not make sense.

Unless you believe in something beyond mathematics. That is what drives the world to madness. Because if Israel is real — if this incredible, ancient, despised nation is somehow still chosen, protected, and flourishing — then perhaps God is not a myth.

Perhaps He is still in history. Perhaps history is not random. Perhaps evil does not have the last word.

Perhaps the Jews are not merely a people... but a testimony.

That is what they cannot bear. Because the moment you acknowledge that Israel's survival is not merely impressive but divine, everything changes. Your moral compass must be reset. Your assumptions about history, power, and justice collapse. You understand that you are not witnessing the end of an empire. You are witnessing the beginning of something eternal. So, they deny it.

They vilify it. They are furiously against it. Because it is easier to call a miracle a "deception" than to acknowledge the possibility that God keeps His promises. And He still keeps them.

I completed the editing of this book after two years of war (2023–2025), in which not all questions have yet been closed. War is a disrespect for the value of life; it is always a heavy psychic trauma and a fall in morality; inevitably the death of soldiers, and much else besides. This war was imposed upon us. I hope this madness will end soon and we shall be able to restore and complete the building of our country.

Prayer for the Soldiers of the IDF

Mi she-berach avoteinu Avraham Yitzhak ve-Ya'akov, hu yevarech et chayalei tzva ha-hagana le-Yisrael, ha-omdim al mishmar artzeinu ve-arei Eloheinu, migvul ha-Levanon ve-ad midbar Mitzraim, umin ha-yam ha-gadol ad levo ha-arava, ba-yabasha, ba-avir uva-yam. Yiten Adonai et oiveinu ha-kamim aleinu nigafim lifneihem. Ha-Kadosh Baruch Hu yishmor ve-yatzil et chayaleinu mikol tzara ve-tzuka, umikol nega u-machala, ve-yishlach bracha ve-hatzlacha bechol ma'asei yedeihem. Yadber son'einu tachtehem, vi-ya'atrem be-keter yeshu'a uva-ateret nitzachon. Ve-yikuyam ba-hem ha-katuv (Devarim 20:4): "Ki Adonai Eloheichem ha-holech imachem, le-hilachem lachem im oiveichem le-hoshi'a etchem." Ve-ne'emar Amen.

May He Who blessed our fathers Abraham, Isaac, and Jacob bless the soldiers of the Israel Defense Forces, who stand guard over our land and the cities of our God, from the border of Lebanon to the desert of Egypt, from the great sea to the approach of the Arabah — on land, in the air, and at sea. May the Lord turn our enemies, who rise against us, to flee before us. May the Holy One, Blessed be

He, guard and deliver our soldiers from all trouble and distress, from all affliction and illness, and may He send blessing and success in all the work of their hands. May He cast our enemies down before them and crown our soldiers with the crown of salvation and the diadem of victory. And may there be fulfilled in them that which is written (Deuteronomy 20:4): "For the Lord your God is He who goes with you, to fight for you against your enemies, to deliver you." And let us say: Amen.

"May this prayer become a symbol of our shared hope and faith in a better future."

About the Author

Dr. Michael Ritsner is a psychiatrist, scientist, and writer. He has more than 40 years of experience in clinical practice, research, and teaching. Since 1989 he has lived and worked in Israel.

Professor Ritsner headed clinical departments at the Talbieh Mental Health Center (Jerusalem) and at the Sha'ar Menashe Mental Health Center. He is a world-renowned expert in the fields of schizophrenia, molecular genetics, quality of life, and neuroprotection. He is the author of more than 220 scientific publications, monographs, and the editor of a series of 14 books on neuropsychiatry. Dr. Ritsner is also the author of works of fiction: 'Not Free, for Infrequent Meetings' (2017), 'Goodbye, Russia' (2019), 'Jerusalem, Haifa and Beyond' (2021), 'My Name is Dr. Levitt' (2022), 'The Split in Israel: Through a Psychiatrist's Eyes' (2026), 'Shadow of Doctor Landau: Dialogues of Minds' (2026), 'Windows of Memory' (2016), and 'Capgra'as mirror. Digital doubles' (2026). His hobbies are symphonic music and chanson, travel, cheesemaking, alpine skiing, chess, table tennis, and swimming. He is currently an Emeritus Professor at the Technion and a leading consultant at the National Insurance Institute of Israel in Haifa.

www.ingramcontent.com/pod-product-compliance
Lightning Source LLC
LaVergne TN
LVHW051918051126
851858LV00008B/129
* 9 7 8 1 8 0 8 5 7 9 8 3 7 *